P9-BYA-513

William Faulkner
Biographical and
Reference Guide

GALE AUTHOR HANDBOOK 1

William Faulkner
Biographical and Reference Guide

A Guide to his Life and Career—with a
Checklist of his Works, a Concise Biography,
and a Critical Introduction
to each of his Novels

Edited by
LELAND H. COX

A BRUCCOLI CLARK BOOK
GALE RESEARCH COMPANY
DETROIT, MICHIGAN 48226

*To My Father
and
To The Memory Of My Mother*

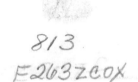

*813
F263ZCOX*

Copyright © 1982 by
Gale Research Company

Library of Congress Cataloging in Publication Data

Cox, Leland H.
    William Faulkner, biographical and reference guide.

    (Gale author handbook; 1)
    "A Bruccoli Clark Book."
    Bibliography.
    1. Faulkner, William, 1897-1962—Handbooks, man-
uals, etc. 2. Faulkner, William, 1897-1962—Bibliography.
I. Title. II. Series.
PS3511.A86Z773   1982   813'.52   82-9262
ISBN 0-8103-1117-8   AACR2

213856

Contents

Publisher's Note

Readers who seek in-depth information about an author's life and work are frequently faced with the frustrating and time-consuming chore of assembling research materials. For many authors, there are only partial bibliographies published in various journals; biographical information is often elusive or unreliable; and the principal critical studies must be gathered from a large body of publications. My objective in planning the Gale Author Handbook Series has been to remedy this troublesome condition, for at least the most noteworthy figures, by organizing reliable biographical and bibliographical information, together with the best critical assessments. I believe that these companion volumes demonstrate the convenience and usefulness this editorial rationale provides. Users are invited to nominate authors for future volumes in the series.

Frederick G. Ruffner, Jr.
Publisher

Foreword

Each *Gale Author Handbook* is a self-contained companion to the study of a major author. *Biographical and Reference Guides* provide the essential information about an author's life and career while explicating his works. *Critical Collections* organize materials for an independent assessment of an author.

In addition to a checklist of the author's works and a chronology of his life, *Biographical and Reference Guides* include two major sections: a concise biography and a book-by-book discussion of the major works. The biography is a chronological account of the major events in the author's life, with emphasis on his professional achievements and his literary relationships. The discussions of the works are intro-ductory—reviewing the subject of each work, its literary techniques, the author's intentions, and its place in the author's canon. Both the contemporary reception and subsequent criti-cal judgments are summarized. The most useful critical studies are cited at the end of each discussion.

The *Critical Collections* include three main sections in addi-tion to the checklist of the author's works. The first, "Back-ground," gathers statements by the author that establish his literary perspectives. The second, "Critical Assessments," provides a selection of the most useful evaluative articles about each of the author's major works and general essays that dis-cuss the author's primary themes. The third section, "Recom-mended Readings," is a topically arranged secondary checklist of the principal critical works.

Gale Author Handbooks serve students as well as good general readers by assembling essential reference materials that reveal the richness of literary masterpieces and the genius of their creators. Thus the series aims to achieve two goals: first, to make our literary heritage more accessible; and second, to enhance the reader's understanding of literary art, to enable him to feel what Vladimir Nabokov described as "the pure satisfaction which an inspired work of art gives."

x

Acknowledgments

I would like to thank my friend and colleague, Prof. James B. Meriwether, for reading portions of this manuscript and especially for making available to me the resources of the Faulkner Reading Room in Thomas Cooper Library at the University of South Carolina. Access to the Reading Room, and particularly to its impressive collection of secondary materials, greatly facilitated the compilation of these two volumes. I would also like to thank the members of the South Carolina Committee for the Humanities for granting a period of sabbatical leave during the latter stages of this project.

Works by Faulkner

Books:

The Marble Faun (Boston: Four Seas, 1924);

Soldiers' Pay (New York: Boni & Liveright, 1926; London: Chatto & Windus, 1930);

Mosquitoes (New York: Boni & Liveright, 1927; London: Chatto & Windus, 1964);

Sartoris (New York: Harcourt, Brace, 1929; London: Chatto & Windus, 1932); original, uncut version, *Flags in the Dust*, edited by Douglas Day (New York: Random House, 1973);

The Sound and the Fury (New York: Cape & Smith, 1929; London: Chatto & Windus, 1931);

As I Lay Dying (New York: Cape & Smith, 1930; London: Chatto & Windus, 1935);

Sanctuary (New York: Cape & Smith, 1931; London: Chatto & Windus, 1931); unrevised version, *Sanctuary: The Original Text*, edited by Noel Polk (New York: Random House, 1981);

These 13 (New York: Cape & Smith, 1931; London: Chatto & Windus, 1933);

Idyll in the Desert (New York: Random House, 1931);

Miss Zilphia Gant (Dallas: Book Club of Texas, 1932);

Salmagundi, edited by Paul Romaine (Milwaukee: Casanova Press, 1932);

Light in August (New York: Smith & Haas, 1932; London: Chatto & Windus, 1933);

A Green Bough (New York: Smith & Haas, 1933);

Doctor Martino and Other Stories (New York: Smith & Haas, 1934);

Pylon (New York: Smith & Haas, 1935; London: Chatto & Windus, 1935);

Absalom, Absalom! (New York: Random House, 1936; London: Chatto & Windus, 1937);

The Unvanquished (New York: Random House, 1938; London: Chatto & Windus, 1938);

The Wild Palms (New York: Random House, 1939; London: Chatto & Windus, 1939);

The Hamlet (New York: Random House, 1940; London: Chatto & Windus, 1940);

Go Down, Moses and Other Stories (New York: Random House, 1942; London: Chatto & Windus, 1942);

The Portable Faulkner, edited by Malcolm Cowley (New York: Viking, 1946);

Intruder in the Dust (New York: Random House, 1948; London: Chatto & Windus, 1949);

Knight's Gambit (New York: Random House, 1949; London: Chatto & Windus, 1951);

Collected Stories of William Faulkner (New York: Random House, 1950; London: Chatto & Windus, 1951);

Notes on a Horsethief (Greenville, Miss.: Levee Press, 1951);

Requiem for a Nun (New York: Random House, 1951; London: Chatto & Windus, 1953);

A Fable (New York: Random House, 1954; London: Chatto & Windus, 1955);

Big Woods (New York: Random House, 1955);

The Town (New York: Random House, 1957; London: Chatto & Windus, 1958);

New Orleans Sketches, edited by Carvel Collins (New Brunswick, N.J.: Rutgers University Press, 1958; London: Sidgwick & Jackson, 1959; augmented edition, New York: Random House, 1968);

The Mansion (New York: Random House, 1959; London: Chatto & Windus, 1961);

The Reivers (New York: Random House, 1962; London: Chatto & Windus, 1962);

Early Prose and Poetry, edited by Collins (Boston: Little, Brown, 1962; London: Cape, 1963);

The Marble Faun and A Green Bough (New York: Random House, 1965);

Essays, Speeches & Public Letters, edited by James B. Meriwether (New York: Random House, 1966; London: Chatto & Windus, 1967);

The Wishing Tree (New York: Random House, 1967; London: Chatto & Windus, 1967);

A Faulkner Miscellany, edited by Meriwether (Jackson: University Press of Mississippi, 1974);

The Marionettes (Charlottesville: University Press of Virginia, 1977);

Mayday (Notre Dame, Ind.: University of Notre Dame Press, 1977);

Uncollected Stories of William Faulkner (New York: Random House, 1979);

Helen: A Courtship and Mississippi Poems (New Orleans & Oxford, Miss.: Tulane University/Yoknapatawpha Press, 1981).

Produced Screenplays:

Today We Live, screen story and dialogue by Faulkner, MGM, 1933;

The Road to Glory, by Faulkner and Joel Sayre, Twentieth Century-Fox, 1936 (Carbondale: Southern Illinois University Press, 1981);

To Have and Have Not, by Faulkner and Jules Furthman, Warner Brothers, 1945 (Madison: University of Wisconsin Press, 1980);

The Big Sleep, by Faulkner, Leigh Brackett, and Furthman, Warner Brothers, 1946 (New York: Irvington, 1971);

Land of the Pharoahs, by Faulkner, Harry Kurnitz, and Harold Jack Bloom, Warner Brothers, 1955.

Biography

I. 1897-1927

Recognized by many critics as one of this country's greatest novelists, William Faulkner was a very private man who resented uninvited intrusions into his private and professional life. Thus, when questioned on personal matters, Faulkner gave himself full license to respond according to his own imaginative whims and his assessment of the interviewer. Asked about his childhood in a 1931 interview with Marshall J. Smith, Faulkner jokingly replied that he was "born in 1826 of a negro slave and an alligator—both named Gladys Rock. I have two brothers. One is Dr. Walter E. Traprock and the other is Eaglerock—an airplane. . . . Quit school after five years in seventh grade. Got job in grandfather's bank and learned medicinal value of his liquor."[1]

Actually, William Cuthbert Faulkner was born on 25 September 1897 in the town of New Albany, Mississippi. He was the oldest of four sons born to Murry Cuthbert and Maud Butler Falkner: Murry Charles, Jr., was born in 1899; John Wesley Thompson III in 1901; and Dean Swift in 1907. Though it is true that William Faulkner did not graduate from high school, he did progress beyond the seventh grade and on into the eleventh grade of the Oxford High School, which was the final grade offered by the school at the time. He did work for a brief period, in 1916, in his grandfather's bank. The Falkners were a large and close-knit family. Many of the values he would carry with him throughout his life were transmitted through family channels; family history and lore provided him with models of behavior as well as the subject matter that would find its way into his novels and stories. For these reasons, the early period of Faulkner's life deserves close attention.

Parts of this family history are shrouded in mystery, in-

cluding the derivation of the name *Falkner*. With the exception
of John, who used his older brother's surname for his own
eight novels, William was the only member of the family to
change the spelling of the name from *Falkner* to *Faulkner*.
Writing to Malcolm Cowley in 1945, he gave the following
explanation for the spelling of his name:

> My first recollection of the name [Falkner] was, no
> outsider seemed able to pronounce it from reading it, and
> when he did pronounce it, he always wrote the "u" into
> it. So it seemed to me that the whole outside world was
> trying to change it, and usually did. Maybe when I began
> to write . . . I secretly was ambitious and did not want to
> ride on grandfather's coat-tails,[2] and so accepted the "u,"
> was glad of such an easy way to strike out for myself. I
> accept either spelling. In Oxford it usually has no "u"
> except on a book. The above was always my mother's and
> father's version of why I put back into it the "u" which
> my greatgrandfather, himself always a little impatient of
> grammar and spelling both, was said to have removed. I
> myself really dont know the true reason. It just seemed to
> me that as soon as I got away from Mississippi, I found
> the "u" in the word whether I wished it or not. I still think
> it is of no importance, and either one suits me.[3]

Concerning the transatlantic background of the Falkner
family, there are varying accounts. One source gives the
Falkners a Welsh background. Faulkner's father placed the
family's origins in Ulster while his uncle, John Wesley
Thompson Falkner, Jr., claimed they were all descended from
French Huguenots. The patriarch of the Falkner clan in
Mississippi—William Clark Falkner, who was also known as
the Old Colonel from his Civil War service—was never known
to have offered an opinion.[4]

For his own accounts, Faulkner drew freely on all of the
sources available to him, which included one version that
placed Falkner antecedents in Scotland with the name of *Fal-*

coner. Faulkner also possessed a large family Bible and genealogy that was passed down the family line from Faulkner's great-great-great-uncle, John Wesley Thompson, to William Clark Falkner (the Old Colonel, and Faulkner's great-grandfather), to John Wesley Thompson Falkner (the Young Colonel), to Murry Falkner, and finally to William Faulkner himself.[5] Various adaptations from these sources are to be found in Faulkner's fiction and nonfiction, and in his responses to interviewers and letter writers. In a 1955 interview, Faulkner stated that "my people were Scottish. They fought on the wrong side, and they came into America, into Carolina, and my grandfather chose the wrong side again in 1861. . . ."[6] As man and artist, Faulkner placed great importance on the values manifested by a sense of family and place, insofar as this sensibility might heighten one's understanding of more general and eternal values.[7]

Though William Faulkner never knew his great-grandfather, the personality and deeds of Col. William Clark Falkner maintained a stronger hold on Faulkner's imagination than did the achievements of his father or grandfather. It was the character of Colonel Falkner upon whom the fictional character of Col. John Sartoris in *The Unvanquished* would largely be based. The deeds of the Old Colonel were certainly dramatic. Born in Knox County, Tennessee, in 1825, William Clark Falkner arrived in Mississippi in 1842; by 1851 he had become a successful lawyer, had helped to capture a murderer named McCannon—whose life story he printed and then sold at the man's execution—had served as a lieutenant and been wounded by guerillas in the Mexican War, and had been married, produced a son, and been widowed. He had, in self-defense, stabbed one man to death and shot and killed another, had published two literary works at his own expense, and in October 1851 had remarried.[8] During the Civil War he was first an infantry captain, then a colonel in command of the Second Mississippi Infantry—his unit distinguished itself at the first battle of Bull Run—and finally the organizer of a group of partisan rangers.[9]

Though little is known of W. C. Falkner's activities between 1863, when he retired from the war, and the end of hostilities, by 1867 he was back in Ripley and actively engaged in restoring his fortunes. His chief effort in this respect was the construction of the Ripley Railroad, on which work was first started in 1871 and which was supported initially by subscriptions from local farmers. Like Col. Thomas Sutpen in *Absalom, Absalom!*, Colonel Falkner had a grand design: to create a railroad that would make the Gulf Coast a port for the Great Lakes. Among the prominent stockholders in the company was a man named R. J. Thurmond, with whom Colonel Falkner was almost constantly at odds, both over personal matters and as a result of a power struggle for control of the railroad. Falkner bought him out in 1886.

While Colonel Falkner's entrepreneurial activities centered on the railroad—the name of which was successively changed from the Ripley Railroad to the Ripley, Ship Island, and Kentucky Railroad, and finally to the Gulf and Chicago Railroad; but because it was constructed on a narrow-gauge track, it was generally called the "doodle-bug" railroad—this did not define the full scope of his interests. His bent for literature led him to write several works, the most notable being *The White Rose of Memphis*, which was serialized in the *Ripley Advertiser* and then published in New York in 1881;[10] and in 1889 Colonel Falkner offered himself as a candidate for the Mississippi legislature. Throughout this entire period Falkner and Thurmond had been quarreling, and in October 1889 Colonel Falkner was told that Thurmond intended to kill him. Falkner refused to arm himself. Reacting much like Col. John Sartoris when he is told that Ben Redmond intends to kill him, Colonel Falkner is said to have reasoned that he "had killed enough men already, and he was not going to shed any more blood."[11] The reported threat became a reality on the fifth of November when Thurmond accosted Colonel Falkner near the Ripley courthouse and shot him in the head, at close range, with a .44 caliber pistol. Thurmond was able to use his wealth and influence, which were considerable, in getting himself acquitted of the charge of manslaughter. J. W. T. Falkner, now the Young Colonel and a successful lawyer in Oxford, was dissuaded from avenging his father's death by taking Thurmond's life in turn and took charge of the railroad that would for a time provide his son Murry, as well as other family members, with employment.[12]

Even then the family was still to be visited by more violence. In 1891 Murry was working out of Pontotoc as a conductor on one of the family's trains. Following a fistfight with a man named Elias Walker—whose sister had offended a young lady Murry was then seeing—Walker sought Murry out, shot him in the back with a 12-gauge shotgun, and then, to make certain the job would be a complete one, he shot him once more in the mouth with a pistol. Miraculously, Murry survived; but J. W. T. Falkner, though he had forsworn vengeance for his father's death, vowed that he would kill Walker and only failed to do so because his navy revolver misfired six times in succession, giving Walker time to draw his own weapon and shoot Falkner in the hand before fleeing.[13]

Growing up, young William Faulkner's imagination was fed by a rich family history, one that abounded in lessons, not always flattering, of pride, arrogance, humility, honor, courage, rapacity, ingenuity, shrewdness, and love. It showed him something of the darker side of human nature and also gave him a sense of place, of rootedness, that was to remain with him throughout his life. If he drew heavily at times on family lore for his Sartorises and Compsons, he drew even more widely from his knowledge of his region and from his own sharp insights into human nature.

A little more than a year after Faulkner's birth, in the waning part of December 1898, the family moved to Ripley where

Murry served as the auditor and treasurer of the railroad until its sale in 1902. It was also in Ripley that Murry, Jr. (known as Jack), and John Wesley Thompson III (called Johncy) were born. After the railroad was sold the family moved to Oxford. Murry, Sr., working closely with his father, had a hand at several different occupations; in turn, he ran a cottonseed-oil mill and an ice plant, a livery stable, a Standard Oil agency, and a hardware business before becoming the business manager for the University of Mississippi shortly after World War I.[14] For his part, J. W. T. Falkner continued to prosper as a lawyer, politician, banker, and businessman. It was in Oxford that the last of the four sons, Dean Swift Falkner, was born.

Living in Oxford gave all the boys an opportunity to know their grandfather, as well as family members on their grandmother's, Sally Murry's, side. Another important influence came from a member of a different race. Caroline Barr came to work in the household of Maud Falkner shortly after the Falkners arrived in Oxford and stayed with the family until her death in 1940. No one knew her exact age, though it was believed she had been born a slave sometime in the 1840s. Delivering her funeral oration, Faulkner described her as:

> one of my earliest recollections, not only as a person, but as a fount of authority over my conduct and of security for my physical welfare, and of active and constant affection and love. She was an active and constant precept for decent behavior. From her I learned to tell the truth, to refrain from waste, to be considerate of the weak and respectful to age. I saw fidelity to a family which was not hers, devotion and love for people she had not borne.[15]

Growing up in a small Mississippi town in the first decade of the twentieth century, Faulkner was never far removed from the country. His love of the outdoors and his knowledge of guns and hunting were developed at an early age, and these activities helped to develop a strong sense of independence, sometimes interpreted as aloofness. In a 1945 letter to Malcolm Cowley, Faulkner wrote that he "more or less grew up in my father's livery stable. Being the eldest of four boys, I escaped my mother's influence pretty easy, since my father thought it was fine for me to apprentice to the business."[16] In the same letter he reported that he "graduated from grammar school, went two years to high school, but only during the fall to play on the football team. . . ."[17]

Whatever his mother's influence during his early years may have been, William Faulkner occupied a position of leadership as far as his brothers were concerned. He evidently had no difficulty persuading Johncy to attempt an experimental flight using corn shucks for wings and arm power for thrust; or in persuading John, Jack, and his cousin Sally Murry to touch their tongues to a freezing iron hitching rack, where of course they stuck.[18] For more innocent entertainment, there were live shows and, later, movies at the Opera House, which was owned by Faulkner's grandfather. There were still traces of violence and lawlessness in community life from time to time. In September 1908, a Negro, Nelse Patton, was lynched for the murder of Mattie McMillan, whose head he nearly cut off with a razor. After being arrested at the end of a dramatic chase—in which one of Faulkner's school friends was involved—Patton was shot and killed in the jail by an angry mob that over-powered the sheriff. "When the body was thrown out of the jail it was quickly castrated and the head mutilated. By means of a rope tied to the neck, it was dragged by car to the Square. Then it was hung, naked, from a tree."[19]

Faulkner's formal education was spotty at best, but he was an avid reader from an early age; by the time he was in his teens he was reading and writing poetry, and sometimes engaging in literary discussions with Estelle Oldham, who in 1929 would become his wife. Evidently, he was also writing some prose fiction at this point in his life, though no examples of it survive, and he had long had a lively interest in the graphic arts.[20] By the age of fourteen, Faulkner had made a discovery of Herman Melville's *Moby-Dick*, telling his brother Jack, "It's one of the best books ever written."[21] However, Faulkner's growing interest in literature and writing was paralleled by increased truancy from school, and in the eighth grade he was not present for the required number of days.[22]

In the three intervening years between the eighth and eleventh grades, William Faulkner continued his reading and writing; but he was not bookish in the sense that he had no interests in outside activities. He did, and these included football, from which he received a broken nose, scouting, hunting, and Estelle Oldham. In June 1914, before entering his final full year of high school, Faulkner began to come under the influence of Phil Stone, who was four years older than Faulkner and whose family had been friends with the Falkners for years. This friendship would prove to be an important influence and would have a significant bearing on Faulkner's early development as a writer.[23]

Stone received B.A. degrees from both the University of Mississippi and Yale. Reading early samples of Faulkner's poetry in 1914, Stone became excited. "Anybody could have seen that he had a real talent," he said years later. "It was perfectly obvious."[24] Thus began a tutelage that was to last until just before Faulkner published *Soldiers' Pay*, his first novel, in 1926. Stone, who was as garrulous as he was precocious, was a willing teacher, and Faulkner's natural quietness made him seem, at least in Stone's eyes, an ideal student. However, as Michael Millgate has pointed out, it does not appear that Stone ever really grasped the true quality of Faulkner's genius. It was a relationship, says Millgate, which "undoubtedly led Stone to exaggerate in his own mind, and in public and private statements, the real extent of his influence on Faulkner and on Faulkner's work."[25] Stone felt that Faulkner's talents were exclusively poetic, and it is true that in these early years Faulkner saw himself primarily as a poet. His first published works were poems and translations of poems, and his first book, *The Marble Faun* (1924), was a book of poetry. In later years Faulkner would describe himself as a failed poet, and critics would sometimes make the mistake of interpreting these remarks literally.

Phil Stone was probably less important to Faulkner as a literary guide than he was as a provider of literary manna— books. Stone may have preached literary theory; but, as Faulkner's brother Jack has pointed out, William "was perfectly capable of making his own selections" as far as theory and taste were concerned.[26] The real service that Stone performed at this time was to order large numbers of books from the Brick Row Bookshop in New Haven, Connecticut, and these he made available to Faulkner. Stone also subscribed to some of the "little" magazines of the period—the *Little Review*, the *Dial*, and *Poetry*—which were important forums for modernistic and avant-garde literary trends. Books made available to Faulkner included novels by Joseph Hergesheimer, F. Scott Fitzgerald, Aldous Huxley, D. H. Lawrence, and Willa Cather. Poetry purchases included works by William Butler Yeats and various Symbolist poets. John Faulkner remembered that during this time "The Stones had a big old Studebaker touring car. . . . Phil loaded it with books for Bill to read and turned the car over to him. Bill would go out on some country road . . . and spend the day reading."[27]

At the same time that he appeared to be coming more and more under the sway of Stone, Faulkner's intentions regarding Estelle Oldham were growing increasingly serious. But the Oldham family discouraged any thoughts of marriage. Eventually, Estelle became engaged to Cornell Franklin, whom she married in April 1918.[28] It was at this point that Faulkner put Oxford, Mississippi, behind him for a while. Undoubtedly he was upset and hurt over Estelle's marriage; but there was also a war raging in Europe, and he wanted to play a part in it. In the same month that Estelle was married, Faulkner traveled to

New Haven, where he stayed for a time with Phil Stone and worked as a clerk for the Winchester Repeating Arms Company.[29] Concerning his desire to become involved in the war, Faulkner later wrote, "This was 1915 and '16; I had seen an aeroplane and my mind was filled with names: Ball, and Immelman and Boelcke, and Guynemer and Bishop, and I was waiting, biding, until I would be old enough or free enough or anyway could get to France and become glorious and beribboned too."[30]

Though Faulkner was successful in becoming a cadet in the Canadian RAF, he never did see combat in France. The war ended before he completed his pilot's training. Just how much flight training Faulkner received during his time as a cadet is not certain. He intimated to friends, relatives, and later to interviewers that he had received injuries from a crash; and in New Orleans during the mid-1920s he obviously led some people—including Sherwood Anderson—to believe that he carried a metal plate in his head as the result of a wound received during World War I.[31]

By December 1918 Faulkner was back in Oxford, and it is at this point that his early career as a writer began to take shape and gather momentum. Stone provides the following description of Faulkner during this stage of his development:

> He had an aristocratic, superior appearance—which most people considered an affectation—and an aloof reserve and an arrogant snappishness when someone tried to get familiar. So he was considered affected, peculiar, a crank, or a harmless ne'er-do-well. And thus he became "Count No Count."
>
> The old families of Oxford tolerated him because, after all, he was a member of the Faulkner family. . . . But they did not invite him to their houses . . . and my frequent statements that he was a writer of ability and would one day be more famous than Stark Young (another native son) and would cause many people to come to Ox-

ford because it was the home of William Faulkner—such statements provoked guffaws from the general public and polite, derisive smiles from the old families.[32]

Faulkner the "ne'er-do-well" enrolled as a special student at the University of Mississippi, though he was no more interested in formal education now than he had been in grammar and high school. On 6 August 1919 a poem by Faulkner entitled "L'Apres-Midi D'un Faune" appeared in the *New Republic*. Later, in October, a slightly different version of the same poem was published in the *Mississippian*, the student newspaper at the University of Mississippi. Between 1919 and 1925 a number of poems, critical pieces, drawings, and two prose sketches would appear in the newspaper. One story, "Landing in Luck," which appeared in the 26 November 1919 issue of the *Mississippian*, apparently was an imaginative by-product of Faulkner's experiences in the Canadian RAF. A lesser amount of work appeared in the local newspaper, the *Oxford Eagle*. Contributions to the *Misissippian* were signed both *Falkner* and *Faulkner*. The poems, some of which are translations, contain echoes of Housman, Swinburne, and Yeats and reflect the depth of Faulkner's reading among various Symbolist and Imagist poets.

Faulkner's critical pieces provide insights into his own theories about literature and foreshadow the direction in which his career was heading. Reviewing Joseph Hergesheimer's *Linda Condon* (1919), *Cytherea* (1922), and *The Bright Shawl* (1922), Faulkner admires the writer's technique: "the tricks of the trade were never employed with better effect, unless by Conrad. The induction to The Bright Shawl is good—he talks of the shawl for a page or so before one is aware of the presence of the shawl as a material object. . . ."[33] Faulkner is more critical of Hergesheimer's characterization: "His people are never actuated from within; they do not create life about them; they are like puppets assuming graceful but meaningless postures in answer to the author's compulsions, and holding these attitudes until he arranges their limbs again in other gestures as graceful and meaningless."[34] He sums up modernistic trends in poetry as "the fog generated by the mental puberty of contemporary American versifiers while writing inferior Keats or sobbing over the middle west. . . ."[35] Faulkner had concluded at an early point that, to be convincing, a writer must address himself to subjects he knows well. In a critical essay on American drama he expressed his belief "that art is preeminently provincial . . . it comes directly from a certain age and a certain locality."[36] Later, in another 1922 essay on American drama—and thinking perhaps of his great-grandfather—he wrote that "We have, in America, an inexhaustible fund of dramatic material. Two sources occur to any one: the old Mississippi river days, and the romantic growth of railroads."[37] In the same piece he held up the American language as "One rainbow we have on our dramatic horizon. . . ." Beside it, "British is a Sunday night affair of bread and milk."[38]

Faulkner also became involved with a drama group, the Marionettes, and late in 1920 he wrote out six hand-lettered copies of a verse play entitled *Marionettes*.[39] Like his poetry, it is highly stylized, and sets up a stark contrast between human passions and compulsions acted out against a visual background that is artificial in the extreme. The plot, which is deliberately slight, revolves around the seduction and abandonment of Marietta by Pierrot. Technically and thematically it is much more complex and foreshadows techniques and themes that would appear abundantly in the author's later work.[40] It was also during this period that Faulkner attempted to get his first book of poetry published. To the Four Seas Company of Boston he sent a manuscript entitled "Orpheus, and Other Poems." The publishers reacted favorably to the manuscript, but said that they could not undertake publication without some subsidy from the author. This Faulkner was unable to provide, so he requested the return of the manuscript, writing to Four Seas in November 1923, "I cannot very well guarantee the initial cost of publishing this mss.; besides, on re-reading some of the things, I see that they aren't particularly significant. And one may obtain no end of poor verse at a dollar and twenty-five cents per volume."[41]

Faulkner withdrew from the University of Mississippi in November 1920. What little money he needed he picked up by working at odd jobs. He enjoyed working with his hands and was a good carpenter and painter. He also continued his work with the Boy Scouts in Oxford, taking advantage of the opportunities it gave him to be out of doors. This was a style of life that seemed to suit him quite well, "to be a tramp, a harmless possessionless vagabond."[42] Following the tramp's urge—as well as the suggestion of Phil Stone that he try to develop some contacts that might aid his career—Faulkner left Oxford in the fall of 1921 for New York, where he stayed for a time as the guest of Stark Young. For livelihood, he worked as a salesman in the Doubleday Bookshop at Lord & Taylor's, which was managed by Elizabeth Prall, soon to become Mrs. Sherwood Anderson. Faulkner was back in Oxford in December 1921 where, with the assistance of Estelle Franklin's father, Lemuel Oldham, he became postmaster at the University of Mississippi. He held the job through October 1924, when the mounting complaints of customers claiming that they were not receiving their mail forced his resignation. Faulkner himself later supplied a humorous summary of this period in his life: "Family got job: postmaster. Resigned by mutual agreement on part of two inspectors; accused of throwing all incoming mail into garbage can. How disposed of outgoing mail never proved."[43] George Healy recalled a slightly different reaction at the time of Faulkner's dismissal. Asked by a friend how he felt about leaving the post office, Faulkner replied, "You know, all my life I probably will be at the beck and call of somebody who's got money. Never again will I be at the beck and call of every son-of-a-bitch who's got two cents to buy a stamp."[44]

It was also in 1924 that Faulkner had another go at the Four

Seas Company, this time with a manuscript entitled *The Marble Faun*. Stone agreed to suppy a $400 subsidy, and the work was published on 15 December 1924. *The Marble Faun* is a single narrative poem of fifty-one pages. Dramatic tension in the poem is supplied by the fawn, who is caught between two worlds. He is aware of the life of nature around him, and of its seasonal movements from the death of winter to the rebirth of spring. Sentient, he is yet marble, and cannot participate in the life about him:

> That quick green snake
> Is free to come and go, while I
> Am prisoner to dream and sigh
> For things I know, yet cannot know,
> 'Twixt sky above and earth below.
> The spreading earth calls to my feet
> Of orchards bright with fruits to eat,
> Of hills and streams on either hand;
> Of sleep at night on moon-blanched sand:
> The whole world breathes and calls to me
> Who marble-bound must ever be.[45]

In its style and derivativeness—the influences of Faulkner's reading remain evident in this work—*The Marble Faun* is much like the poetry Faulkner had been writing for the *Mississippian*. Though he was still committed to poetry, he continued to write occasional prose compositions as well, and there are a number of unpublished stories that date generally from this period.

In the fall of 1924 Faulkner and Stone traveled to New Orleans, where Elizabeth Prall introduced Faulkner to Sherwood Anderson, now her husband. He and Anderson got on well together, and apparently Anderson based a short story entitled "A Meeting South" on his first meeting with Faulkner. The central character is a Southerner named David who drank to combat pain and sleeplessness from wounds received during

World War I and who had a metal plate in his head.

In January 1925 Faulkner was back in New Orleans, ostensibly for the purpose of boarding a ship that would take him to Europe where the young poet would travel, study, and improve his craft for "two or three years."[46] Instead, Faulkner settled into an apartment at 624 Orleans Alley (now a tourist thoroughfare known as Pirate's Alley) and lived in New Orleans for six months. There he resumed his friendship with Anderson and continued his own writing. It was an important six months, at the end of which time Faulkner sailed for Europe not as a poet but as a writer of prose fiction with a completed, if unpublished, novel to mark his transition from poet to novelist.

Faulkner did not "discover" New Orleans in 1924 and 1925. He had traveled there with friends as early as 1918 and had made more frequent visits, sometimes with Stone, since 1921. It is not surprising, then, that there were channels of publication available to Faulkner in 1925. What is surprising is the quality of writing that started to pass through those channels. In February 1925 a prose piece by Faulkner entitled "New Orleans" appeared in the *Double Dealer*, a little magazine edited by Julius Weis Friend, John McClure, and Basil Thompson. It was not Faulkner's first contribution to the magazine, for in the June 1922 issue a poem, "Portrait," had appeared; and while he was in New Orleans in 1925 two more poems and two critical essays were published in the *Double Dealer*.[47]

Also in February 1925 a series of prose sketches, most of which were grouped under the collective "running" title of "Another 'Mirror of Chartres Street,' " began appearing in the Sunday supplement section of the *New Orleans Times-Picayune* newspaper, and for which Faulkner was paid a modest sum.[48] Recent evidence has shown that these were not random, independent submissions, but rather that almost all of them belonged to a numbered sequence of stories that had their own internal unity. Faulkner's running title for early type-script versions of these stories was "Sinbad in New Orleans."

Moreover, unpublished typescripts from the period indicate further how actively Faulkner was pursuing his craft. Bearing directly upon the New Orleans experience are two typescript versions of a story entitled "Don Giovanni," the latter draft of which was incorporated into Faulkner's second novel, *Mosquitoes* (1927), and "Peter," another New Orleans story that shows the young writer experimenting simultaneously with a number of expository, dramatic, and poetic techniques.[49] "Nympholepsy" is not a New Orleans story, but rather is a prose narrative related to a 1922 composition by Faulkner entitled "The Hill." One particular section of an undated and untitled typescript of twenty-three pages contains a verbatim rendering of the main action found in the "Frankie and Johnny" subnarrative in "New Orleans."[50] To these materials must be added two typescript versions of *Soldiers' Pay*. The first is a loose draft of over 300 pages that differs greatly from the later 476-page typescript and from the published text of the 1926 book.

Between January and July 1925, when he finally sailed for Europe, Faulkner was engaged in a number of different activities. He continued to write poetry, and to this can be added two critical essays ("On Criticism" and "Verse Old and Nascent") that were published, respectively, in the January-February and the April issues of the *Double Dealer*, a review of *Ducdame* (a novel by John Cowper Powys) that appeared in the 22 March issue of the *Times-Picayune*, and an unpublished essay entitled "Literature and War."[51] In the neighboring state of Texas an essay by Faulkner on Sherwood Anderson appeared in the *Dallas Morning News* on 26 April.[52] In none of these nonfictional pieces did Faulkner show any basic change in his critical views. Writing of his earlier experience with poetry, Faulkner made an obvious reference to Stone: "I was subject to the usual proselyting of an older person, but the strings were pulled so casually as scarcely to influence my point of view."[53]

Independent of Stone, and now writing far more prose than poetry, the major achievement at the end of Faulkner's New Orleans experience was the writing of *Soldiers' Pay*. One of Faulkner's versions of how he wrote *Soldiers' Pay* and became a novelist—which was always the same basic story given with a number of minor variations, and which is a good example of one of the ways in which Faulkner protected his privacy—was given to Jean Stein in 1955:

> I was living in New Orleans, doing whatever kind of work was necessary to earn a little money now and then. I met Sherwood Anderson. We would walk about the city in the afternoon and talk to people. In the evenings we would meet again and sit over a bottle or two while he talked and I listened. In the forenoon I would never see him. He was secluded, working. . . . I decided that if that was the life of a writer, then becoming a writer was the thing for me. So I began to write my first book. At once I found that writing was fun. I even forgot that I hadn't seen Mr. Anderson for three weeks until he walked in my door. . . . and said "What's wrong? Are you mad at me?" I told him I was writing a book. He said "My God" and walked out. When I finished the book . . . I met Mrs. Anderson on the street. She asked how the book was going and I said I finished it. She said, "Sherwood says that he will make a trade with you. If he doesn't have to read your manuscript he will tell his publisher to accept it." I said "Done" and that's how I became a writer.[54]

Of course Faulkner had decided long before he came to New Orleans that he was going to be a writer; and he wrote *Soldiers' Pay* because he was confident of his talent, a talent that had been taking him more and more in the direction of prose fiction.

Knowing that Sherwood Anderson had at least recommended *Soldiers' Pay* for publication, Faulkner finally set sail for Europe on board the freighter *West Ivis* on 7 July 1925. Traveling with him was the artist William Spratling, with whom Faulkner had developed a strong friendship in New Orleans. Landing at Genoa, Italy, on 2 August, Spratling and Faulkner were together for a while in Italy before going their separate ways. Meeting again in Stresa, the two traveled to Paris where they found residence in separate quarters. Faulkner settled into a dwelling at 26 rue Servandoni, near the Luxembourg Gardens. Spratling left for home on 6 September; and though Faulkner would remain in Paris a while longer, his entire trip abroad was a sojourn of roughly three months, not two or three years. Among the places Faulkner visited in Paris were the Louvre and the Luxembourg galleries, where he had opportunities to view the paintings of Cezanne, Degas, Manet, and a variety of other modern and postimpressionist artists. He also wrote home of having seen, in private collections, paintings by Matisse and Picasso.

Of course he continued to write. Some of the material he was working on would appear in later stories and novels. In a letter to his mother postmarked 6 September he wrote, "I have just written such a beautiful thing that I am about to bust— 2000 words about the Luxembourg gardens and death. It has a thin thread of plot, about a young woman, and it is poetry though written in prose form."[55] Here Faulkner may have been referring to the same piece he described to his aunt, Alabama McLean, in a letter postmarked four days later: "I have just finished the most beautiful short story in the world. So beautiful that when I finished it I went to look at myself in a mirror. And I thought, Did that ugly ratty-looking face, that mixture of childishness and unreliability and sublime vanity, imagine that? But I did. And the hand doesn't hold blood to improve on it."[56] No immediate use was made of this material; but if in fact the two references are to the same piece, he may have turned back to it later in writing the 445-word description of Temple Drake in the Luxembourg Gardens that concludes *Sanctuary* (1931). The conclusion itself ends with Temple looking at "the sky lying prone and vanquished in the embrace of the season of rain and death."[57] Speculation aside, Faulkner's letters leave little doubt concerning his self-confidence in his writing at the time.

Faulkner also seems to have been at work for a time on two different novels: one entitled "Mosquito," which would appear in 1927 as *Mosquitoes*; and one entitled "Elmer," which, despite the fact that Faulkner attempted to cast the material in both novel and short-story forms and continued working with it over several years, was never published. Again, there is a relationship here between short-story and novelistic material. An uncompleted short story by Faulkner entitled "Growing Pains" pictures the character of Elmer Hodge as a four-year-old growing up in Jefferson, Mississippi—the town that, in *Flags in the Dust* (first published in edited form as *Sartoris* in 1929), would be developed as the county seat of Faulkner's Yoknapatawpha County. "Elmer" itself was never completed as a novel, though a typescript of 130 pages, not always sequential, does survive. Drawing on this material Faulkner completed an unpublished short story entitled "Portrait of Elmer Hodge," which is set in Paris and uses flashbacks to fill the reader in on Elmer's background.

Both the uncompleted novel and the finished but unpublished short story represent an attempt on Faulkner's part to render a comic portrait of Elmer Hodge as a young artist. (Elmer is a painter.) Faulkner told James B. Meriwether in 1958 that "Elmer" was "funny, but not funny enough."[58] The work on "Elmer" was not in vain, for as Thomas L. McHaney points out, "many characters, themes, and even patches of dialogue and imagery from 'Elmer' found a way into the novels which followed, especially *Mosquitoes* and *Sartoris* [*Flags in the Dust*]. Then, much later, and with a high degree of seriousness, Faulkner took up the romantic—and apparently personal—elements of 'Elmer' and gave them form in his 1939 novel *The Wild Palms*, where the love story of Harry and Charlotte echoes the affair between Elmer and Ethel in the 1925 attempt."[59] In addition to "Elmer," Faulkner's European sojourn provided him with material that would result later in published short stories. These include "Divorce in Naples" (1930), "The Leg" (1930), and "Mistral" (1930).[60] A final unpublished piece that dates from this period is a humorous poem entitled "Ode to the Louver."[61]

It is not surprising that Faulkner made Elmer a painter. As has already been pointed out, he had a strong interest in graphic arts from an early age, contributed several pen-and-ink drawings to the *Mississippian*, and maintained a strong interest in painting all his life. In Paris, he was much impressed with the paintings he saw exhibited. Writing to his mother in a September letter, he remarked that Cézanne had "dipped his brush in light like Tobe Caruthers would dip his in red lead to paint a lamp-post. . . ."[62]Two other things impressed him: the small amount of money that it cost him to live in Paris ($1.50 or less per day), and the general rudeness of American tourists. "I am quite disgusted with my own nationality in Europe," he wrote to his Aunt Bama in September. "Imagine a stranger coming in your home, spitting on your floor and flinging you a dollar. That's the way they act."[63]

After a brief trip to London, which he found frightfully expensive, he returned to Paris, and by 9 December he was on his way home. He had learned prior to his departure that Boni & Liveright was going to follow Anderson's recommendation to publish his first novel, not under Faulkner's original title of "Mayday,"[64] but as *Soldiers' Pay*. Faulkner was much on the move in 1926. He was in Oxford from time to time, but he spent the winter months of that year in New Orleans— where he roomed with William Spratling and collaborated with him on *Sherwood Anderson & Other Famous Creoles*[65]—and

the summer months on the Gulf Coast of Mississippi. *Soldiers'
Pay* was published on 25 February 1926.

Soon afterward, despite Anderson's role in getting *Soldiers'
Pay* published, the friendship between the two writers termi-
nated abruptly. In April 1926, Anderson wrote to Horace
Liveright that he had seen a favorable review of the novel. "If I
were you," he told Liveright, "I would do what I could to
encourage him to keep at work. If you want to do so, why
don't you write him a letter telling him some of the things I
have said about him. . . . He was so nasty to me personally
that I don't want to write him myself, but would be glad if you
were to do it in this indirect way, as I surely think he is a good
prospect."[66]

Neither the exact causes nor the precise time of the break
between Anderson and Faulkner is known, though many explanations have been offered. Michael Millgate makes a very
plausible suggestion that the two may still have been on
friendly terms when Faulkner left for Europe in July. It may
well be that there was not one single event that drove the two
men apart, but rather an accretion of disagreements that ultimately produced irreconcilable differences. It should also be
pointed out that even though Faulkner had immense respect
for Anderson as a man and as an artist, he was not uncritical of
his talent. He rated Anderson's "I'm a Fool" as one of the best
stories he had ever read; but in his *Dallas Morning News* piece
he characterized *Many Marriages* as evidence of "a bad ear" on
Anderson's part, described *A Story Teller's Story* as uneven,
and indicated that Anderson, who was forty-eight years old at
the time, had not yet matured as a writer.[67] Just as Faulkner
ultimately had to assert his independence from Phil Stone, so
he may have felt the need to put some kind of professional
distance between himself and Anderson.

It was in Pascagoula, Mississippi, that Faulkner's second
novel, *Mosquitoes*, was written. The last page of the carbon
typescript of the novel bears the inscription, "Pascagoula,

Miss / 1 Sept 1926." As *Soldiers' Pay* is a novel about people trying to come to terms with life in postwar America, so *Mosquitoes* is a novel about the role of art and artists in society. In *Soldiers' Pay*, the main action of the novel takes place within the microcosm of a small Georgia community, Charlestown. In *Mosquitoes*, the action is confined to a yacht, the *Nausikaa*, where a number of New Orleans artists and dilettantes spend a long weekend talking about art and sex, and accomplishing very little of either. Though the reviews of *Soldiers' Pay* were mixed, Boni & Liveright decided to stay with their young author, and on 30 April 1927 *Mosquitoes* was published.

II.   1928-1931

The work and energy that Faulkner put into his first two novels gave him a tremendous amount of momentum. Independently from the impressions and ideas he had gathered during his European tour, he seems to have been working—certainly by 1926 and perhaps even earlier—on story lines involving two of his principal fictional families: the Sartorises and the Snopeses. The Snopes material appears in a manuscript entitled "Father Abraham" that, as Millgate has indicated, was to have served as the first chapter of *The Hamlet* (1940).[68] The Sartoris family was first developed in *Flags in the Dust*, a novel in which the Snopeses also appeared; but the sections of the novel that developed the Snopes clan were the ones that were hacked out of the work for its publication as *Sartoris* in 1929. It was Phil Stone who, in an unpublished article that was to have appeared in the *Oxford Eagle* in 1926 or 1927, mentioned the dual work in progress:

> Since his return from Europe Faulkner has been here at home playing golf and writing two new novels which are already under contract. Both are Southern in setting. One is something of a saga of an extensive family connection of

typical "poor white trash" and is said by those who have seen that part of the manuscript completed to be the funniest book anybody ever wrote. The other is a tale of the aristocratic, chivalrous and ill-fated Sartoris family, one of whom was even too reckless for the daring Confederate cavalry leader, Jeb Stuart. Both are laid in Mississippi.[69]

Laying the Snopes material aside, Faulkner concentrated on the Sartorises and *Flags in the Dust*. Writing to Horace Liveright in an October 1927 letter, Faulkner proclaimed, "I have written THE book, of which those other things were but foals. I believe it is the damdest best book you'll look at this year, and any other publisher." The letter also contained some mild complaint about overediting, though Faulkner, perhaps wishing to be tactful, uses the term *printer* rather than *editor* in saying that "He's been punctuating my stuff to death; giving me gratis quotation marks and premiums of commas that I dont need." He concluded by claiming, "I dont think that even the bird who named 'Soldiers' Pay' can improve on my title."[70]

Thus, seeming to have made some tough-minded evaluations of his earlier work, and ready now to step up to a higher plateau, Faulkner mailed his manuscript to Boni & Liveright. It was rejected; and though Faulkner must have been considerably surprised, he seemed in control of himself when he wrote Liveright on 30 November: "It's too bad you dont like Flags in the Dust. . . . I still believe it is the book which will make my name for me as a writer."[71] *Soldiers' Pay* and *Mosquitoes* had been published with comparative ease. Now things got tougher; and it was not until November 1928—after the manuscript had been submitted and rejected several times—that the firm of Harcourt, Brace agreed to undertake publication of a heavily cut and edited version entitled *Sartoris*, which Faulkner agreed to but did not edit himself. *Sartoris* was published 31 January 1929; the novel Faulkner wrote, *Flags in the Dust*, would not be published until 1973, eleven years after his death.

In the meantime, a fundamental change was about to take place in Faulkner's life. The marriage between Estelle and Cornell Franklin had not gone well; Estelle, with her two children Malcolm and Victoria, had returned to Oxford. In April 1929 she was legally divorced. For his part, Faulkner was spending a good deal of time with Estelle and the children, and on 10 June he and Estelle were married. Up to this point, it had not made much difference to Faulkner that *Soldiers' Pay* and *Mosquitoes* had produced very little in the way of revenue. *Sartoris* would not prove to be much of a money-maker either; and he would not record his first short-story sale until 1930 when "A Rose for Emily" appeared in *Forum*. With his marriage to Estelle in June he immediately became responsible for the welfare of a family of four, though Franklin would provide some support money for Malcolm and Victoria. Pressure on him increased rather than decreased over time as he took on financial obligations for other members of his family.

Despite these problems, and the difficulties in finding a publisher for *Sartoris*, the period of 1928-1929 was an extremely productive one for Faulkner. Following the initial rejection of that novel, Faulkner—perhaps reexamining what he had accomplished thus far in a brief career and considering what he wanted to accomplish in his lifetime—made an important decision about his work. In an introduction written for *The Sound and the Fury*, but not published until after his death, Faulkner wrote:

> Previous to it [*The Sound and the Fury*] I had written three novels, with progressively decreasing ease and pleasure, and reward or emolument. The third one was shopped about for three years, during which I sent it from publisher to publisher with a kind of stubborn and fading hope of at least justifying the paper I had used and the time I had spent writing it. This hope must have died at last, because one day it suddenly seemed as if a door had

clapped silently and forever to between me and all publishers' addresses and booklists and I said to myself, Now
I can write. Now I can just write. Whereupon I, who had
three brothers and no sisters and was destined to lose my
first daughter in infancy, began to write about a little
girl.[72]

The little girl is Caddy Compson, whose story, along with
that of the rest of her family, is told in *The Sound and the Fury*.
Faulkner on numerous occasions said that his treatment of
Caddy began as a short story but could not be contained within
such limits. The manuscript of the novel, the first page of
which was dated 7 April 1928, originally carried the title of
"Twilight" and began, as does the published novel, with
Benjy's narration. Faulkner continued working on the novel in
Oxford and finished the final typescript in New York in 1928,
where he was sharing a room with his friend Ben Wasson, a
Mississippian who had known Faulkner in Oxford and who
was then acting as his literary agent. When he finished the
typescript, he handed it to Wasson saying "Read this, Bud. It's
a real sonofabitch."[73]

Whatever Faulkner may have thought of the finished product, he certainly had his doubts as to whether anyone in New
York would be willing to publish it. To Alfred Harcourt,
whose firm had published *Sartoris* in January, Faulkner wrote
in February 1929: "About the Sound & Fury ms. That is all
right. I did not believe that anyone would publish it; I had no
definite plan to submit it to anyone. I told Hal[74] about it once
and he dared me to bring it to him. And so it really was to him
that I submitted it, more as a curiosity than aught else. I am
sorry it did not go over with you all, but I will not say I did not
expect that result."[75] The manuscript did "go over" with
Harrison Smith, who would soon be leaving Harcourt, Brace
to become a partner in the firm of Jonathan Cape and Harrison
Smith, and he asked Harcourt to let him have *The Sound and
the Fury* manuscript. Harcourt agreed, telling Smith "You're

the only damn fool in New York who would publish it."[76] Subsequently, *The Sound and the Fury* was published by Cape and Smith on 7 October 1929.

Thus, 1929 saw the publication of two novels by Faulkner, and before the end of the year he would write two more: the first version of *Sanctuary* (1931), completed in May 1929, and *As I Lay Dying* (1930), which was written between October and December of the same year. Though Faulkner was certainly not unknown before 1929—his first three novels had each received a number of positive reviews—*The Sound and the Fury* received more critical attention, much of it highly favorable, than any of his previous work. It would not be a money-maker, however.

Following their honeymoon in Pascagoula, William and Estelle Faulkner returned to Oxford where they rented an apartment. No short stories had been sold, and Faulkner took a job that fall in the University of Mississippi power plant where, as a supervisor on the night shift, he wrote *As I Lay Dying*. Financially, things began looking up in 1930, since Faulkner began to meet with some success—owing in part to the critical reception of *The Sound and the Fury*—in getting his short stories published. Using the evidence supplied by the data contained in the short-story sending schedule Faulkner kept for about two years between 1930 and 1932,[77] Millgate notes that Faulkner "succeeded in placing no less than thirty of the forty-two stories which he tried to sell to magazines during that period."[78] Millgate continues:

> In a note dated January 1, 1931, which appears on the back of a page from . . . "The Brooch," Faulkner jotted down some of the money he had earned in 1930. From *Scribner's*, presumably as an advance payment for "Dry September" . . . he had received $200; from the *Saturday Evening Post* he had had two payments of $750 each, for "Thrift" . . . and "Red Leaves." . . . Thus these last two stories each brought Faulkner more money than either of

his first two novels, for which he apparently received advances of $200 and $400 respectively, and it seems extremely unlikely that he received anything like $750 for *Sartoris* or *The Sound and the Fury*.[79]

Faulkner would have need of all the revenue he could lay his hands on, for in June 1930 he purchased a home, built by Robert B. Shegog in the 1840s, though it was in bad need of repair and without modern fixtures. (The work of modernization and restoration would be carried out over a number of years, principally by Faulkner himself.) The house and the four acres of land he purchased to go with it cost $6,000. The Faulkners took up residence in June, and Faulkner christened the house Rowan Oak, after the tree symbolizing peace and security.[80] The satisfaction derived from settling in at Rowan Oak was undermined by grief a few months later when the Faulkners' first daughter, Alabama—named after Faulkner's Aunt Bama, Mrs. Alabama McLean, a direct descendant of the Old Colonel's—died just nine days following her birth on 11 January 1931.

As I Lay Dying, the novel that Faulkner would claim repeatedly was written in six weeks' time but that actually took just over ten weeks, was published on 6 October 1930. Though there is no direct line of descent from the "Father Abraham" material that Faulkner had been working on since the mid-1920s and the specific contents of the novel, there are some general similarities in terms of the names of characters who would be developed in *The Hamlet* and in reference to the sale of a herd of wild Texas ponies that would be one of the main lines of action in the 1940 novel. Also, a version of "Spotted Horses" submitted to *Scribner's Magazine* in 1928 bore the title "As I Lay Dying." *As I Lay Dying* was also Faulkner's first novelistic treatment of the social and economic world of the poor white farmer. Faulkner's knowledge of this class of people may have been increased appreciably during the time in 1928 when he accompanied his uncle J. W. T. Falkner II, who was running for the office of district attorney, on campaign trips. Faulkner later said, "I would go around with him and sit on the front galleries of country stores and listen to the talk that would go on. . . . it was interesting and I remembered most of it. . . ."[81]

As I Lay Dying also added to Faulkner's critical reputation, but not in quite the same way that *The Sound and the Fury* had. While some critics would give the novel serious treatment, others could not get over their initial shock at its morbid subject matter: the transportation, by wagon, of a three-day-old corpse for burial in the town of Jefferson, a trip that ends up taking six days in itself. This subject matter would give rise to charges of sensationalism and poor taste, charges that would be embellished and carried to even greater extremes with the publication of *Sanctuary*, and which would be responsible for a misreading of Faulkner's fiction for years to come. Even in 1950, when Faulkner had received the Nobel Prize, the *Jackson Daily News* proclaimed Faulkner to be "a propagandist of degradation" who "properly belongs in the privy school of literature."[82] What *As I Lay Dying* and *The Sound and the Fury* did have in common was an undistinguished sales record.

Though Faulkner finished the writing of *Sanctuary* in May 1929, this would not be the text of the novel that was published 9 February 1931 because he considered the 1929 version to be artistically unsound. Though again there would be favorable reviews acknowledging the novel's power, other critics would decry its sadism, cruelty, morbidity, and general unpleasantness. The brutal rape of Temple Drake with a corncob would be battened on by the more sensationalistic reviews. Even if misunderstood, the novel sold well and the thirty-three-year-old author suddenly found himself to be a celebrity and a marketable commodity.

Faulkner's celebrity status, owing not just to *Sanctuary* but to his general critical reputation as well, was indicated in an invitation extended by Prof. James Southall Wilson, who asked Faulkner to attend an informal writers' conference at the University of Virginia in October. Other attendees were to include Sherwood Anderson, Ellen Glasgow, James Branch Cabell, and Allen Tate. Faulkner's reservations about such gatherings, bound up, as always, with his sense of privacy, are reflected in his response to Professor Wilson:

> Thank you for your invitation. I would like very much to avail myself of it, what with your letter's pleasing assurance that loopholes will be supplied to them who have peculiarities about social gambits. You have seen a country wagon come into town, with a hound dog under the wagon. It stops on the Square and the folks get out, but that hound never gets very far from that wagon. He might be cajoled or scared out for a short distance, but first thing you know he has scuttled back under the wagon; maybe he growls at you a little. Well, that's me.[83]

Faulkner did in fact attend the conference, arriving in Charlottesville by train on 21 October. Apparently, he drew quite a bit of attention. In a letter written at the end of the conference, on 24 October, Anderson reported that "Bill Faulkner had arrived and got drunk. From time to time he appeared, got drunk again immediately, & disappeared. He kept asking everyone for drinks. If they didn't give him any, he drank his own."[84] From Charlottesville, Faulkner traveled on to New York where he stayed for about seven weeks; again, social and business pressures resulted in heavy drinking.

Though alcohol was sometimes a problem in Faulkner's life, accounts of his drinking and the factors that produced it have been frequently misconstrued. Millgate's assessment of this aspect of Faulkner's life is as accurate as it is levelheaded: "He drank heavily at times, with disastrous results which occasionally necessitated hospital treatment. But these unhappy periods apparently represented the occasional surrenders of a man who was otherwise possessed of tremendous powers of will, determination, and endurance—qualities which alone enabled him to survive the extraordinary personal and practical pressures to which he was subjected for most of his adult life."[85] These pressures would include coping with problems of acute alcoholism among members of his immediate family.

The year that saw the publication of *Sanctuary* was also the year that saw the publication of Faulkner's first collection of short stories, *These 13*, on 21 September 1931. The short-story volume was divided into three parts. Part one consisted of "Victory," "Ad Astra," "All the Dead Pilots," and "Crevasse"—all World War I stories. Part two contained "Red Leaves," "A Rose for Emily," "A Justice," "Hair," "That Evening Sun," and "Dry September"—all dealing with local material. Part three brought the collection to an end with "Mistral," "Divorce in Naples," and "Carcassonne," which were foreign in setting and obviously owed something to Faulkner's 1925 trip. *These 13* was not just a loose assemblage of stories, but was put together by Faulkner with a definite artistic structure.

With 1931 drawing to a close, Faulkner's new publishers had every reason to be pleased. The firm of Jonathan Cape and Harrison Smith had published three novels and one collection of short stories by the young Mississippian. *The Sound and the Fury* had generally received high praise from all corners. *As I Lay Dying* and *Sanctuary* had received serious, if sometimes sensationalistic attention; and *Sanctuary* was a bona fide commercial success, quickly attracting the attention of moviemakers. *These 13* received favorable treatment from the reviewers, though some, like Granville Hicks, felt that Faulkner's strength lay in the writing of novels and that he should keep his energies focused in that direction. The reviews notwithstanding, *These 13* also sold quite well and had to go into a second printing before the end of September.[86]

Thus, when Faulkner and Smith traveled to New York in

October 1931, they would find on their arrival a number of people who were very much interested in publishing books with Faulkner's name on them. The combination of intense lobbying and celebrity treatment contributed to heavy drinking on Faulkner's part; and other events that unfolded during his fall and winter stay in New York would be indicative of certain kinds of problems, mostly of a business nature, that would crop up from time to time during his career.

The Viking Press, Alfred A. Knopf, and especially Random House applied strong pressure on Faulkner. Bennett Cerf wanted to publish *Sanctuary* in the firm's Modern Library series; and Ben Wasson, who had not been able to sell Faulkner's "Idyll in the Desert" to the magazines, thought that Random House might bring it out as a special publication, which they did on 10 December.[87] Faulkner's response to the whole situation was to drink. Smith, anxious to get his author off the firing line, bought two boat tickets and engaged Milton Abernethy—a student at the University of North Carolina who, along with Anthony J. Buttitta, was editing the little magazine *Contempo* and who had driven up from Charlottesville with Smith and Faulkner—to sail with Faulkner to Jacksonville, Florida. After a short stay in Jacksonville, Abernethy and Faulkner traveled to Chapel Hill where Faulkner met Anthony Buttitta and was provided with a room. During all this time—since Faulkner left Oxford—he had been carrying the manuscript of *Light in August* with him.

Faulkner was feeling much better by the time he and Abernethy arrived back in New York in November, having been gone a little more than a week. He was still interested in improving his economic situation as much as possible; and in early November he wrote to his wife: "I have the assurance of a movie agent that I can go to California, to Hollywood and make 500.00 or 750.00 a week in the movies. . . . Hal Smith will not want me to do it, but if all that money is out there, I might as well hack a little on the side and put the novel off. . . .

I have taken in about 300.00 since I got here. It's just like I was some strange and valuable beast, and I believe that I can make 1000.00 more in a month."[88] Though Faulkner was enjoying more economic prosperity than he ever had before from his writing efforts, he was not so firmly in the black that he did not need to be concerned about future income. Some of his recent earnings would be applied to what he had drawn as advances on royalties, and a $440 check he wrote to Mrs. Sallie Bryant on 3 November, one day before his letter to Estelle was post-marked, not only covered his current mortgage payment on Rowan Oak, but made up for the previous six months when he had been able to pay nothing at all.[89]

After the partnership of Jonathan Cape and Harrison Smith dissolved, Smith went into business with Robert Haas, the two forming the publishing company of Smith and Haas. This firm would publish two novels, a collection of verse, and a collection of short stories by Faulkner before he began to be published regularly by Random House in 1936. A problem arose early in 1932 when Faulkner and Haas were proceeding with their plans to bring out a collection of verse, published as *A Green Bough* in 1933. Following up on Faulkner's invitation, Buttitta had visited him at Rowan Oak in early January 1932 and had come away with one short story and ten poems, ostensibly for publication in *Contempo*. But when Smith learned that a limited edition of the *Contempo* poems was being planned, he wrote to Faulkner and received a prompt reply:

> Got your letter. Wired Abernethy at once: he answers that the paper has already gone to press. I'm sorry. I didn't realize at the time what I had got into. Goddamn the paper and goddamn me for getting mixed up with it and goddamn you for sending me off . . . in the shape I was in. I dont think it will happen again. But if I should do so, for God's sake find Ben [Wasson] and turn me on to him next time, for your sake and mine too.[90]

At about the same time Faulkner wrote a letter to Wasson that goes a long way toward explaining his reasons—which had nothing to do with alcohol this time—for cooperating with Buttitta:

> You know that state I seem to get into when people come to see me and I begin to visualise a kind of jail corridor of literary talk. I dont know what in hell it is, except I seem to lose all perspective and do things, like a coon in a tree. As long as they dont bother the hand full of leaves in front of his face, they can cut the whole tree down and haul it off.[91]

Faulkner told Wasson in the same letter that he had not intended to give Buttitta permission to print a limited edition of the poems he gave him, that he understood the material was simply to appear in *Contempo* "without any fuss about it."[92] He concluded with a rueful and somewhat bitter acknowledgment: "But anyway, my country innocence has been taken advantage of. Which is no one's fault except mine, of course. I think I am madder at that than I am at the financial part of it. . . . And I solemnly swear that after this I'll never promise anyone anything without first asking your permission."[93] As if to salvage some of his pride, he wrote very soon after this to Smith concerning the poetry Buttitta had taken from Rowan Oak: "I didn't look at what he chose, having a certain faith in the infallibility of his poetic judgment. i.e., I believed that he would pick the bum ones without my help."[94] Despite these assurances that Faulkner had learned his lesson from the *Contempo* affair, Smith discovered a short time later that Casanova Press of Milwaukee was preparing a special edition entitled *Salmagundi* by William Faulkner. Faulkner explained to Smith that the edition consisted only of material that had been published in the New Orleans *Double Dealer* in 1925. He apologized and once again promised not to become involved in such transactions without discussing them with Smith.

Faulkner did not get himself into professional binds and make bad business deals because of his drinking, but he did have a problem of "innocence" in a way. He would trust people whom he would have been better off not trusting. He would attempt to conduct business on the basis of unwritten, and sometimes unspoken, assumptions. He would divide transactions between literary agents—Ben Wasson, Morton Goldman, and finally Harold Ober—with whom he dealt concerning short-story sales and the publishers and agents with whom he dealt concerning books and motion picture contracts and properties. Yet the dividing line between these various functions was not always clear, and sometimes Faulkner himself got involved in transactions without telling either his agent or publisher what he was up to. These were situations that could produce unhappiness, worry, anxiety, and stress and might therefore contribute to periods of hard drinking. The culmination of unfortunate business arrangements would occur in the 1940s when Faulkner became involved in a long-term contract with Warner Brothers that would drain him emotionally and financially.

III.   1932-1945

In the first months of 1932, Faulkner concerned himself with *Light in August*. As his work on the novel was drawing to a close, he cautiously signed a contract with Smith and Haas to publish his book, which was completed in February. He thought he might make some money by arranging serialization of the novel, and in a letter that demonstrates his confidence as a writer, Faulkner instructed Wasson to be firm in his dealings. "I will not want to take less than $5000.00 for it, and not a word to be changed. This may not sound only hard, but a little swell-headed. But I can get along somehow if it is not serialised. But I will take five thousand and no editing."[95] Wasson was unable to sell serial rights to the novel, but Faulkner was able to make another deal that brought him money quickly. MGM had inquired about his availability as a screen-writer, and, with the help of Wasson's boss Leland Hayward and the Selznick-Joyce Agency in Hollywood, Faulkner got a six-week contract for $500 a week.

On 7 May 1932 Faulkner arrived for his first tour of duty in Hollywood. Questioned about his motion picture work in 1955, he replied: "If I didn't take, or felt I was capable of taking, motion picture work seriously, out of simple honesty to motion pictures and myself too, I would not have tried. But I know now that I will never be a good motion picture writer; so that work will never have the urgency for me which my own medium has."[96] At the same time, Faulkner did not feel that working for the motion pictures would necessarily harm a writer's talent or the integrity of his work. "Nothing can injure a man's writing if he's a first rate writer," he told the same interviewer. "If a man is not a first rate writer, there's not anything can help it much. The problem does not apply if he is not first rate, because he has already sold his soul for a swim-ming pool."[97] "There's some people who are writers who believed they had talent," he commented in 1957, "they get offers to go to Hollywood where they can make a lot of money, they begin to acquire junk swimming pools and im-ported cars, and they can't quit their jobs because they have got to continue to own that swimming pool and the imported cars."[98] Faulkner was never one of these. Even in 1932 he considered himself one of the best writers in America, as he explained to Clark Gable on a dove-hunting expedition with motion picture director and producer Howard Hawks. When Gable showed some interest in modern literature and inquired who the best living writers were, Faulkner gave him a direct answer: "Ernest Hemingway, Willa Cather, Thomas Mann, John Dos Passos, and William Faulkner."[99]

In addition to the frustrations of working in a medium that was not naturally his own, Faulkner was put off by the notoriety attached to him as the author of *Sanctuary*. He did not like living for long periods of time in California, and he continued to like it less and less on each return visit. Doggedly, he tried to protect his privacy as best he could. Joseph Blotner reports that on one social occasion a woman with more curiosity than tact remarked to Faulkner, "I understand that an author always puts himself in his books. Which character are you in *Sanctuary*?" Faulkner replied, "Madam, I was the corncob."[100]

One of the good things that happened to William Faulkner during this time was the development of a strong personal and professional relationship with Hawks. Each man had a deep respect for the other's abilities, and it was Hawks who understood how best to use Faulkner's talents in terms of motion picture scripts. Working with Hawks, Faulkner became what he himself termed a "script doctor." That is, rather than being charged with complete responsibility for developing the treatment of a property, Faulkner would be called on to help strengthen, clarify, or sometimes substantially rewrite portions of scripts that were proving to be problematic. At times, this would actually entail rewriting scenes on set, with actors in their costumes waiting for their new lines. Of course, this is not the only kind of script writing that Faulkner was assigned to during his various periods of employment in Hollywood; but it was in the capacity of "script doctor" that he did his best work in the medium.

Faulkner's contract with MGM provided him with a salary which gave him, he said, "enough momentum to coast a while."[101] In addition, Paramount Corporation had paid $750 for a four-month option on rights to *Sanctuary*, which would be filmed and released in 1933 as *The Story of Temple Drake*. Once that option was exercised, Faulkner stood to gain over $6,000 more.[102] His immediate money problems over, Faulkner was not eager to stay in Hollywood, nor was MGM impressed with his work. He was offered a new contract at

$250 a week, half of his 1932 salary, and he refused it. Hawks wanted Faulkner in Hollywood, though, and asked him to write a screen treatment for his story "Turn About," which Hawks had only recently read. Faulkner was interested in the possibilities of the project and agreed to attempt it. ("I would have made this script for nothing," he told Wasson.) The job completed, Hawks took the script to MGM head Irving Thalberg, who read it and said, "I feel as if I'd make tracks all over it if I touched it. . . . Shoot it as it is."[103] Thus, by 26 July Faulkner was back on the MGM payroll, at a salary of $250 per week. Faulkner remained in Hollywood until 10 August, when he returned to Oxford because of his father's death on the seventh. Jack Falkner remembered that after Murry Falkner died, "Bill considered himself as head of our clan, and so did we. It was a natural role for him, and he assumed it at once, without fanfare, but with dignity and purpose."[104] Faulkner would not be assuming just moral responsibilities, but economic ones as well. As he wrote to Wasson in September 1932, "Dad left mother solvent for only about 1 year. Then it is me."[105] Ultimately, this kind of responsibility would extend beyond Faulkner's and his mother's immediate households.

In the meantime, Faulkner had arranged with MGM before leaving California to continue working on "Turn About" in Oxford. (This was a much more congenial arrangement as far as Faulkner was concerned, and he would attempt similar arrangements in subsequent business dealings with Hollywood.) Faulkner continued to receive his $250 weekly checks, and he received another $2,250 when the option on "Turn About" was taken up by MGM. (The movie, retitled *Today We Live*, was released in April 1933.) He read proofs on *Light in August* in Oxford, and on 3 October, three days before the novel was published, he left for a three-week stay in Hollywood that would end with another termination of his contract. It had not been a bad experience; but he was left with a distinctly sour taste concerning Hollywood agents, who, he felt, took 10 percent of his income and rendered him no service. In November 1932 Faulkner confided to Wasson that he had had another offer from MGM, through Hawks—this time for $600 a week, though his salary was later cut to $300—and that Hawks's brother would represent him as agent, though he expected that the Selznick-Joyce Agency might try to claim a commission if they heard about the deal. Faulkner finished up his work with Hawks in May 1933 without incident, though this early experience contained a foreboding of bad things to come in later dealings with agents and the movie world.

Back at home, with family finances on steady ground at least for the present, Faulkner turned his attention to other things than his own writing. From his days as an aviation cadet in Canada, Faulkner's interest in flying remained undiminished, and in February 1933, while working on film treatments of his own short story "Honor" and of Elliot White Springs's *War Birds*, he began taking flying lessons; by December he was a licensed pilot as well as the owner of a single engine Waco cabin aircraft.

In April 1933 *A Green Bough* was published by Smith and Haas. These were not new poems, but rather a collection of verse dating largely from the 1920s, some of which had been previously published. Faulkner, however, did not just throw together a loose collection of poems; he was too much of a craftsman for that. Rewriting of poetic material was involved, and poems were selected to give the volume a definite structure. "I chose the best ms and built a volume just like a novel," he told Smith.[106] This would be the last volume of original verse by Faulkner to be published.

The chief event of Faulkner's life in 1933 involved neither the movies, aviation, nor writing. It was the birth of a daughter, Jill, on 24 June. Happily, he wrote to Ben Wasson, "Well, bud, we've got us a gal baby named Jill. Born Saturday and both well."[107] In the same letter, Faulkner gave Wasson permission to pursue a very interesting publishing project. Earlier in the year Bennett Cerf, with the permission of Smith and Haas, proposed to Faulkner the publication of a special edition of *The Sound and the Fury* for which Faulkner would write an introduction. Faulkner declined. Now, with his household recently expanded—and having bought three lots bordering his property at Rowan Oak[108]—he became interested in the project once more. He told Wasson, "About Bennett and 'Sound & F.' All Right. Let me know about it, if he will use the colored ink. I like that. I will need time to lay it out again. How many different colors shall I be limited to? Just what does he want in the introduction? I'm ready to start right away. $750.00 is right, is it?"[109] Faulkner was to be paid $750 for writing the introduction to the special edition, which was to be published by the Grabhorn Press in San Francisco. The reference to the use of colored inks in printing the volume concerns an idea Faulkner had had when he was first preparing the novel for publication. That is, rather than italics Faulkner had wanted to use colors to indicate time shifts within the stream-of-consciousness portions of the narrative, particularly Benjy's section. In a 1929 letter to Wasson he had complained, "I wish publishing was advanced enough to use colored ink for such"[110]; now it appeared that at least one publisher was. Accordingly, Faulkner marked up the Benjy section of his own copy of *The Sound and the Fury* in three different colors and sent it to Cerf, who was to have the Grabhorn Press set the section in type. Unfortunately, the project fell through; and even more unfortunately, neither the marked-up book nor the pages set by the press survive. While the project was still alive, though, Faulkner worked steadily at the introduction, an extremely important document. By the middle of August it was ready to be sent to Wasson. "I have worked on it a good deal," Faulkner said in the letter that was enclosed with the manuscript, "like on a poem almost, and I think that it is all right now."[111]

During all this time, Faulkner had continued to think about his Snopes book, but the material had not yet come together in his mind. Concerning work in progress, he wrote to Smith in October 1933 that he was "at the Snopes book, but I have another bee now, and a good title, I think: REQUIEM FOR A NUN."[112] (This novel, after much further work and rethinking, but with the title unchanged, would not be published until 1951.) Smith had also inquired about another collection of short stories, to which Faulkner replied that he would examine his existing files and "see if we can get a book we wont be ashamed of."[113] As it turned out, Faulkner did not get very far with the Snopes book, which he thought would take about two years of steady work, or with *Requiem for a Nun*. Early in 1934 he told Hal Smith that he was working on an altogether different novel. "I have put both the Snopes and the Nun one aside," he said. "The one I am writing now will be called DARK HOUSE or something of that nature. It is the more or less violent breakup of a household or family from 1860 to about 1910. . . . The story is an anecdote which occurred during and right after the civil war; the climax is another anecdote which happened about 1910 and which explains the story."[114] The story Faulkner wanted to tell would eventually become *Absalom, Absalom!*, a novel that would chronicle the rise and eventual destruction of Thomas Sutpen and his family, and which would be published by Random House in 1936. But again, as is the case with the Snopes and *Requiem for a Nun* material, the germ of the story in Faulkner's imagination dates from an earlier period.

Among the materials that Faulkner developed out of his European trip in 1925 were some stories involving a narrator and a traveling companion named Don. One of these stories, dating from about 1930 or 1931, was entitled "Evangeline," but it had a Mississippian rather than a European setting. Between them, the narrator and Don would try to come to terms with the attempts of a character named Colonel Sutpen to create a family dynasty. Carried through many revisions, this is the same story that Quentin Compson would try to explain to Shreve McCannon, his Canadian roommate at Harvard, in *Absalom, Absalom!* By the time in 1934 when Faulkner wrote Smith of his plans for "Dark House," he had already decided that Quentin Compson, of *The Sound and the Fury*, would tell the story.

In November 1933 after Wasson left the American Play Company to go to California, Morton Goldman became Faulkner's agent in New York. While Goldman was responsible for handling short-story sales, Faulkner continued to deal directly with Smith and Haas regarding his novel and collected short-story manuscripts. Faulkner was also looking for some source of economic relief that would enable him to concentrate on a novel—be it the Snopes book, *Requiem for a Nun*, or "Dark House"—for Smith. He was trying to raise money by writing short stories, the returns on which were impossible to predict. His only other alternatives were to draw in advance on his royalties from Smith and Haas or return to Hollywood. Concerning the specific financial responsibilities he had to meet, he explained to Smith that "I have my own taxes and my mother's, and the possibility that Estelle's people will call on me before Feb. 1, and also my mother's and Dean's [Faulkner's youngest brother, Dean Falkner] support, and occasional demands from my other two brothers which I can never anticipate. Then in March I have $700.00 insurance and income tax of about $1500.00."[115] Faulkner's attitude toward writing short fiction for quick magazine sales is not as simple as has sometimes been made out. In many respects the attitude reflected in one of his statements to Goldman—"while I have to write trash, I dont care who buys it, as long as they pay the best price I can get"[116]—is an accurate one. Faulkner's letters amply document his willingness to shape his short-story material to the taste of a particular magazine's readership as long as there was a reasonable chance for a sale. But there were some lines concerning personal and artistic principles he would not cross. For example, transmitting a message through Goldman, he wrote, "Vanity Fair I think it was wrote me for a lynching article. Tell them I never saw a lynching and so couldn't describe one."[117] Faulkner would also draw the line at jeopardizing the integrity of material for which he might have later use in his main fiction.

There is also a sharp distinction to be made between the short stories Faulkner submitted to magazines and the creative energy he expended in putting together short-story collections. Faulkner's second collection of short stories, *Dr. Martino and Other Stories*, was published on 16 April 1934. It contained two stories—"Black Music" and "Leg"—that had not been previously published. The remaining stories in the volume ("Beyond," "Death Drag," "Doctor Martino," "Elly," "Fox Hunt," "Honor," "The Hound," "Mountain Victory," "Smoke," "There Was a Queen," "Turnabout," and "Wash") had appeared in magazines. This collection does not seem to have been as deliberately structured as *These 13*, and generally the reviews were not as favorable as they had been for the first collection. It is a fairly strong collection of individual stories, however, and some of them are among Faulkner's best. As he had promised Smith, there was nothing to be ashamed of in the volume.

Faulkner's interest in flying took him to New Orleans in February 1934 to attend the dedication of Shushan Airport. The events there were dramatic to say the least. One pilot was killed while, flying at night, he failed to complete a loop in his "comet plane"; there were several nonfatal mishaps during the air races; and a harrowing double death occurred when a parachutist's shroud lines became entangled in the aircraft he was to jump from, causing the airplane to crash in Lake Ponchartrain, dragging the parachutist behind it, instantly killing both jumper and pilot.[118] These events sparked Faulkner's imagination, and he soon produced a short story that he called

"This Kind of Courage."[119] Later, in October 1934, he asked
Goldman to return the story to him, explaining, "I am writing
a novel out of it."[120] Faulkner worked rapidly on this project,
and he started mailing chapters of *Pylon* to Smith in
November, completing the task by mid-December. The novel
was published on 25 March 1935.

Faulkner may have turned to *Pylon* in part because of the
difficulties he was having with *Absalom, Absalom!* In the late
summer of 1934 he had written Smith that "the book is not
quite ripe yet. . . . I have not gone my nine months. . . . I
have a mass of stuff, but only one chapter that suits me."[121] He
did say that he had finally settled on a title: "ABSALOM,
ABSALOM; the story is of a man who wanted a son through
pride, and got too many of them and they destroyed
him. . . ."[122] Faulkner had continued to work on *Absalom,
Absalom!* when he was in Hollywood on a brief assignment for
Howard Hawks in July, and by October he may well have
been frustrated over his lack of progress on any novel, *Absalom, Absalom!*, *Requiem for a Nun*, or Snopes. Nonetheless,
Faulkner was able to write *Pylon* in a remarkably short time.

The published sum of Faulkner's creative output in 1933 and
1934 is deceptive. His only published books were *A Green
Bough* and *Doctor Martino and Other Stories*, neither of which
had involved original or new writing. He published three short
stories in 1933 and nine in 1934. This does not, however,
indicate the degree to which his imagination had been engaged.
He wrote more stories than were actually published, and he
put considerable energy into writing the introduction for *The
Sound and the Fury*. He continued to sweat over the Snopes
material, he developed the conception for *Requiem for a Nun*,
he became deeply involved with *Absalom, Absalom!*, and he
wrote *Pylon*.

With the exception of 1937, Faulkner would average one
published novel per year between 1935 and 1940. As was true
of his entire writing career, he continued to produce work of

very high quality in the face of some extreme pressures. One tragic event in 1935 had both personal and economic implications. This was the death of Faulkner's youngest brother, Dean Falkner.

As head of the general Falkner household, Faulkner had been concerned for some time—in much the same way that Faulkner's father and grandfather had been concerned about him—that Dean, who had a reputation for being a bit on the wild side, find something constructive to do with his life, something that he could commit his talents and energies to. It appeared that flying might provide the answer, and Faulkner encouraged Dean in this pursuit. With financial help from Faulkner and with lessons, advice, and encouragement from Memphis pilot Vernon Omlie, who had given Faulkner his flying lessons, Dean was soon qualified as an instructor and was making his living as a professional pilot. In November 1935, Dean was conducting an air circus in Pontotoc. Flying Faulkner's Waco aircraft, he had taken three farmers who wanted to see what their farms looked like from the air for a short ride. Shortly after taking off, the airplane lost a portion of its left wing and crashed, killing everyone on board. Aside from intense grief, Faulkner felt a strong measure of culpability for the accident. Dean's wife, Louise, was four months pregnant at the time of his death. Faulkner discharged the responsibility he felt toward his brother's family in the only way he knew how. He took an active interest in the raising of Dean's daughter, who was also named Dean, and he took upon himself the financial responsibility for her education.

Events involving romance and tragedy were juxtaposed in the same year. In December 1935, Faulkner was hired by Twentieth Century-Fox under a four-week contract that would pay him $1,000 a week, though his employment was extended and Faulkner worked in Hollywood for much of the period until August 1937.[123] He was hired specifically at the request of Howard Hawks, who wanted to have Faulkner's assistance in developing a story line based on a French World War I film entitled *Les Croix des Bois* and which contained documentary combat footage. The tentative title for the American film that would be developed out of the French source was *Wooden Crosses*. The film was released in September 1936 as *Road to Glory* and Faulkner received cocredit with Joel Sayre for the screenplay. Faulkner contributed additional dialogue and wrote the screen story for *Slave Ship* (released in 1937), but though he worked on a number of other produced screenplays during the period (including *Banjo on My Knee*, *Four Men and a Prayer*, *Submarine Patrol*, *Gunga Din*, and *Drums Along the Mohawk*), he was not credited for his work.

It was during this time that Faulkner met Meta Carpenter, a script supervisor and general girl Friday for Howard Hawks. She was born in Memphis, Tennessee, and grew up in Tunica, Mississippi. Beginning in 1935 she and Faulkner had an affair that would last, with many interruptions and long periods of separation, until the 1950s. Carpenter was not the only woman with whom Faulkner had an intimate relationship during his life; but she does appear to be the only one for whom Faulkner seriously considered leaving Estelle, thereby risking his family life in general and custody of his daughter Jill in particular. Faulkner's love affair with Carpenter also seems to have been more durable than any of his other relationships. She is very emphatic in her memoir when she records that Faulkner told her many times that she "was the girl he would surely have married if our paths had only crossed before 1929, when he had taken Estelle as his wife. He was as sure of that as he was of his hand before his face and the fingers attached to it."[124]

Not surprisingly, the early part of their affair was the most intense, and before he left Hollywood to return to Oxford, Faulkner told Carpenter, "When Jill was born, from that time on, Estelle and I have not had anything to do with each other as man and woman. Soon as she could, she moved upstairs at

Rowan Oak to a room of her own. I swear to you . . . we have not had male-female sex since then. Estelle goes to her bed at night, I go to mine."[125] At several points during the early phase of their relationship, Faulkner indicated that he had hopes that Estelle would agree to a divorce. However, it later became obvious that Faulkner would not get custody of Jill and that Estelle would make the divorce proceedings as messy as possible. Shortly after reaching this impasse, Carpenter married the German pianist Wolfgang Rebner in 1936; but the event would not mark the end of her relationship with Faulkner.

Faulkner continued to work on *Absalom, Absalom!* while he was in Hollywood. He finished the job in Oxford in spring of 1936, and the novel was published by Faulkner's new publisher, Random House, on 26 October 1936. The change in publisher resulted from a kind of merger between Smith and Haas and Random House; that is, in late 1935 Robert Haas suggested to Bennett Cerf that Random House buy Smith and Haas, and in January 1936 the deal was completed. Haas and Harrison Smith joined Random House as senior partners.[126] What Random House got was William Faulkner. To Cerf, Faulkner seems to have been primarily a status symbol that he wanted badly for his firm. As Cerf remarked later, "We didn't think he'd *ever* be a commercial success, but he would be the greatest possible adornment to the Random House list."[127]

While Faulkner was still in California in February 1937, he corresponded with Maurice Coindreau, whose work as a critic and translator was largely responsible for Faulkner's high reputation in France, and who now wanted to undertake a challenging job, a French translation of *The Sound and the Fury*. Faulkner's attitude toward the project is enlightening. He respected Coindreau's work, and he was pleased that Coindreau was planning to translate *The Sound and the Fury*, though apparently there were reservations as to how well this could be done:

After reading 'As I Lay Dying' in your translation, I am happy that you are considering undertaking S & F. I want to see this translation, indeed, because I feel that it will probably be a damned poor book, but it may be a damned good one (in French, I mean, of course) but in either case, particularly in the latter, it will be Coindreau and not Faulkner, just as the Rubaiyat which English speaking people know is a little more Fitzgerald than Khayyam.[128]

Faulkner had a very definite notion of what constituted *his* work; namely, that which bore the stamp of his own sweat and blood. The same attitude would surface a few years later when Faulkner and Malcolm Cowley began their correspondence concerning the Viking Press's *Portable Faulkner*.

The next of Faulkner's books to be published by Random House were *The Unvanquished* (1938) and *The Wild Palms* (1939). Faulkner's work on both volumes dates from an earlier time. Writing to Morton Goldman in the summer of 1937, Faulkner reported that "Random House is going to collect the Civil War stories we sold the Post into a book. They needed one more story to finish them, which I have just completed, named 'An Odor of Verbena.' "[129] Three of the stories Faulkner referred to in his letter were published in the *Saturday Evening Post* in 1934. The fourth and fifth were published in the *Post* in 1936, and the sixth story in the series appeared in *Scribner's Magazine* in 1935. "An Odor of Verbena" was tried out on the *Post* but was rejected; thus its first appearance in print was as the last chapter of *The Unvanquished*. *The Unvanquished* was published on 15 February 1938, and the screen rights to the novel were purchased by MGM for $25,000, leaving Faulkner with $19,000 after commissions.

In the winter of 1937-1938 Faulkner made two important land purchases calculated to provide him increased privacy and a more reliable base of income from timber and farming. First, he bought the four lots adjoining Rowan

Oak that comprised Bailey's Woods. Two months later, in February, he bought a 320-acre tract which he later named Greenfield Farm. This last purchase proved to be more of an economic liability than an asset. Once he had made the purchase, though, Faulkner had no intention of selling, for the farm was valuable to him in other ways. As Michael Millgate observed, "its main importance was that it gave him an opportunity to acquire the kind of knowledge about farming—about the crops, the animals, the seasons, the weather, the land, and, not least, the tenants—without which he could scarcely have written such books as *The Hamlet* and *Go Down, Moses*. It also provided minimal justification for one of his favourite tongue-in-cheek remarks, that he was not a literary man at all, but a farmer."[131]

The sale of the movie rights to *The Unvanquished* also produced some misunderstanding between Faulkner and his agent, Goldman. The lack of any previous written understanding between the two men was a significant factor in their dealings. Goldman felt that as Faulkner's agent he was owed 10 percent of the sale price of the seven stories that had appeared in *The Unvanquished* that MGM bought. After Random House's 20 percent share, this would have amounted to $2,000. Faulkner had a different understanding, and he wrote to Goldman in February 1938 that he construed short-story and novel sales, even when short-story material was involved, to be two different matters. They finally agreed that Goldman would get a $1,000 commission from the MGM sale, but Faulkner had acute regrets that there had not been a clearer understanding on the matter. "But that was my fault," he wrote Goldman, "and I am grateful for your offer to compromise, even though I do feel I have been screwed about 600.00 worth. But then, you probably feel you have been screwed 1,000.00, which is worse, I reckon."[132]

Part of his work on the volume had taken him to New York

in October 1937 where he saw Meta Carpenter, now married to Wolfgang Rebner, once more. She and her husband were living in New York. Faulkner telephoned, and Rebner suggested that they all three meet later in the evening. The reunion seemed to be pleasant enough, and arrangements were made for the Rebners to meet Faulkner at his hotel the following evening for dinner. When they arrived at the lobby of Faulkner's hotel, the Algonquin, there was no sign of their host. Told at the desk that Faulkner was ill, they went up to his room to see if there was anything they could do. The Rebners found Faulkner in a semiconscious state and in great pain. He explained to Carpenter that he had started drinking very heavily after seeing her the previous evening. At some point he had gone into his small hotel bathroom, had fallen with his back against a hot steam pipe, and had been unable to move himself from it. He had been found by a friend, Jim Devine, who discovered him lying face down and unconscious on the floor of his hotel room. Exactly how long he lay against the steam pipe is not known, but the result was painfully clear: "In the small of his back, on the left side in the area of the kidney, was a third-degree burn the size of the palm of a hand," which would require skin grafting and a long, uncomfortable healing process.[133]

Years later, Faulkner told Joan Williams that he wrote *The Wild Palms* "to stave off what I thought was heart-break."[134] Though Blotner holds up Helen Baird—an artist and sculptress Faulkner met in Pascagoula in 1925 and to whom he dedicated *Mosquitoes*—as a model for the character of Charlotte Ritenmeyer in *The Wild Palms*, the sequence of events points to Carpenter, not necessarily as a specific character model, but at least as a catalyst and source of inspiration. On the day *The Wild Palms* was published in 1939, Faulkner asked Cerf to send a copy of the book to Mrs. Wolfgang Rebner, who remembered being struck by Harry Wilbourne's last lines: "*between grief and nothing I will take grief.*"[135] And in a letter written to Carpenter in the late 1940s, Faulkner elaborated on the quality of grief: "I know grief is the inevitable part of it, the thing that makes it cohere; that grief is the only thing you are capable of sustaining, keeping; that what is valuable is what you have lost, since then you never had the chance to wear out and so lose it shabbily. . . ."[136]

If Carpenter's recollections are accurate, Faulkner was working on the novel that would be published as *The Wild Palms* as early as 1936. The earliest documentary reference to the novel is in a November 1937 letter to Haas. Faulkner reports, "I have got into the novel. It has not begun to move very fast yet, but I imagine it will soon and that I will be able to send it in by May first [1938]."[137] Faulkner's own title for the novel (*If I Forget Thee, Jerusalem*) was scriptural, and he fought a losing battle to have it kept as the title of the published book. A July 1938 letter to Haas concerned the deletion of objectionable words from the novel, and Faulkner proposed a compromise:

> why not let me swap you the objectionable words for the title? you to do as you see fit about the words, and let the title stand? The movies could change it as they did Sanctuary, and I think it is a good title. It invented itself as a title for the chapter in which Charlotte died and where Wilbourne said "Between grief and nothing I will take grief" and which is the theme of the whole book . . . just as "The Unvanquished" was the title of the story of Granny's struggle between her morality and her children's needs, which was the theme of that book and which we extended to cover the whole book successfully. Dont you think this title might do the same?[138]

Though persuasive, Faulkner's argument was not quite persuasive enough, and the novel was published as *The Wild Palms* on 19 January 1939.

By the latter part of 1938 the Snopes material Faulkner had

had on his mind for so long had started coming together. He wrote to Haas in December that the Snopes story would be divided into three books, though he was not certain whether or not these would be separate volumes. The first book, or volume, was to be called *The Peasants*, the second *Rus in Urbe*, and the third *Ilium Falling*. The outline of the main action, as he described it to Haas, was essentially the same as that which would be developed in *The Hamlet, The Town*, and *The Mansion*.[139] Work on the first book moved along at a good pace and early in February 1939 Haas received word from Faulkner that he had completed some 215 pages. By March, Faulkner was still calling the first volume *The Peasants* and was planning to structure the work in four books.[140] In the same month he decided that the entire Snopes story would be told in three volumes, and he was apparently working at the project with energy, enthusiasm, and confidence. He continued to shape and reshape the first volume, and in April he reported to Haas that "The book was getting too thin, diffuse. I have tightened it up, added some more here and there to give it density, make the people stand up. As you can see, the portion you have, as corrected, constitutes but *one* book, which is BOOK ONE, Chapters 1-5. There will be two books in the first volume." In pen, Faulkner added a postscript: "I am the best in America, by God."[141] When published, *The Hamlet* consisted of four books—"Flem," "Eula," "The Long Summer," and "The Peasants"—and by the fall of 1939 Faulkner had pretty well decided on the titles for the three volumes constituting the trilogy: *The Hamlet, The Town*, and *The Mansion*.[142] Faulkner was not always a careful proofreader, and his handling of the galleys for *The Hamlet* is a case in point. Returning proof to Haas in early February 1940, he wrote: "I read carefully only about halfway through galley, after that I merely answered indicated queries. But it seems to be a very clear printing, and from what of it I did read word for word, the mss. was followed to the letter. So I am sure it's all right."[143] The novel was published on 1 April 1940.

Apparently, the revenue Faulkner cleared from the sale of *The Unvanquished* was quickly eaten up by taxes, the purchase of Greenfield Farm, operating expenses for Rowan Oak, and family. In addition, Faulkner's erstwhile mentor, Phil Stone, was deeply in debt, which was compounded by the fact—as Faulkner later told James B. Meriwether—that "a mean woman here in Oxford was foreclosing on him."[144] Concerning Stone's problems, Faulkner had written to Haas in March 1939, "I have a friend here, I have known him all my life, never any question of mine and thine between us when either had it. His father died a few years ago, estate badly involved, is being sued on $7000.00 note, which will cause whole business to be sold up. He must have money in 3 weeks."[145] Faulkner got $3,000 from Random House—not a gift, of course, but an advance on royalties—and estimated that he could get another $3,300 by cashing in his life insurance policy. He also gave a Memphis bank an assignment on his royalties; and if necessary, he said he would be willing to sell some of his manuscripts, which he had viewed as a primary source of financial security for Jill.

The toll that financial worries took on Faulkner's peace of mind and creative energy is impossible to measure. The more he was pressured to write short stories to produce income, the more frustrated he became. "I have written 4 short stories this year," he told Haas in April 1940, shortly after *The Hamlet* had been published, "and I would have been all right if they sold as I wrote them. But maybe a man worrying about money cant write anything worth buying. . . ."[146] At times he resented deeply that as an artist—"a sincere one and of the first class"—he nevertheless found himself as "the sole, principal and partial support—food, shelter, heat, clothes, medicine, kotex, school fees, toilet paper and picture shows—of my mother . . . brother's widow and child, a wife of my own and two step children, my own child; I inherited my father's debts and his dependents, white and black without inheriting yet from anyone one inch of land or one stick of furniture or one cent of money. . . ."[147] Yet despite these pressures, Faulkner seems not to have lost completely his sense of humor. In the same letter to Haas he suggests:

> What I need is some East Indian process to attain to the nigger attitude about debt. One of them is discussing the five dollars he must pay before sunset to his creditor, canvasses all possibilities, completes the circle back to the point of departure, where there is simply no way under heaven for him to get five dollars, says at last, "Well, anyway, he (the creditor) cant eat me." "How you know he cant?" the second says. "Maybe he wont want to," the first says.[148]

Despite flashes of a healthy wit and humor, Faulkner's frustrations were nevertheless real and long lasting. His aggregate family continued to be an emotional and financial responsibility. As he told Harold Ober, who replaced Goldman as Faulkner's literary agent in 1942, "I have been trying for about ten years to carry a load that no artist has any business attempting: oldest son to widowed mothers and inept brothers and nephews and wives and other female connections and their children, most of whom I dont like and with none of whom I have anything in common, even to make conversation about. I am either not brave enough or not scoundrel enough to take my hat and walk out. . . ." But here again there was a dividing line that Faulkner was determined not to cross: "if it's really beginning to hurt my work, I will choose pretty damn quick," he added.[149] Thus the period of the 1940s, until after World War II, generally was not a pleasant one for Faulkner. Nonetheless, as Millgate has pointed out, there is no apparent decline in the quality of Faulkner's work, though the specter of flagging powers was one that occasionally raised itself in Faulkner's mind during periods of depression.[150]

Faulkner attempted a number of different ploys to keep from having to mortgage or sell off part of his property. He let banks take assignments on his royalties, and he proposed drawing royalties in advance on books he had not yet written. In May 1940 he outlined to Haas a plan for "a sort of Huck Finn" book,[151] which would be published as *The Reivers* in 1962. Later in 1940 he even considered leaving Random House and moving to the Viking Press when it appeared that he might be better off financially with Viking.

The most immediate solution to his financial problems seemed to be a return to Hollywood, where, in part because of past drinking problems, he was not particularly marketable. Faulkner would eventually get to Hollywood; but, again due to lack of attention to business details, it would not be a very satisfactory arrangement. A Hollywood agent, William Herndon, had been contacted by Stephen Longstreet, a screenwriter Faulkner liked and with whom he spent time when in Hollywood. With Faulkner's permission, Herndon started trying in May 1941 to land a screenwriting job for his client, and to sell any properties in which he might be able to interest a studio. Later, in July 1942, having heard nothing about a studio job from Herndon and presuming him to have been unsuccessful, Faulkner began dealing with H. N. Swanson, Ober's representative on the West Coast. Herndon learned that Swanson was about to close a deal with Robert Buckner at Warner Brothers. He told Faulkner he had approached Warner Brothers first and would take legal action if Faulkner dealt through anyone but him. Faulkner explained the Herndon matter in a July 1942 letter to Ober: "Even if he had nothing to do with this particular deal and perhaps never even thought of me again until he heard somebody else was trying to sell me, there is still the fact that he brought me to Buckner's notice and the former business did exist, of which this may be a byproduct."[152] He wanted to go ahead and pay Herndon's full commission and so, he thought, wipe the slate clean. The letter ended with instructions to Ober to hold any checks that might be coming to him until he had arrived in California. "I do not want checks to come here [Oxford] in my absence," Faulkner explained, "as they will be misapplied."[153] Faulkner arrived in California in late July, thinking that he was facing nothing more than a thirteen-week contract. What he discovered was that Herndon had obligated him to a seven-year contract at a starting salary of only $300 per week, a very low figure for a man of Faulkner's stature and experience. Despite the fact that Ober and Swanson generously withdrew any claims they might have made for a commission, and though Ober advised Faulkner to close directly with the studio, he signed the contract that Herndon had negotiated, explaining to Ober that he had been promised that once he had proved himself to the studio, the present contract would be torn up and a new one written. Not surprisingly, this promise, which existed as an oral understanding only, was never fulfilled. Even though Faulkner was eventually able to arrange to go off pay from the studio for periods of time and work in Oxford, and even though he finally managed a release from the contract, it was an unpleasant situation, one that increased rather than relieved his frustrations, and which had a negative impact on his writing.

Nonetheless, Faulkner was involved in two of Howard Hawks's most notable movies of the period, both starring Humphrey Bogart and Lauren Bacall. With Jules Furthman Faulkner wrote the screenplay for *To Have and Have Not* (released 20 January 1945), adapted from Hemingway's novel; and with Furthman and Leigh Brackett he wrote the screenplay for *The Big Sleep* (released 31 August 1946), adapted from Raymond Chandler's novel. He also worked on at least six projects that were never produced, including a film treatment of *Absalom, Absalom!*

America's involvement in World War II produced ambivalent feelings for Faulkner. At times he felt that "what will be left after this one will certainly not be worth living for";[154] but this does not seem to have been a dominant feeling. Faulkner tried several times, unsuccessfully, to obtain a commission in the armed services, and he told his stepson, Malcolm Franklin, that he intended to do "as much as anyone else can to make secure the manner of living I prefer and that suits my kin and kind."[155] In the same letter, written shortly before Franklin himself entered service, Faulkner stressed, "We must see that the old Laodicean smell doesn't rise again after this one. But we must preserve what liberty and freedom we already have to do that." Once the struggle had been won in the field, he said, "perhaps the time of the older men will come, the ones like me who are articulate in the national voice, who are too old to be soldiers, but are old enough and have been vocal long enough to be listened to, yet are not so old that we too have become another batch of decrepit old men looking stubbornly backward at a point 25 or 50 years in the past."[156]

It would be grossly incorrect to assume that World War II represented an awakening in Faulkner's social consciousness of principles he did not already hold. It is true, however, that in his letters he begins speaking of certain issues more explicitly than he had before; and after the war, particularly in the 1950s, he became quite vocal on issues of privacy, race, justice, and education. One event affected Faulkner very deeply. He learned in 1943 that Haas's only son, who was serving as a pilot on an aircraft carrier, had been killed in action. The letter of sympathy Faulkner wrote to Haas is as moving as it is brief. He mentioned the pride that "belongs to all the ex-airmen whom time has altered into grounded old men, and some of the grief is theirs too whose blood flies in this war." He told Haas that his nephew was being trained as a carrier pilot, and then wrote: "who knows? the blood of your fathers and the blood of mine side by side at the same long table in Valhalla, talking of glory and heroes, draining the cup and banging the empty pewter on the long board to fill again, holding two places for us maybe, not because we were heroes or not heroes, but because we loved them."[157] Three days later, on 4 July 1943, Faulkner wrote a very different kind of letter about Haas to Malcolm Franklin, telling him at first what a generous friend the senior Haas had always been:

> He had an only son, and a daughter. In '40, the son withdrew from Yale and became a Navy pilot. In '41, the girl about 20, joined that Women's Ferry Squadron, is now flying, ferrying aeroplanes from factories to bases. The boy was flying torpedo planes off carriers . . . in the Pacific. He was killed last week. The girl is still flying. All Jews. I just hope I dont run into some hundred percent American Legionnaire until I feel better.[158]

Faulkner then expanded from this particular event to a more general issue. He reflected that on the same day that a squadron of Negro pilots risked their lives in the air, white policemen killed twenty black people in Detroit. He ended the letter emphatically; positive social change would have to emerge from the war. "If it doesn't," Faulkner declared, "if the politicians and the people who run this country are not forced to make good the shibboleth they glibly talk about freedom, liberty, human rights, then you young men who live through it will have wasted your precious time, and those who dont live through it will have died in vain.[159]

There were, however, some positive occurrences during this time. *Go Down, Moses*—which, along with *The Hamlet*, is considered by some critics as one of the two masterpieces of Faulkner's maturity—was published on 11 May 1942. In 1944 he began the correspondence with Cowley that led to the publication of the Viking *Portable Faulkner*. Out of an informal partnership with two Hollywood movie men, William Bacher and Henry Hathaway, he began working on an idea for a film that would become, some years later, his sixteenth novel, *A Fable*. And earlier, in July 1941, he received a kind of recognition that pleased him greatly. Warren Beck published three articles on Faulkner that year in which he made a strong and lucid case for the moral base of Faulkner's fiction and attempted to explain the relationships between the writer's subject matter and his style.[160] He sent copies of the articles to Faulkner, and Faulkner's response to Beck is significant because it is one of the few times that he ever bothered to "explain" his own work:

> I have been writing all the time about honor, truth, pity, consideration, the capacity to endure well grief and misfortune and injustice and then endure again, in terms of individuals who observed and adhered to them not for reward but for virtue's own sake, not even merely because they are admirable in themselves, but in order to live with oneself and die peacefully with oneself when the time comes. . . . I believe there are some, not necessarily many, who do and will continue to read Faulkner and say, "Yes. It's all right. I'd rather be Ratliff than Flem Snopes. And I'd still rather be Ratliff without any Snopes to measure by even."[161]

Despite the frustrations and doubts that shadowed Faulkner through a rough time in his life, he emerged with the principles and convictions expressed in his letter to Beck unshaken.

IV.   1946-1950

By September 1945, Faulkner was entirely frustrated by his contract with Warner Brothers, which he considered oppressive. He felt that his work for the studio was demanding too much of his time and was keeping him from completing his new novel, *A Fable*. He applied for a leave of absence to work in Oxford on the novel and was informed by Finlay McDermid, the head of Warner's story department, that a six-month leave could be arranged if Faulkner would guarantee the studio

first refusal on motion picture rights. Faulkner declined. "I've
got ink poisoning,"[162] he protested.

On 18 September, Faulkner left the studio without permission and returned to Oxford, but he did not leave his contract
problems with Warner Brothers behind. On 15 October 1945,
he wrote to Jack Warner, head of the studio, to make a direct
plea for release from his obligations to the studio: "I feel that I
have made a bust at moving picture writing and therefore have
mis-spent and will continue to mis-spend time which at my age
I cannot afford. . . . And I dont dare mis-spend any more of
it."[163] Warner refused Faulkner's request, and the matter went
unresolved through the winter, while Ober, Haas, and Cerf, a
personal friend of Warner's, tried to negotiate for Faulkner the
time he needed to finish his book, without further obligating
him to the studio. Throughout this period, Faulkner had resigned himself to returning to Hollywood and stayed in Oxford
only as a result of the frequent assurances of Ober and Haas
that they would do all they could to get his contract voided.
Moreover, Random House provided him with a $2,000 ad-
vance on *A Fable* to ease his financial problems as he was
writing the novel. Finally, on 28 March 1946, Ober, Haas, and
Cerf were successful. Jack Warner said he was no longer
interested in rights to Faulkner's novel and agreed to release
Faulkner until the novel was finished.

One month later, in April 1946, a book was published that
contributed significantly to a critical reevaluation of Faulkner's
work. The book was *The Portable Faulkner*, edited by Cowley. Cowley had first written Faulkner in spring 1944. He
observed that Faulkner's reputation among other writers was
high: "there you hear almost nothing but admiration," he said,
"and the better the writer the greater the admiration is likely to
be. Conrad Aiken, for example, puts you up at the top of the
heap."[164] According to Cowley, the "academic and near-
academic critics" had generally misunderstood and misstated
the importance of Faulkner's work.[165] And in another letter he

gave Faulkner an indication of his critical reputation in France by quoting Jean-Paul Sartre: *"Pour les jeunes en France, Faulkner c'est un dieu."* (For the youth of France, Faulkner is a god.)[166]

Cowley had edited a *Portable Hemingway* for the Viking Press and persuaded the publishers to undertake a *Portable Faulkner*, which would be a collection—not a complete one, of course—of Faulkner's work, taking material from both the short stories and the novels dealing with Yoknapatawpha County. Faulkner endorsed the idea, writing Cowley in the summer of 1945, "By all means let us make a Golden Book of my apocryphal county. I have thought of spending my old age doing something of that nature."[167] Faulkner appreciated what Cowley was trying to do, and he cooperated every way he could; at the same time he had a very definite idea about whose book it was. He wrote to Cowley late in 1945, "It's not a new work by Faulkner. It's a new work by Cowley all right though."[168] There were also some reservations that tempered Faulkner's enthusiasm. Concerning Cowley's introduction to his work, he remarked, "I don't see too much Southern legend in it";[169] and he was as adamant as ever concerning biographical details: "I would have preferred nothing at all prior to the instant I began to write, as though Faulkner and Typewriter were concomitant, conadjutant and without past on the moment they first faced each other at the suitable (nameless) table."[170]

Reservations aside, Faulkner seems to have been genuinely pleased with the final product. Writing to Cowley in April 1946, shortly after the volume had been published, he said, "The job is splendid. Damn you to hell anyway. But even if I had beat you to the idea, mine wouldn't have been this good. By God, I didn't know myself what I had tried to do, and how much I had succeeded."[171] Faulkner also provided Cowley with some original material to be included in the Viking *Portable Faulkner*. This was the "Compson Appendix," a summary (or obituary, as Faulkner later called it) of family members and a few other characters involved with Compson family history. It began with the Indian Ikkemotubbe, "A dispossessed American king," and ended with four black characters: T. P., Frony, Luster, and Dilsey.[172]

At about this same time, Random House was planning a republication of *The Sound and the Fury* and *As I Lay Dying*, combined in one volume. Random House editor Robert Linscott wanted Faulkner to write an introduction for the volume, which Faulkner resisted until that aspect of the project was finally abandoned. Nor was Faulkner overly excited about printing *The Sound and the Fury* and *As I Lay Dying* together. Though he did not try to block the project, Faulkner told Linscott in March 1946, "I dont agree with you about printing TSAF and AS I LAY DYING together. It's as though we were saying 'this is a versatile guy; he can write in the same stream of consciousness style about princes and then peasants,' or 'This is a universal writer; he has written about all the kinds of people in Miss. in the same style.' "[173] But if the volume was going to exist, Faulkner was all in favor of the "Compson Appendix" being part of it, and he had some very definite ideas about what it would contribute to the volume. An introduction, he thought, was no more than "deliberate pandering to those who wont make the effort to understand the book"; whereas the appendix was "the key to the whole book; after reading this, any reader will understand all the other sections."[174] He also felt that the appendix should be placed before the text of *The Sound and the Fury*, and he instructed Linscott: "Viking titled the appendix *The* Compsons. It should be, simply:

COMPSON

1699   1945

Because it's really an obituary, not a segregation."[175]

The work that most consumed Faulkner's interest in the spring of 1946 was *A Fable*, which he worked at for the better part of ten years. In June 1946, he told Haas, "I believe now it's

not just my best but perhaps the best of my time."[176] And in
June of the following year he reported, "It's getting right now.
It was a tragedy of ideas, morals, before; now it's getting to be a
tragedy of people."[177] Late in 1947 he asked Ober, "Will
anybódy read it in the next say 25 years? . . . My own time
doesn't count," he said. "I dont believe I am wasting it or I
would have stopped before now. There is nothing wrong with
the book as it will be, only it may be 50 years before the world
can stop to read it."[178] Up until the time the novel was published, Faulkner continued to speculate. "It is either nothing
and I am blind in my dotage, or it is the best of my time," he
told Saxe Commins in 1953.[179]

Faulkner put his manuscript of *A Fable* aside in the early
part of 1948 and started another project. In February he told
Ober, "I now have 60 pages on an approximate 120 page short
novel set in my apocryphal Jefferson. . . . a Negro in jail
accused of murder and waiting for the white folks to drag him
out and pour gasoline over him and set him on fire, is the
detective, solves the crime because he goddamn has to to keep
from being lynched."[180] The novel would end up a bit longer
than Faulkner had anticipated and would be published as *Intruder in the Dust* on 27 September 1948. It was in some
respects a case of fortunate timing, because MGM purchased
the motion-picture rights to the novel for $50,000, thus giving
Faulkner a measure of financial security (his share amounted to
$40,000) that he had not enjoyed for a long time.[181] It would
also give him a degree of notoriety, which he was not at all
interested in, in the town of Oxford when the film was made on
location there. And the critics, reviewing the novel, picked up
on its political implications and speculated as to whether it
represented an awakening of social conscience on the part of
the author, which assumed, at least by implication, that he had
not had one before or else he would have expressed it in earlier
novels. *Intruder in the Dust* also contained a character—a
Jefferson lawyer named Gavin Stevens, similar in some ways to

Oxford lawyer Stone—who some critics and scholars would incorrectly identify as Faulkner's moral mouthpiece.

Regardless of what other people might be saying about him, Faulkner had his own notions regarding his worth as a writer. In a 1947 class conference at the University of Mississippi, responding to a question asking him to rate who he thought the significant writers of the time were, Faulkner classified the following group, not on the basis of what they had achieved, but on the basis of what they had attempted, or risked, as artists:

> 1. Thomas Wolfe—he had much courage, wrote as if he didn't have long to live. 2. William Faulkner. 3. Dos Passos. 4. Hemingway—he has no courage, has never climbed out on a limb. He has never used a word where the reader might check his usage by a dictionary. 5. Steinbeck—I had great hopes for him at one time. Now I don't know.[182]

Portions of Faulkner's comments were published in the *New York Herald Tribune*, and the use of the term *courage* was misunderstood badly, particularly by Ernest Hemingway. A much more explicit statement concerning what Faulkner regarded as his literary reputation was made in a letter to Ober in 1946. "In France," Faulkner said, "I am the father of a literary movement. In Europe I am considered the best modern American and among the first of all writers. In America, I eke out a hack's motion picture wages."[183]

In 1948 Random House suggested that a collected volume of Faulkner short stories be assembled for publication, and Faulkner enthusiastically endorsed the idea, beginning immediately to think about stories that might be included. "I would like to mull over it," he told Haas, "try to give this volume an integrated form of its own, like the Moses book if possible, or at least These 13."[184] When published on 2 August 1950, the volume contained forty-two stories organized under six section headings: "The Country," "The Village," "The Wilderness," "The Wasteland," "The Middle Ground," and "Beyond." Another volume of stories, however, was collected and published before this one. Faulkner began to have second thoughts about the big collection later in 1948 and wrote to Saxe Commins, who was then his editor at Random House, that perhaps they were being premature in thinking about a collected edition. "I am thinking of a 'Gavin Stevens' volume," he explained, "more or less detective stories . . . in which Stevens solves or prevents crime to protect the weak, right injustice, or punish evil."[185] The volume would also contain one story "in which Stevens prevents a crime . . . not for justice but to gain . . . the childhood sweetheart which he lost 20 years ago."[186] This last story was called "Knight's Gambit," also the title for the collection, which was published on 27 November 1949.

As in previous years, Faulkner continued to be very protective of his privacy. When Cowley informed Faulkner in May 1946 that a visiting Russian writer wanted to see him in Oxford, Faulkner shot back a reply: "Thank you for warning me. What the hell can I do? Goddamn it I've spent almost fifty years trying to cure myself of the curse of human speech, all for nothing. . . . I swear to Christ being in Hollywood was better than this where nobody knew me or cared a damn."[187] In 1949, he stubbornly resisted having a *Life* magazine personality profile done on him; and, when informed in November 1950 that he had won the Nobel Prize for 1949, he downplayed the award—he had earlier said that he would "rather be in the same pigeon hole with Dreiser and Sherwood Anderson [neither of whom ever won the Nobel], than with Sinclair Lewis and Mrs. Chinahand Buck."[188] For a while he indicated that he did not intend to go to Stockholm to receive it. Of course, he did go, taking his daughter Jill, who was then in high school, with him. "I dont at all regret going to Stockholm now," he told Haas's wife after his return, "I realise it was the only thing to do; you can commit mistake and only feel regret, but when you commit bad taste, what you feel is shame."[189]

In some respects, Faulkner's Nobel speech was as widely misinterpreted as some of his fictional works had been. Those who praised it for its humanity and compassion and those who challenged its message as being inconsistent with views expressed in Faulkner's published work missed completely the fact that the address was aimed primarily at other writers, "the young men and women already dedicated to the same anguish and travail" of the writer's craft.[190] He did not predict that man would achieve victory over his material or spiritual environment; he said only that he would "prevail" in the sense that human nature would continue to exist to be dealt with, and that therefore the young writer must learn to write about people, not the conditions that affect people. Failing that, "His griefs grieve on no universal bones, leaving no scars. He writes not of the heart but of the glands."[191]

Even though he had neither asked nor sought it, the recognition given to him by the Nobel Prize seems also to have given Faulkner a sharper sense of public responsibility than he had had before. He continued to protect his privacy from uninvited intrusions, but he also became more vocal in speaking out on public issues. He undertook travel at the request of the State Department, attended conferences, and made occasional addresses. But above all he continued to be a writer.

V.   1951-1962

As Faulkner moved into the post-Nobel period of his life, he would comment from time to time to various people that he felt he must be near the bottom of the barrel, that soon there would be nothing left for him to write. Such sentiments, however, even during periods of depression, do not appear to have lasted very long. Indeed, the entire last period of Faulkner's life, despite some intense personal, physical, and psychological problems, is one that reflects confidence in his talents and a lifelong commitment to his art. "I had thought," he said in 1955, "that perhaps with A FABLE, I would find myself empty of anything more to say, do. But I was wrong."[192] And later in the same year he acknowledged, "I know I wont live long enough to write all I need to write about my imaginary country and county, so I must not waste what I have left."[193] But perhaps his two strongest statements were made to Saxe Commins and to Joan Williams, a young writer of whom Faulkner was enamored. Writing to Commins in 1953 about his progress with *A Fable* — it was going well and he was excited about it — he said, as though striking his fist on a table for emphasis, "Damn it, I did have genius. . . . It just took me 55 years to find out. I suppose I was too busy working to notice it before."[194] To Williams, also in 1953, Faulkner expressed a profound sense of amazement over what he had achieved:

> uneducated in every formal sense, without even very literate, let alone literary, companions, yet to have made the things I made. I dont know where it came from. I dont know why God or gods or whoever it was, selected me to be the vessel. Believe me, this is not humility, false modesty: it is simply amazement.[195]

Faulkner also had more than his share of problems during the period of the early and mid-1950s. The cumulative effect of repeated back injuries caused him extreme physical pain; and given the choice between enduring pain and having his spine surgically fused, he chose the pain. Extremely intense and long-lasting physical discomfort is enough in itself to bring on severe depression. With Faulkner this was compounded by his occasional reliance on alcohol and self-dosings of other drugs to combat the pain in his back. In turn, these practices had a generally debilitating effect on his health, and in some cases necessitated hospitalization. Much of this depression, however, was caused not just by Faulkner's physical condition, but also by his observations of the world around him. Racial and other social problems, particularly in his native state, led him to protest on one occasion that "human beings are terrible. One must believe well in man to endure him, wait out his folly and savagery and inhumanity."[196] There were affairs of the heart during this period that would contribute to Faulkner's melancholy. Yet some of Faulkner's most important work was published during this time, and none of it represented a lessening of talent.

Between 1951 and 1962, Faulkner had relationships of different kinds with three women: Jean Stein, Else Jonsson, and Joan Williams. Stein was nineteen years old when Faulkner met her in Switzerland in December 1953, while he was working on a motion-picture assignment for Howard Hawks. She was frequently in his company during the short time he was in Europe, he saw her occasionally in later years in New York, and he wrote to her frequently. Faulkner's relationship with Stein was an intimate one, and it lasted for several years; but its most significant by-product was of a public rather than a personal nature. *Paris Review* editor George Plimpton had long wanted to have an interview with Faulkner published in his magazine. With Stein as the interviewer, Faulkner agreed. The result was a rarity: an interview in which Faulkner was not only a willing and cooperative participant, but for which he may have actually composed the questions.

Jonsson was the wife of Swedish journalist Thorsten Jonsson, who had visited Faulkner in Oxford and predicted that he would be a recipient of the Nobel Prize.[197] Else Jonsson first met Faulkner when he was in Stockholm to receive his award. Subsequently divorced from her husband, she and Faulkner became correspondents, and she was frequently in his company during his later visits to Europe. It was she who arranged an appointment for Faulkner with a masseur in Norway when the author was in Europe in 1952 and was virtually incapacitated by the pain in his back. The masseur's treatment was more successful than any he had received previously, leaving him, as he told friends after his return to Oxford, with "no back pain at all any more, the first time in years, I realise now."[198] In his letters to Jonsson, Faulkner confided some of his most troubling thoughts about his work and life.

The most important of the three women with whom Faulkner was close in his later years was Joan Williams, a young woman from Memphis with aspirations of being a serious writer. Faulkner helped her both personally and professionally and in doing so revealed much about himself. Williams first met Faulkner in 1949 when she was twenty-one and Faulkner was fifty-one.[199] He was strongly attracted to the young woman to the point that he wanted more than just a platonic or teacher-student relationship. He also realized that Williams needed to mature if she were to make good her intent to be a serious writer. Though emotionally involved, he was candid with his criticisms. Writing to her about the story that would eventually be developed into her novel *The Morning and the Evening*, Faulkner commented that he would have to "write almost as many words explaining what I mean, as I would need to write the story itself, which would be much easier."[200] He feared that his letter might discourage her too much:

> You worked hard at this story. I know that. Where you didn't work hard enough was in using the time I was with you to learn from me the best point of view to approach a story from, to milk it dry. Not style: I dont want you to learn my style anymore than you want to, nor do I want to help you with criticism forever anymore than you want me to. I just want you to learn, in the simplest and quickest way, to save yourself from the nervous wear and tear and emotional exhaustion of doing work that is not quite right, how to approach a story to tell it in the manner that will be closest to right that you can do. Once you learn that, you wont need me or anybody.
>
> I learned to write from other writers. Why should you

refuse to? . . . The putting of a story down on paper, the
telling it, is a craft. How else can a young carpenter learn
to build a house, except by helping an experienced carpenter build one? He cant learn it just by looking at
finished houses.[201]

Other advice offered by Faulkner was practical and insightful.
The essence of any compelling human story could "be told in
one sentence," he said in one of his letters.[202] On another
occasion he instructed her, "You have got to write the first
sentence of a story so that whoever reads it will want to read the
second one."[203] Concerning the discipline of writing short
fiction, which Faulkner rated as being second only to poetry in
difficulty, he stated that a "short story is a crystallised instant,
arbitrarily selected, in which character conflicts with character
or environment or itself."[204] In addition to offering specific
criticism, Faulkner gave Williams writing assignments, helped
to get her short fiction published, and suggested collabora-
tion.[205] It was at Faulkner's suggestion that Williams undertook the writing of a novel that was based to a large extent on
her relationship with him. This novel, *The Wintering*, published by Harcourt Brace Jovanovich in 1971, has as its chief
male character a writer who closely resembles Faulkner and
whose name (Almoner) was selected by Faulkner himself.[206]
(At about the same time that the personal side of Faulkner's
relationship with Williams was irrevocably sealed by her marriage to Ezra Bowen in March 1953, Faulkner met Jean Stein.)
    It was also in the early 1950s that Faulkner, in giving a rather
complex but nonetheless honest and complimentary evaluation of Hemingway's work, inadvertently offended the
novelist whose artistic standards he had always respected.
Asked to write a review of Hemingway's *The Old Man and the
Sea* for the *New York Times Book Review*, Faulkner instead
wrote an open letter to *Times* editor Harvey Breit that began
with the following observation:

A few years ago, I forget what the occasion was, Hemingway said that writers should stick together just as doctors and lawyers and wolves do. I think there is more wit in that than truth or necessity either, at least in Hemingway's case, since the sort of writers who need to band together willy nilly or perish, resemble the wolves who are wolves only in pack, and, singly, are just another dog.[207]

Faulkner stated that a man capable of writing *Men Without Women*, *The Sun Also Rises*, *A Farewell to Arms*, and *For Whom the Bell Tolls* needed no protection from a pack of any kind. And he felt certain that no man would be "quicker and harsher to judge what remained" after these major pieces than Hemingway himself, that if "what remained had not been as honest and true as he could make it, then he himself would have burned the manuscript before the publisher ever saw it."[208] From this (Breit sent Hemingway a copy) Hemingway concluded that Faulkner was saying that he was "just another dog."[209] Whether Hemingway saw Faulkner's subsequent review of *The Old Man and the Sea* in the fall 1952 issue of *Shenandoah*, in which Faulkner said that "Time may show it to be the best single piece of any of us," is not known.[210]

After receiving the Nobel Prize in 1950, Faulkner's attitude toward public appearances changed somewhat, but in a way that was perfectly consistent with his character. Concerning his Nobel Prize money, he told his uncle, Judge John Falkner, "I want you to do something with that damned money. I haven't earned it and I don't feel like it's mine."[211] Making good his pledge "to find an aim for the money high enough to be commensurate with the purpose and significance of its origin,"[212] Faulkner designated that $25,000 of the $30,000 prize be used to endow the William Faulkner Foundation whose purpose would be to provide educational scholarships for Mississippi Negroes and to encourage writers in Latin America.[213] Likewise, when presented with awards that honored the work rather than the man, Faulkner seemed to feel that he was obligated to give more than just a pro forma response. The kind of dividing line he drew is indicated by his responses to offers of honorary degrees. To accept such a degree, he felt, "would be an insult to all those who have gained degrees by means of the long and arduous devotion commensurate with what any degree must be always worth."[214]

As would be expected, various awards recognizing Faulkner's achievements were quick to follow the Nobel Prize. In 1950 he received the Howells Medal from the American Academy of Arts and Letters. Though he did not go to receive the award in person, he took time to write an acceptance statement that also contained a straightforward and moving appraisal of what he had accomplished:

> it still seems to me impossible to evaluate a man's work. None of mine ever quite suited me, each time I wrote the last word I would think, if I could just do it over, I would do it better, maybe even right. But I was too busy; there was always another one. I would tell myself, maybe I'm too young or too busy to decide; when I reach fifty, I will be able to decide how good or not. Then one day I was fifty and looked back at it, and I decided that it was all pretty good—and then in the same instant I realised that that was the worst of all since that meant only that a little nearer now was the moment, instant, night: dark: sleep: when I would put it all away forever that I anguished and sweated over, and it would never trouble me anymore.[215]

In 1951 Faulkner received the National Book Award for Fiction and the French government presented him with the Legion of Honor.

Requiem for a Nun—which in its final version featured two female characters: Temple Drake Stevens, picking up her life several years after the events in *Sanctuary*, and Nancy Mannigoe, a black servant in the Stevens home who, believing she has been left no alternative, murders the Stevens's infant—was published on 27 September 1951. This was the fruition of the story line that Faulkner had begun thinking about in 1933 and that he had conceived, at different times, as both a play and a novel. He continued to work on the play version after the novel had been published.

Jill Faulkner graduated from high school in 1951, and Faulkner agreed to address the graduating class. He told the class and the assembled guests that the greatest danger facing the world was fear; not fear of a specific threat such as the atomic bomb that, once used, "will have robbed itself of its only power over us: which is fear of it."[216] In a single, strong, assertive sentence, Faulkner told his audience that "Our danger is the forces in the world today which are trying to use man's fear to rob him of his individuality, his soul, trying to reduce him to an unthinking mass by fear and bribery—giving him free food which he has not earned, easy and valueless money which he has not worked for;—the economies or ideologies or political systems, communist or socialist or democratic, whatever they wish to call themselves, the tyrants and the politicians, American or European or Asiatic, whatever they call themselves, who would reduce man to one obedient mass for their own aggrandisement and power, or because they themselves are baffled and afraid, afraid of, or incapable of, believing in man's capacity for courage and endurance and sacrifice."[217] This was a theme that Faulkner returned to frequently in his public remarks.

Faulkner's next opportunity at speech making came in May 1952 when he was asked to address the Delta Council, a large group of cotton farmers and businessmen, in Cleveland, Mississippi. The speech was a longer one than he had made to his daughter's graduating class, but he again stressed the importance of the individual, freedom, and a sense of responsibility as being necessary for the preservation of freedom. It was the duty of man to be responsible, he said, "not just responsible to and for his fellow man, but to himself . . . to be responsible for the consequences of his own acts, to pay his own score, owing nothing to any man."[218] As a concomitant of one's sense of individual responsibility, one should respect the individuality and privacy of others. Faulkner told his Delta Council audience that "man must assume and maintain and defend his right to be responsible for his freedom";[219] that vigilance was all the more necessary because the enemy who would take his freedom and his right of responsibility from him was now more difficult to identify. "He faces us now from beneath the eagle-perched domes of our capitols and from behind the alphabetical splatters on the doors of welfare and other bureaus of economic or industrial regimentation . . . his artillery is a debased and respectless currency which has emasculated the initiative for independence by robbing initiative of the only mutual scale it knew to measure independence by."[220] Faulkner believed that government, committed to economic controls and the financing of public welfare, and pandering to individual rights rather than responsibilities threatened to undermine the strength and integrity of the country.

In a third address—delivered this time to the graduating class of Pine Manor Junior College, where Jill had gone after graduating from high school—Faulkner continued to develop these same ideas. He clothed his message in the form of a parable, using the story of God's creation of man and of His conflict with Satan. During the time of creation:

> the angels (with one exception; God had probably had trouble with this one before) merely looked on and watched—the serene and blameless seraphim, that white and shining congeries who, with the exception of that one whose arrogance and pride God had already had to curb, were content merely to bask for eternity in the reflected glory of the miracle of man, content merely to watch, uninvolved and not even caring, while man ran his

worthless and unregretted course toward and at last into that twilight where he would be no more. Because they were white, immaculate, negative, without past, without thought or grief or regrets or hopes, except that one—the splendid dark incorrigible one, who possessed the arrogance and pride to demand with, and the temerity to object with, and the ambition to substitute with—not only to decline to accept a condition just because it was a fact, but to want to substitute another condition in its place.[221]

The condition Satan wants might require the subversion and subjection of humankind; but, even so, his individuality and his willingness to risk failure and even oblivion make him more worthy of respect than all the rest of the myriad mindless hosts of heaven. Nevertheless, Satan's desire to encourage man's corruption still must be resisted; "not as groups or classes but as individuals, simple men and women individually free and capable of freedom and decision, who must decide, affirm simply and firmly and forever never to be led like sheep into peace and security."[222]

Faulkner's view of the nation, at its best, was a view that saw America as a land populated by free individuals who themselves saw their freedom not as a gift but as a responsibility that could never be completely discharged, because the moment the individual ceased to bear his responsibility would be the same moment that he lost his freedom. Evidently, Faulkner's sense of responsibility prompted him to carry this message to others, even outside the United States. This may explain his willingness to undertake various State Department assignments, which included visits to South America (1954), Japan, Manila, Europe, and Iceland (all in 1955), Greece (1957), and Venezuela (1961). After the first of these trips, Faulkner wrote to State Department official Harold Howland, "I became suddenly interested in what I was trying to do, once I reached the scene and learned exactly what was hoped from this plan of which I was a part . . . and I shall be in New York this fall and can hold myself available to call on you to make a verbal report or discuss what further possibilities, situations, capacities, etc. in which I might do what I can to help give people of other countries a truer idea than they sometimes have of what the U.S. actually is."[223] Faulkner's longest trip under State Department auspices was to Japan, and apparently this was the trip he enjoyed the most. He respected greatly the courtesy of the Japanese people, and he felt a strong sympathy for a country that had been as badly defeated and devastated as Japan had been in World War II. On his return home, he also had some advice on U.S. foreign policy. In Europe he had gotten the impression that Russia was afraid of there ever being a reunified Germany. "I believe they are convinced," Faulkner said, "that, once Germany is united, the whole nation would stop being communists and be Germans plain and simple."[224] Faulkner then suggested a strategy: "I wonder what would happen if we took publicly a high moral plane and said that a un-unified nation is such a crime against nature and morality both that, rather than be a party to it, we will allow Germany to withdraw from promise of NATO troops, and be unified under any conditions they wish."[225]

In 1953 Random House brought out a collection of stories and novel fragments entitled *The Faulkner Reader* for which Faulkner wrote a foreword, where he stated that the purpose of the artist was to uplift the heart of man, for by doing so the artist was saying "No to death for himself by means of the hearts which he has hoped to uplift."[226] By 1954, the year that *A Fable* was published, Faulkner's stage version of *Requiem for a Nun* still had not been produced. As Faulkner continued to work on the project, he became more and more frustrated over his inability to arrive at a satisfactory dramatic treatment of the novel. He had promised Ruth Ford—who as a graduate student at the University of Mississippi had dated Dean Falkner, and who was among Faulkner's circle of friends in

Hollywood—that she would have the part of Temple Drake; and he continued to protect her interests until the work was finally produced on Broadway in January 1959. In 1955 he received the National Book Award for Fiction for *A Fable*, and he was quite interested in putting together a collection of his hunting stories, *Big Woods*, which was illustrated in a manner much to Faulkner's liking by Edward Shenton. The four stories published in the volume were linked together by narrative passages, set in italics, that Faulkner called "interrupted catalysts."[227] The volume was published on 14 October 1955.

It was also during this period that the Snopes trilogy was brought to completion. Progress on *The Town* was slow, but he worked at it steadily. As *The Hamlet* had followed the ascension of Flem Snopes within the community of Frenchman's Bend, *The Town* described his conquest of Jefferson. At first Faulkner was concerned that there was "no fire, force, passion anymore in the words and sentences,"[228] but he gained confidence along with momentum. Nearing completion of the writing in the summer of 1956, he told Jean Stein, "Each time I begin to hope I am written out and can quit, I discover I am not at all cured and the sickness will probably kill me."[229] By the time he finished the writing he reported, "It breaks my heart, I wrote one scene and almost cried. I thought it was a funny book but I was wrong."[230] *The Town* was published on 1 May 1957 and was followed, a little over two years later, by *The Mansion*, on 13 November 1959.

As *The Mansion* was being completed, it became apparent that there were many factual discrepancies—events, dates, times, ages, etc.—among the three novels. Faulkner agreed to assist in making corrections, though he was not as troubled about the discrepancies as his editors were. Throughout his professional career he always had drawn a sharp distinction between fact and truth. "I dont care much for facts," he told Malcolm Cowley in 1946, "am not much interested in them, you cant stand a fact up, you've got to prop it up, and when you move to one side a little and look at it from that angle, it's not thick enough to cast a shadow in that direction."[231] This attitude applied to discrepancies in his work as well. Concerning the Snopes novels he told Random House editor Albert Erskine, "We should know what and where they are, even if we dont use, correct them. What I am trying to say is, the essential truth of these people and their doings, is the thing; the facts are not too important."[232] Nonetheless, some extreme efforts were made to achieve consistency, including the invention of a new character (a younger brother for Clarence Snopes) who would appear in later printings of *The Town*.[233]

Faulkner's best nonfiction was written during the 1950s. At one point in his life Faulkner was seriously considering writing his memoirs. He told Robert Haas, "it will be a book in the shape of a biography but actually about half fiction, chapters resembling essays about dogs and horses and family niggers and kin, chapters based on actual happenings but 'improved' where fiction would help, which will probably be short stories."[234] The project was never completed; it is not known if it was ever actually started, though in the April 1954 issue of *Holiday* magazine, Faulkner published an essay having many of the attributes described in his letter to Hass. "Mississippi" is one of the most masterful and moving pieces that Faulkner ever wrote about his native state and himself. The essay is launched on a grand scale: "Mississippi begins in the lobby of a Memphis, Tennessee hotel and extends south to the Gulf of Mexico."[235] The essay is narrated from a third person point of view, a novelist writing about himself. But the *he* the narrator is writing about makes his appearance gradually, and the shift of the narrative is subtle. First, the settlement of the country is chronicled. Faulkner's condensed, rich prose gives a sense of rapidity and urgency to the flow of history, as though the events he describes were being watched on a speeded-up film. He describes the Anglo-Saxon as the man who ultimately settled the country that was not yet a state:

the tall man roaring with Protestant scripture and boiled
whiskey, Bible and jug in one hand and like as not an
Indian tomahawk in the other, brawling, turbulent,
uxorious and polygamous: a married invincible bachelor
without destination but only motion, advancement,
dragging his gravid wife and most of his mother-in-law's
kin behind him into the trackless wilderness, to spawn
that child behind a log-crotched rifle and then get her with
another one before they moved again, and at the same
time scattering his inexhaustible other seed in three
hundred miles of dusky bellies: without avarice or compassion or forethought either: felling a tree which took
two hundred years to grow, to extract from it a bear or a
capful of wild honey.[236]

The narrator's own experience of Mississippi is mixed; he is
attracted and repelled at the same time as he comes to understand the nature of humor and compassion as well as bigotry
and injustice. The whole movement of the essay is toward the
acquisition of a mature understanding: "Loving all of it even
while he had to hate some of it because he knows now that you
dont love because: you love despite; not for the virtues, but
despite the faults."[237]

Faulkner also planned at one time to publish a collection of
essays under the title "The American Dream." The material
would be developed first as lectures and would examine "what
has happened to the American Dream which at one time the
whole earth looked up, aspired to."[238] Only two essays of the
projected series were written, "On Privacy" and "On Fear."
"On Privacy" appeared in *Harper's* in July 1955 and was
subtitled "The American Dream: What Happened to It?" In
the essay Faulkner pointed out that freedom from being treated
just as another integer in a powerless mass was one of the
greatest attractions and hopes that the country held out in its
beginnings. He used, by way of example, difficulties he had
experienced in protecting his own privacy, and he believed that

these difficulties were symptomatic of an unhealthy condition:

> in America today any organization or group, simply by
> functioning under a phrase like Freedom of the Press or
> National Security or League Against Subversion, can
> postulate to itself complete immunity to violate the
> individualness—the individual privacy lacking which he
> cannot be an individual and lacking which individuality
> he is not anything at all worth the having or keeping—of
> anyone who is not himself a member of some organiza-
> tion or group numerous enough or rich enough to
> frighten them off.[239]

In his essay "On Fear: Deep South in Labor: Mississippi,"[240] which was published in the June 1956 issue of
Harper's, Faulkner addressed the subject of segregation in
particular and racial problems in general. Speaking on the issue
of segregation in the public schools, Faulkner argued that
Mississippi needed a school system that "would make no distinction among pupils except that of simple ability," because,
he continued, what America needed very badly was that "all
Americans at least should be on the side of America," and that
then "we would not need to fear that other nations and
ideologies would doubt us when we talked of human freedom."[241] Observing that the insistence of the federal government that segregation become a reality in the South, and the
equal resoluteness of many white Southerners to resist segregation at all costs seemed to represent an insoluble impasse,
Faulkner noted that between these two forces:

> there are people in the South, Southerners born, who not
> only believe they can be reconciled but who love our
> land—not love white people specifically nor love Negroes
> specifically, but our land, our country: our climate and
> geography, the qualities in our people, white and Negro
> too, for honesty and fairness, the splendors in our tradi-

tions, the glories in our past—enough to try to reconcile
them, even at the cost of displeasing both sides: the contempt of the Northern radicals who believe we dont do
enough, the contumely and threats of our own Southern
reactionaries who are convinced that anything we do is
already too much.[242]

The fear that Faulkner wrote about was an economic one, a fear
that "the Negro, who has done so much with no chance, might
do so much more with an equal one that he might take the
white man's economy away from him."[243]

As a moderate Southerner, an insider with a responsible and
perceptive view of the racial situation, Faulkner was one of
those who would find himself criticized by liberal and conser-
vative alike. He had little respect for the extreme views of
outlanders like Norman Mailer, who held that the essence of
the white Southern male's fear of the Negro was the Negro's
sexual superiority. Faulkner said of Mailer's hypothesis, "I
have heard this idea expressed several times during the last
twenty years, though not before by a man. The others were
ladies, northern or middle western ladies, usually around 40 or
50 years of age. I dont know what a psychiatrist would find in
this."[244] Faulkner was also being consistent with his own
moderate views when he declined to debate W. E. B. Du Bois,
telling him that they were already in agreement on the moral,
legal, and ethical grounds for integration; and that to debate
between them the practical means for achieving a goal they
both believed in would not be helpful.[245]

Faulkner's public record on segregation and racial matters
helps to put in perspective the remarks that were attributed to
him by Russell Howe in a 1956 interview. Howe was the New
York correspondent for the *Sunday Times* (London). His
interview with Faulkner, which took place on 21 February,
appeared first in the *Sunday Times* on 4 March, and then on
22 March a different, longer version appeared in the *Reporter*.

In the latter version, Faulkner was quoted as saying that "if it came to fighting I'd fight for Mississippi against the United States even if it meant going out into the street and shooting Negroes."[246] This part of the interview was frequently quoted out of context; even then, it might have been recognized as inconsistent with Faulkner's previous statements, to say nothing of the ones he would make later. Faulkner's opinions on public issues had certainly been misunderstood and misquoted before, without one sentence of rebuttal coming from Faulkner himself. This time, however, he issued a strong repudiation, writing in a letter to the editor of the *Reporter* that he had not read the interview before it went to press and that various statements attributed to him were ones "which no sober man would make, nor, it seems to me, any sane man believe."[247] Though Howe claimed that the interview was transcribed from "verbatim shorthand notes,"[248] no copy of these notes was ever produced or is known now to exist.[249]

In the winter of 1957 Faulkner went to the University of Virginia as a writer-in-residence. The date marked the beginning of a lengthy association with the institution, all the more pleasant because his daughter (now Jill Faulkner Summers), grandchildren, and son-in-law (Paul Summers) were living in Charlottesville where Paul Summers was practicing law. Faulkner also found Charlottesville congenial because, as he said jokingly, "Virginians are all snobs, and I like snobs. A snob has to spend so much time being a snob that he has little left to meddle with you."[250] In 1959 Faulkner purchased a house in Charlottesville, and in 1960 he was appointed to a position on the University of Virginia faculty. Despite his back condition and though he suffered a broken collarbone in 1959, Faulkner continued to ride and hunt particularly with various hunt clubs in the area, evidently willing to pay a steep physical price for his pleasure. In the meantime, classroom conferences at the institution and a series of meetings that took place during a visit to the United States Military Academy (Paul Summers's alma mater) provided material for two volumes of published interviews.[251]

It was during this time that Faulkner turned to the writing of his last novel, the "Huck Finn" book that he had outlined for Robert Haas in 1940.[252] His original title for the work was "The Stealers," but it subsequently was changed to "The Reavers," "The Rievers," and finally *The Reivers*.[253] These and other revisions were made after he had completed the manuscript of the novel, and the book was published on 4 June 1962. In the summer of that year Faulkner was back in Oxford, and he was arranging for the purchase of a home outside Charlottesville in Albemarle County situated on 250 acres of land.[254] Faulkner had been injured in a horse fall in June, and perhaps as a result of the accident, his back began hurting him again. It was a severe case. The medication Faulkner took to ease the pain physically debilitated him and he had to be hospitalized on the fifth of July. The next day he died of a heart attack. The career was over; and if its curtailment was abrupt and unexpected, it had at least come at a time when Faulkner was still in command of his creative powers, before the wellspring of his imagination had run dry. It was the end of a life which, given the exigencies of circumstance and responsibility he had coped with, had been lived to a remarkable degree on Faulkner's own terms.

---

[1]*Lion in the Garden: Interviews with William Faulkner 1926-1962*, edited by James B. Meriwether and Michael Millgate (New York: Random House, 1968), p. 7. See also p. 9. Referred to hereafter as *Lion*.

[2]The reference is actually to Faulkner's great-grandfather, William Clark Falkner, who was the author of several books including a novel entitled *The White Rose of Memphis*.

[3]Jospeh Blotner, ed., *Selected Letters of William Faulkner* (New York: Random House, 1977), p. 212. Referred to hereafter as *Letters*.

[4]See Blotner, *Faulkner: A Biography* (New York: Random House, 1974), pp. 4-7. Referred to hereafter as Blotner.

[5]See Blotner, p. 6.

[6]*Lion*, p. 101.

[7]For an accurate and concise overview of Falkner family history and its relationship to William Faulkner's fiction, see Thomas L. McHaney, "The Falkners and the Origins of Yoknapatawpha County: Some Corrections," *Mississippi Quarterly*, 25 (Summer 1972): 249-264.

[8]See McHaney, "The Falkners and the Origins of Yoknapatawpha County," pp. 251-252. Most of the information on Colonel Falkner is based on Donald P. Duclos's "Son of Sorrow: The Life, Works, and Influence of Colonel William C. Falkner, 1825-1889," Ph.D. dissertation, University of Michigan, 1962. See Blotner, pp. 14-19.

[9]See McHaney, "The Falkners and the Origins of Yoknapatawpha County," p. 255; and Blotner, pp. 20-32.

[10]See McHaney, "The Falkners and the Origins of Yoknapatawpha County," p. 256; and Blotner, pp. 37-38. See also Millgate, *The Achievement of William Faulkner* (New York: Random House, 1966), pp. 1-2. Referred to hereafter as Millgate.

[11]Blotner, p. 46. See also *The Unvanquished* (New York: Random House, 1938), p. 266, where Colonel Sartoris tells his son Bayard, "I am tired of killing men, no matter what the necessity nor the end. Tomorrow, when I go to town to meet Ben Redmond, I shall be unarmed."

[12]See Blotner, pp. 46-47; and McHaney, "The Falkners and the Origins of Yoknapatawpha County," pp. 258-259.

[13]See Blotner, pp. 53-54.

[14]See Blotner, pp. 79-80, 150, 233; and Millgate, p. 3.

[15]Meriwether, ed., *Essays, Speeches and Public Letters by William Faulkner* (New York: Random House, 1966), p. 117. Referred to hereafter as *Essays, Speeches and Public Letters*.

[16]*Letters*, p. 212.

[17]*Letters*, p. 212.

[18]Blotner, pp. 111-112.

[19]Blotner, p. 114.

[20]Blotner, pp. 120, 140-142.

[21]Blotner, p. 146.

[22]Blotner, p. 147.

[23]See Millgate, pp. 3-4; and Blotner, pp. 161-162.

[24]Quoted in Robert Coughlan, *The Private World of William Faulkner* (New York: Harper, 1954), p. 48.

[25]Millgate, p. 4.

[26]Murry C. Falkner, *The Falkners of Mississippi: A Memoir* (Baton Rouge: Louisiana State University Press, 1967), p. 18.

[27]John Faulkner, *My Brother Bill* (New York: Trident Press, 1963), p. 130.

[28]See Blotner, pp. 193-197.

[29]See Millgate, p. 6; and Blotner, pp. 201-204.

[30]*The Faulkner Reader* (New York: Random House, 1953), p. x.

[31]See Millgate, "William Faulkner, Cadet," *University of Toronto Quarterly*, 35 (January 1966): 117-132.

[32]Phil Stone, "William Faulkner and His Neighbors," *Saturday Review*, 25 (19 September 1942): 12.

[33]Carvel Collins, ed., *William Faulkner: Early Prose and Poetry* (Boston: Little, Brown, 1962), p. 102. Referred to hereafter as *Early Prose and Poetry*.

[34]*Early Prose and Poetry*, pp. 101-102.

[35]*Early Prose and Poetry*, p. 74.

[36]*Early Prose and Poetry*, p. 86.

[37]*Early Prose and Poetry*, p. 94.

[38]*Early Prose and Poetry*, p.95.

[39]See Millgate, p. 8; Blotner, pp. 295-298; and Noel Polk, "William Faulkner's *Marionettes*," *Mississippi Quarterly*, 26 (Summer 1973): 247-280. *The Marionettes* was edited by Polk and published by the University Press of Virginia in 1977.

[40]See Polk, "William Faulkner's *Marionettes*," p. 248.

[41]*Letters*, p. 6.

[42]*Essays, Speeches and Public Letters*, p. 21.

[43]*Letters*, p. 47.

[44]James W. Webb and A. Wigfall Green, *William Faulkner of Oxford* (Baton Rouge: Louisiana State University Press, 1965), p. 58.

[45]*The Marble Faun* (Boston: Four Seas, 1924), p. 12. Faulkner's borrowings from Robert Nichols's *Ardours and Endurances* is discussed in Martin Kreiswirth, "Faulkner's *The Marble Faun*: Dependence and Independence," *English Studies in Canada*, 6 (Fall 1980): 333-344.

[46]Millgate, p. 12.

[47]The poems were "Dying Gladiator" (January-February 1925 issue) and "The Faun" (April 1925 issue). The critical essays were "On Criticism" (January-February 1925 issue) and "Verse Old and Nascent: A Pilgrimage" (April 1925 issue). They are all reprinted in *Early Prose and Poetry*.

[48]See Collins, ed., *William Faulkner: New Orleans Sketches* (New Brunswick, N.J.: Rutgers University Press, 1958), p. 25. Blotner (pp. 395, 61-62) reports that Faulkner was paid an average of $5.00 for his first four contributions to the *Picayune*.

[49]"Don Giovanni" and "Peter" are published in Blotner, ed., *Uncollected Stories of William Faulkner* (New York: Random House, 1979). "Don

Giovanni" was first published in *Mississippi Quarterly*, 32 (Summer 1979): 484-495.

⁵⁰"Nympholepsy" was first published in *Mississippi Quarterly*, 26 (Summer 1973): 403-409, and is also printed in Blotner, ed., *Uncollected Stories*. "The Hill" is reprinted in *Early Prose and Poetry*. "Frankie and Johnny" was first published in *Mississippi Quarterly*, 26 (Summer 1973): 403-409. It also appears in Blotner, ed., *Uncollected Stories*.

⁵¹See Millgate, "Faulkner on the Literature of the First World War," *Mississippi Quarterly*, 26 (Summer 1973): 387-393.

⁵²Reprinted in Collins, ed., *William Faulkner: New Orleans Sketches* (1968 edition).

⁵³*Early Prose and Poetry*, p. 116.

⁵⁴*Lion*, pp. 248-249.

⁵⁵*Letters*, p. 17.

⁵⁶*Letters*, p. 20.

⁵⁷*Sanctuary* (New York: Cape & Smith, 1931), p. 309.

⁵⁸See Meriwether, *The Literary Career of William Faulkner* (Columbia: University of South Carolina Press, 1971), p. 81; and McHaney, "The Elmer Papers: Faulkner's Comic Portraits of the Artist," *Mississippi Quarterly*, 26 (Summer 1973): 281-311. The short story "A Portrait of Elmer" is published in Blotner, ed., *Uncollected Stories*.

⁵⁹McHaney, "The Elmer Papers," pp. 282-283.

⁶⁰"Divorce in Naples" and "Mistral" were published in *These 13* (New York: Cape & Smith, 1931), and "The Leg" (published as "Leg") first appeared in *Doctor Martino and Other Stories* (New York: Smith & Haas, 1934).

⁶¹Published in *Mississippi Quarterly*, 27 (Summer 1974): 333-335.

⁶²*Letters*, p. 24.

⁶³*Letters*, p. 19.

⁶⁴Faulkner wrote two works which he entitled *Mayday*. One was an allegorical "quest" narrative, dated 27 January 1926, that was not published during his lifetime, and the other was the manuscript of his first novel. The allegorical *Mayday* was published in a facsimile edition by the University of Notre Dame Press in 1976.

⁶⁵The work was published in a limited edition by the Pelican Bookshop Press in 1926 in New Orleans. The introduction by Faulkner is a parody of Anderson's style.

⁶⁶Howard Mumford Jones and Walter B. Rideout, eds., *Letters of Sherwood Anderson* (Boston: Little, Brown, 1953), p. 155.

⁶⁷Collins, ed., *William Faulkner: New Orleans Sketches* (1968 edition), pp. 135, 137-139.

⁶⁸See Millgate, pp. 24, 180-181.
⁶⁹Meriwether, "Sartoris and Snopes: An Early Notice," *Library Chronicle of the University of Texas*, 7 (Summer 1962): 36-37.
⁷⁰*Letters*, p. 38.
⁷¹*Letters*, p. 39.
⁷²Meriwether, ed., "An Introduction to *The Sound and the Fury*," *Mississippi Quarterly*, 26 (Summer 1973): 412-413.
⁷³Millgate, pp. 26-27.
⁷⁴Harrison Smith.
⁷⁵*Letters*, p. 43.
⁷⁶Blotner, p. 603.
⁷⁷See Meriwether, *The Literary Career of William Faulkner*, pp. 167-180.
⁷⁸Millgate, p. 28.
⁷⁹Millgate, p. 28.
⁸⁰See Blotner, pp. 653, 657, 660-661.
⁸¹Frederick L. Gwynn and Blotner, eds., *Faulkner in the University: Class Conferences at the University of Virginia, 1957-1958* (New York: Vintage, 1965), p. 233. Referred to hereafter as *Faulkner in the University*.
⁸²Blotner, p. 1344.
⁸³*Letters*, p. 51.
⁸⁴Jones and Rideout, eds., *Letters of Sherwood Anderson*, p. 252.
⁸⁵Millgate, p. 31.
⁸⁶See Blotner, p. 705.
⁸⁷See Blotner, pp. 722-723.
⁸⁸*Letters*, pp. 52-53.
⁸⁹See Blotner, pp. 689, 727.
⁹⁰*Letters*, p. 55.
⁹¹*Letters*, p. 56.
⁹²*Letters*, p. 57.
⁹³*Letters*, p. 57.
⁹⁴*Letters*, p. 58.
⁹⁵*Letters*, p. 61.
⁹⁶*Lion*, p. 241.
⁹⁷*Lion*, p. 240.
⁹⁸*Faulkner in the University*, p. 102.
⁹⁹Blotner, p. 787.
¹⁰⁰Blotner, p. 777.
¹⁰¹Blotner, p. 767, and *Letters*, p. 62.
¹⁰²See Blotner, pp. 778, 786.
¹⁰³Blotner, p. 780.
¹⁰⁴Falkner, *The Falkners of Mississippi*, pp. 200-201.
¹⁰⁵*Letters*, p. 65.

[106]*Letters*, p. 67.

[107]*Letters*, p. 71.

[108]See Blotner, p. 803.

[109]*Letters*, p. 71.

[110]*Letters*, p. 44.

[111]*Letters*, p. 74.

[112]*Letters*, p. 75.

[113]*Letters*, p. 75.

[114]*Letters*, pp. 78-79.

[115]*Letters*, p. 78.

[116]*Letters*, p. 84.

[117]*Letters*, p. 89.

[118]See Blotner, pp. 832-837.

[119]See Blotner, pp. 860-861, 865.

[120]*Letters*, p. 85.

[121]*Letters*, p. 83-84.

[122]*Letters*, p. 84.

[123]See Blotner, p. 922.

[124]Meta Carpenter Wilde, *A Loving Gentleman* (New York: Simon & Schuster, 1976), p. 24.

[125]Wilde, *A Loving Gentleman*, p. 52.

[126]See Blotner, pp. 928-929.

[127]Blotner, p. 929.

[128]*Letters*, p. 99.

[129]*Letters*, p. 100.

[130]See Blotner, pp. 954, 984-985.

[131]Millgate, p. 39.

[132]*Letters*, p. 105.

[133]Blotner, p. 975; see Wilde, *A Loving Gentleman*, pp. 220-225.

[134]*Letters*, p. 338.

[135]See *Letters*, p. 109; Wilde, *A Loving Gentleman*, p. 230; and *The Wild Palms* (New York: Random House, 1939), p. 324. For additional discussion of Helen Baird as a model for Charlotte Rittenmeyer, see Collins, "Biographical Background for Faulkner's *Helen*, in *Helen: A Courtship and Mississippi Poems* (New Orleans & Oxford, Miss.: Tulane University/ Yoknapatawpha Press, 1981), pp. 86-88.

[136]Wilde, *A Loving Gentleman*, p. 317.

[137]*Letters*, p. 102.

[138]*Letters*, p. 106.

[139]See *Letters*, pp. 107-108.

[140]See *Letters*, pp. 109-110.

[141]*Letters*, p. 113.

[142]See *Letters*, p. 115.

[143]*Letters*, p. 117.

[144]Blotner, pp. 1020, *143-144*.

[145]*Letters*, p. 111.

[146]*Letters*, p. 121.

[147]*Letters*, p. 122.

[148]*Letters*, p. 123.

[149]*Letters*, p. 153.

[150]See Millgate, p. 41.

[151]*Letters*, p. 123.

[152]*Letters*, p. 159.

[153]*Letters*, p. 159.

[154]*Letters*, p. 125.

[155]*Letters*, p. 166.

[156]*Letters*, p. 166.

[157]*Letters*, p. 175.

[158]*Letters*, p. 175.

[159]*Letters*, p. 176.

[160]The articles were "Faulkner's Point of View," *College English*, 2 (May 1941): 736-749; "Faulkner and the South," *Antioch Review*, 1 (March 1941): 82-94; "William Faulkner's Style," *American Prefaces*, 6 (Spring 1941): 195-211.

[161]*Letters*, p. 142.

[162]Blotner, p. 1191.

[163]*Letters*, p. 204.

[164]Malcolm Cowley, *The Faulkner-Cowley File: Letters and Memories, 1944-1962* (New York: Viking, 1966), p. 10. Referred to hereafter as *Faulkner-Cowley File*.

[165]*Faulkner-Cowley File*, p. 10.

[166]*Faulkner-Cowley File*, p. 24.

[167]*Letters*, p. 197.

[168]*Letters*, p. 211.

[169]*Letters*, p. 215.

[170]*Letters*, p. 222.

[171]*Letters*, p. 233.

[172]*The Sound and the Fury* (New York: Modern Library, 1966), p. 403.

[173]*Letters*, p. 228.

[174]*Letters*, p. 228.

[175]*Letters*, p. 237.

[176]*Letters*, p. 237.

[177]*Letters*, p. 250.

[178]*Letters*, pp. 261-262.

[179]*Letters*, p. 352.

[180]*Letters*, p. 262.

[181]See Blotner, p. 1257.

[182]*Lion*, p. 58.

[183]*Letters*, pp. 217-218.

[184]*Go Down, Moses* (New York: Random House, 1942), *These 13* (New York: Random House, 1931). See *Letters*, p. 273.

[185]*Letters*, p. 280.

[186]*Letters*, p. 280.

[187]*Letters*, p. 234.

[188]*Letters*, p. 299.

[189]*Letters*, p. 311.

[190]*Essays, Speeches and Public Letters*, p. 119.

[191]*Essays, Speeches and Public Letters*, p. 120.

[192]*Letters*, p. 378.

[193]*Letters*, p. 387.

[194]*Letters*, p. 352.

[195]*Letters*, p. 348.

[196]*Letters*, p. 382.

[197]See Blotner, p. 1207.

[198]*Letters*, p. 332.

[199]See Blotner, pp. 1291-1292.

[200]*Letters*, pp. 349-350.

[201]*Letters*, p. 350.

[202]*Letters*, p. 323.

[203]*Letters*, p. 327.

[204]*Letters*, p. 345.

[205]Unpublished interview with Joan Williams, conducted by the Southern Studies Program, University of South Carolina, 6-8 December 1978. See also *Letters*, pp. 337, 338-340, 342-343, 349-352.

[206]Unpublished interview with Joan Williams.

[207]*Letters*, p. 333.

[208]*Letters*, p. 334.

[209]Carlos Baker, *Ernest Hemingway: A Life Story* (New York: Scribners, 1969), p. 504.

[210]*Essays, Speeches and Public Letters*, p. 193.

[211]Blotner, p. 1370.

[212]*Letters*, p. 309.

[213]See Millgate, p. 49, and Blotner, p. 1374.

[214]*Letters*, p. 394.

[215]*Essays, Speeches and Public Letters*, p. 206.

[216]*Essays, Speeches and Public Letters*, p. 123.

[217]*Essays, Speeches and Public Letters*, p. 123.

[218]*Essays, Speeches and Public Letters*, p. 129.

[219]*Essays, Speeches and Public Letters*, p. 131.

[220]*Essays, Speeches and Public Letters*, p. 132.

[221]*Essays, Speeches and Public Letters*, pp. 136-137.

[222]*Essays, Speeches and Public Letters*, pp. 138-139.

[223]*Letters*, p. 369.

[224]*Letters*, p. 388.

[225]*Letters*, p. 388.

[226]*The Faulkner Reader*, p. xi.

[227]Blotner, p. 1522.

[228]*Letters*, p. 391.

[229]*Letters*, p. 402.

[230]*Letters*, p. 402.

[231]*Letters*, p. 222.

[232]*Letters*, p. 422.

[233]See *Letters*, p. 424.

[234]*Letters*, pp. 320-321.

[235]*Essays, Speeches and Public Letters*, p. 11.

[236]*Essays, Speeches and Public Letters*, p. 14.

[237]*Essays, Speeches and Public Letters*, pp. 42-43.

[238]*Letters*, p. 372.

[239]*Essays, Speeches and Public Letters*, p. 70.

[240] Subtitled "The American Dream: What Happened to It?"

[241]*Essays, Speeches and Public Letters*, p. 94.

[242]*Essays, Speeches and Public Letters*, p. 95.

[243]*Essays, Speeches and Public Letters*, p. 96.

[244]*Letters*, p. 411.

[245]See *Letters*, p. 398.

[246]*Lion*, p. 261.

[247]*Lion*, p. 265.

[248]*Lion*, p. 265.

[249]When he was approached by the editors of *Lion in the Garden* in 1967, Howe said that he did not know where the original notes were.

[250]*Faulkner in the University*, p. 12.

[251]*Faulkner in the University* (Charlottesville: University of Virginia Press, 1959; reprinted, New York: Vintage, 1965; previously cited), and Joseph L. Fant and Robert P. Ashley, eds., *Faulkner at West Point* (New York: Random House, 1964).

[252]See *Letters*, p. 123.

[253]See *Letters*, p. 456.

[254]See *Letters*, p. 461-462.

Soldiers' Pay

In a 1953 essay on Sherwood Anderson, William Faulkner, writing of the time he had known the older writer in New Orleans in the mid-1920s, remembers Anderson telling him, "You're a country boy; all you know is that little patch up there in Mississippi where you started from. But that's all right too. It's America too."[1] This view—that the writer, to be convincing, should know what he is writing about; that universal themes can be found in one's own particular surroundings—was one that Faulkner himself had advanced in his early literary criticism in 1922. Though *Soldiers' Pay*, Faulkner's first novel, was set neither in the fictional county of Yoknapatawpha nor even in Mississippi, it was set in the South and dealt with people and events about which Faulkner thought he knew a great deal. As several critics have observed, the novel foreshadows many of the important themes and technical motifs that Faulkner would develop and strive to perfect throughout his career.

Faulkner also uses the structure of the novel to emphasize the disjointed nature of life in the postwar world. There is no smooth and logical flow of events, and outcomes do not fit conveniently into neat cause-and-effect formulas. The nine chapters of the novel are divided into separate sections; the shortest chapter consists of five sections and the longest has fifteen. The structure is episodic; that is, there is little in the way of smooth narrative transition from section to section or from chapter to chapter. This structure helps to emphasize the isolation of the characters in the novel and the fragile tenuousness of the few contacts that are made between people. Time is fragmented; it is not a continuum that man, by relying on reason, can adapt himself to. The fragmenting of time has also separated man from the world of nature, which *is* pictured as a continuum. In nature's world human reasoning becomes specious because nature is not logical; it is compulsive, repetitive, and indifferent to the condition of man.

The setting of *Soldiers' Pay* is post-World War I America. The time is late March 1919,[2] and soldiers are being returned home following the cessation of hostilities in November 1918. Though peace has come, the times are far from peaceful; Faulkner skillfully uses the microcosm of a railroad train in the first chapter to show the turbulence of the times. The soldiers that appear in the opening scene are drunk and for the most part uncontrollable. Julian Lowe is an air cadet who did not finish his training in time to see action. At nineteen, he still has romantic notions about the glory of combat in the sky; and, since he has not had his illusions dashed by the realities of war, he is bitterly disappointed that the war is over. Joe Gilligan, who figures as a major character in the novel, is a discharged private. He is older (thirty-two), more experienced with the ways of the world, and, though not an outright cynic, he looks at people and their motives with a healthy skepticism. Introducing himself as "Number no thousand no hundred and naughty naught Private (very private) Joe Gilligan,"[3] he does not see himself as a returning hero (he was not in combat and evidently did not miss it) and has no idealistic illusions about the war.

A conductor who tries to quell the drinking and the boisterous behavior is totally frustrated by Gilligan. Feigning indignation, he complains, "this is the reward we get for giving our flesh and blood to our country's need. Yes, sir, he don't want us here; he begrudges us riding on his train, even. Say, suppose we hadn't sprang to the nation's call, do you know what kind of a train you'd have? A train full of Germans. A train full of folks eating sausage and drinking beer, all going to Milwaukee" (p. 12). The more the conductor tries to restore order, the more conditions deteriorate into a kind of comic madhouse. Gilligan throws a suitcase belonging to a soldier named Hank White off the train and almost succeeds in pushing White through the window of the moving train as well. When the melee subsides, the conductor asks two businessmen to watch Gilligan and Lowe until the train reaches its destination (Buffalo, New York) and the conductor is able to turn the two soldiers over to the police. A sharp contrast is thus made between the soldiers and the civilians who stayed at home while the war was being fought. Mr. Schluss, a seller of ladies' underwear, asserts, "They ain't no one respects the uniform like I do. Listen, I would of liked to fought by your side, see? But someone got to look out for business while the boys are gone. Ain't that right?" (pp. 17-18). In fact, the civilians have no understanding of the soldiers at all, are uncomfortable around them, and wish to be rid of them as soon as possible. This is a theme that is developed consistently throughout the novel. As the first section ends, with Gilligan and Lowe having left the train at Buffalo, they are aware that "spring was somewhere in the world. . . . Caught both in the magic of change they stood feeling the spring in the cold air" (p. 22). It is one of the major ironies of *Soldiers' Pay* that while the world of nature moves inexorably through its cycle of renewal from the death of winter to the new life of spring, there is no corresponding renewal in the world of man. Faulkner, like many novelists of the time, saw World War I as a monumental watershed, on the postwar side of which was a spiritual and moral wasteland where old values and standards of behavior were no longer applicable.

The day after leaving their train in Buffalo, Gilligan and Lowe board another train that will take them to Cincinnati. It is on this train that they encounter a wounded and dying airman, Donald Mahon, and Margaret Powers, who has been widowed by the war and who decides to assist Gilligan in getting Mahon home to Charlestown, Georgia.

Themes and motifs introduced in the first section are expanded and new material is introduced. Though Margaret is an attractive woman, there is an element of violence and ugliness in the imagery that describes her, indicating that she too has been wounded by the war. She feels guilty because her husband, Richard Powers, whom she married on an impulse and had lived with for only three days, was killed in action before he received the letter from Margaret telling him that the marriage, which was not founded on love, should be dissolved. Thus, she reasons he died "still believing in her" (p. 36). Margaret introduces one of the major themes of the novel, the complex relationship between sex and death, in her troubled thoughts about her dead husband:

> Dick, Dick. Dead, ugly Dick. Once you were alive and young and passionate and ugly, after a time you were dead, dear Dick: that flesh, that body, which I loved and did not love; your beautiful, young, ugly body, dear Dick, become now a seething of worms, like new milk (p. 44).

It is not simply her natural compassion, but also her feelings of guilt that make her want to help Donald Mahon.

Another of the novel's major themes introduced in the first chapter is that of injustice. Gilligan predicts—accurately, as it turns out—that if Mahon has a girl at home she will throw him over. To Lowe's protest he replies, "You don't know women. Once the new has wore off it'll be some bird that stayed at home and made money, or some lad that wore shiny leggings and never got nowheres so he could get hurt" (p. 30). After he reads a letter among the wounded man's effects from Cecily Saunders, Mahon's fiance, he tells Margaret that it contained "all the old bunk about knights of the air and the romance of battle, that even the fat crying ones outgrow soon as the excitement is over and uniforms and being wounded ain't only not stylish no more, but it is troublesome" (p. 41). The point raised here, and throughout the novel, is central: what is soldiers' pay? The answer is not very much nor very good; their reward for enduring the horrors of war is not gratitude but oblivion. Like all mankind, soldiers cannot expect just recompense for their labors.

The foursome stop at a hotel in Cincinnati before proceeding further south. Lowe is sent home by Margaret, and she and Gilligan decide to accompany Mahon to Charlestown, hoping to see that he is treated justly there. It is April by the time the second chapter opens in Charlestown. The rest of the novel's main characters are introduced and the plot, that has already been prefigured, begins to unfold. Indeed, from this point on the novel contains relatively little action; rather, what we see is the gradual working out of the conditions established in the first chapter. The first two characters to appear are Januarius Jones and Reverend Mahon, Donald's father. Jones is a selfish and self-serving rake who cares only for the satisfaction of his own appetites, both sexual and gastronomic. Jones thinks and talks about sex far more than he actually engages in it, and he seems less interested in its sensual aspects than in using sex as a means of achieving dominance over women. Reverend Mahon, an Episcopalian minister, has pretty much withdrawn from the world. He takes pride in his impressive but stiffly formal garden that shows him to be essentially ill at ease with the world of spontaneous nature, as he is interested only in those aspects of it that he can control. The centerpiece of the garden is his rosebush which he describes as "my son and my daughter, the wife of my bosom and the bread of my belly" (p. 61). The housekeeper, Emmy, who had a brief romance with Donald Mahon before he left for the war, is introduced in the first section, as is Cecily Saunders, who turns out to be as shallow as Gilligan guessed she would be. Though there is immediate conflict between her and Jones, the two characters share at least one significant trait: they both regard sex as a device that will help them achieve other ends, a concept of sex that fits logically into the postwar world that Faulkner describes in *Soldiers' Pay*.

Seeing what the war has done to Donald, Cecily declares that she cannot bear to think about seeing him anymore. Reverend Mahon is convinced that she can work a miraculous cure for his son, while her father—a well-meaning but weak man, described as "Cecily in the masculine and gone to flesh: the same slightly shallow good looks and somewhere an indicated laxness of moral fiber" (p. 96)—only wants his daughter to do the right thing, though he is not quite certain what that is. Mrs. Saunders is much more pragmatic; she wants her daughter to marry well and not be a fool. Margaret also thinks that Cecily can be helpful, though hers is a more rational view. She does not believe that Cecily should be pressured into fulfilling her engagement to Donald; only that she should consent to see him, with the question of marriage put aside for the moment. When Cecily does go to see Donald the next day for her own reasons (her father's arguments and his forbidding her to see her present boyfriend, George Farr, carry little weight with her), she succeeds only in making a fool of herself. Covering her eyes so she does not have to see Donald's scarred face, she sinks to her knees and makes an impassioned speech to Januarius Jones, thinking he is Donald. Her humiliation is compounded by the fact that Margaret witnesses the entire scene. When she returns home she is more resolved than ever not to see Donald any more, and illogically blames him for humiliating her. Telling her father that she is "sick and tired of men" (p. 142), she gives herself the next night to George, not out of love but out of frustration and defiance. Later Cecily decides to marry George to escape responsibility for making decisions about what her moral obligations to Donald should be.

Within the Mahon household, an uneasy status quo prevails. The rector does not know what to do nor how to care for his son, so this responsibility falls primarily to Gilligan. To-gether, he and Margaret shield Donald from the intrusions of curious townspeople. Donald seems to be suspended in time; while all around him seasonal changes are taking place, his condition remains static. As the specialist from Atlanta who comes to examine Donald observes, "He is practically a dead man now. More than that, he should have been dead these three months were it not for the fact that he seems to be waiting for something. Something he has begun but has not completed, something he has carried from his former life that he does not remember consciously" (pp. 154-155). As nature moves through its seasonal cycles, so is Donald sustained temporarily by some inner cycle. Once it has been completed he will die.

One group from which Donald does not need to be protected is Charlestown's returned veterans. Gilligan senses this and tells Margaret, "You'll notice them soldiers don't bother him, specially the ones that was over-seas. They just kind of call the whole thing off. He just had hard luck and whatcher going to do about it? is the way they figure" (p. 150). The most vehement antiwar passages of the novel are in chapter 5, which deals almost exclusively with the soldiers of Charlestown. The chapter contains flashbacks to combat scenes and also reveals the ironic nature of Richard Powers's death. Sergeant Madden, a native of Charlestown, was Richard Powers's platoon sergeant, and it was while their unit was going on line for the first time that Powers was killed. At the rumor of gas attack, some of the men in the platoon panic and Dewey Burney, also a Charlestown native, accuses Powers of getting them all killed and shoots him in the face at point-blank range (p. 179). Now Burney's mother upbraids the other men in Charlestown who were in his unit for not taking better care of her son, whom she regards as a hero.   *213856*

It is during a party scene in Charlestown, though, that most of the novel's antiwar sentiment is expressed. With the war over, society has little use for soldiers.

This, the spring of 1919, was the day of the Boy, of him
who had been too young for soldiering. For two years he
had had a dry time of it. Of course, girls had used him
during the scarcity of men, but always in such a detached
impersonal manner. Like committing fornication with a
beautiful woman who chews gum steadily all the while (p.
188).

Shortly before Donald's death, it suddenly dawns on
Margaret that the person who can do the most for Donald is
Emmy, the housekeeper, not Cecily. Emmy has told Margaret
of her relationship with Donald before the war. It was a
relationship that was natural, spontaneous, and therefore in
harmony with the world of nature. Donald and Emmy had
made love after Donald had become engaged to Cecily. It was
an idyllic scene, at night under soft moonlight, on a hill over-
looking the place they used to swim together. Emmy remembers, "I couldn't see anything except the sky, and I don't know
how long it was when all of a sudden there was his head against
the sky, over me, and he was wet again and I could see the
moonlight kind of running on his wet shoulders and arms, and
he looked at me. . . . I could hear him panting from running,
and I could feel something inside me panting, too" (p. 127).
Margaret realizes, too late, that this is the world that Donald
needs to be reconnected with, that Emmy is the logical one to
marry Donald. Emmy, however, refuses; her pride does not
permit her to "take another's leavings" (p. 273). Margaret then
decides to marry Donald herself, more as a consolation to
Reverend Mahon than for any good it will accomplish.

The novel draws rapidly to a close after this point. The
circuit of memory within Donald is completed as he finally
remembers the day of the preceding year when he was shot
down. Remembering this, he dies. Januarius Jones takes advantage of Emmy's grief to achieve a seduction of sorts. Margaret leaves Charlestown, and Gilligan, unable to persuade

Margaret to marry him, decides to stay with Reverend Mahon for the time being.

Soldiers' Pay was well received when it was published in 1926, and, unlike a number of Faulkner's novels, it has benefited from sound and thoughtful criticism. Cleanth Brooks rates the novel highly for a first attempt: "It is written up to the hilt. As one would expect in the early work of a talented young writer, the style is uneven. But in general, the writing shows an enormous vitality. It is never languid or tepid."[4] Michael Millgate, with some qualifications, praises the book's structure, pointing out that the "repetitions of motifs, of images, of whole phrases and sentences may sometimes seem lacking in immediate point, but there is little doubt that they were designed to function within an elaborate but perhaps inadequately realised formal conception governing the whole book."[5] There are no profound differences of opinion among critics regarding the meaning of the novel, and the student may turn to a number of useful essays offering perceptive insights into different aspects of Faulkner's achievement.

Several critics have commented on Faulkner's use of mythical figures and mythical references in *Soldiers' Pay*. Margaret Yonce has written an illuminating study of Faulkner's use of the Atthis myth (Jones refers to Cecily Saunders as Atthis, a kind of bird goddess), and examines some of the sources Faulkner may have relied on. These include Sappho, the Greek poet of antiquity whose home was the island of Lesbos, and the British poet Algernon Charles Swinburne.[6] Faulkner clearly does not use mythological or classical allusions in *Soldiers' Pay*, nor in any of his later works, merely for purposes of adornment. As Brooks states it, Faulkner's interest in various nature myths reflects his deep concern over

> the oddly divided nature of man. Man was obviously a part of nature like other natural creatures, equipped with much the same biological mechanisms and subject to

animal appetites and needs. Yet he was also—with his memory, reason, and imagination—somehow outside nature as the other creatures were not. One might regard Man as a sort of amphibian, swimming in the sea of nature and unable to live outside it, and yet with his head lifted above the surface of that sea.[7]

Faulkner also uses as source material for *Soldiers' Pay* some of his own published and unpublished work. The language that Reverend Mahon uses to describe his rosebush is taken from one of Faulkner's contributions to a New Orleans literary magazine, the *Double Dealer*. Some of the poetry quoted by Januarius Jones is from poetry by Faulkner that was unpublished at the time. The circumstances of Donald Mahon's wounding and the fragmentation of personality that follows are prefigured in Faulkner's "The Lilacs," which was first published in the June 1925 issue of the *Double Dealer* and later appeared as poem I of *A Green Bough*. The significance of this early treatment of a fragmented personality has been noted by Margaret Yonce:

> In "The Lilacs" Faulkner had experimented with an aviator whose mind had been fragmented by the war so that he has multiple memories of his wounding. In *Soldiers' Pay*, mind and body are somehow separated at the moment of the wounding, and the death-in-life state persists until the two are reunited. In *Flags in the Dust* [published in heavily edited form as *Sartoris* in 1927], the divided psyche is symbolized in terms of twinship, the death of one twin dooming the other. Finally, in *The Sound and the Fury* (1929) Faulkner carries the division of personality to its furthest advance in the Compson brothers.[8]

Were the novel not as good as it is, the weaknesses of *Soldiers' Pay* would stand out more prominently than they do.

The various characters are sometimes overly given to speechifying, and as a result they are occasionally dwarfed by the ideas they debate. Concern over moral and ethical ideas and social conditions permeates the novel, and an array of subjects is discussed, including utopianism, the meaning of youth, the nature of God, and man's duty to man. What prevents the novel from becoming a dry intellectual exercise is Faulkner's concern for his characters. From his first novel Faulkner "comes down on the side of civilization and the full community."[9] Margaret Powers may ruefully regret that the whole business in Charlestown "had got on without any particular drain on any intelligence" (p. 271), and Gilligan may be right in his judgment that "I tried to help nature make a good job out of a poor one without having no luck at it" (p. 303). Both characters, however, are willing to take risks for what they regard as a higher cause. *Soldiers' Pay* is ultimately a novel of people, not of ideas, and that is its primary strength.

---

[1]*Essays, Speeches and Public Letters*, p. 8.

[2]See the chronology of the novel in Cleanth Brooks, *William Faulkner: Toward Yoknapatawpha and Beyond* (New Haven: Yale University Press, 1978), pp. 366-370.

[3]*Soldiers' Pay* (New York: Boni & Liveright, 1926), p. 8. Subsequent references are placed within text.

[4]Brooks, *Toward Yoknapatawpha and Beyond*, p. 93.

[5]Millgate, "Starting Out in the Twenties: Reflections on *Soldiers' Pay*," in R. G. Collins and Kenneth McRobbie, eds., *Mosaic: The Novels of William Faulkner* (Winnipeg: University of Manitoba Press, 1973), p. 6.

[6]See "Faulkner's 'Atthis' and 'Attis': Some Sources of Myth," *Mississippi Quarterly*, 23 (Summer 1970): 289-298.

[7]Brooks, *Toward Yoknapatawpha and Beyond*, p. 68.

[8]" 'Shot Down Last Spring': The Wounded Aviators of Faulkner's Wasteland," *Mississippi Quarterly*, 31 (Summer 1978): 368.

[9]Brooks, *Toward Yoknapatawpha and Beyond*, p. 72.

Mosquitoes

William Faulkner's second novel, *Mosquitoes*, is a satire designed to expose human folly and the pretensions of man's intellectual abstractions, his love of "ideas." As Mary Dunlap has pointed out, Faulkner satirizes "civic groups, organized religion, war, education, women, boredom," and in so doing launches a headlong "attack on words, sex, and art, interrelating the last three topics with the theme of sterility."[1] If it is as satire that *Mosquitoes* enjoys its greatest success, that is also its most glaring weakness. As a novel of ideas, *Mosquitoes* outdoes *Soldiers' Pay*. The result is an arid book, at least in terms of action; yet it is a work that has its moments. There are flashes of rich humor, individual scenes that are vivid and forceful, and some penetrating characterizations.

Both *Soldiers' Pay* and *Mosquitoes* are modern novels—the only two that Faulkner would ever write—insofar as they represent responses to a particular set of social conditions. But whereas *Soldiers' Pay* was concerned with the moral and physical condition of postwar America in the year after the signing of the Armistice, *Mosquitoes* is preoccupied with the world of art, artists, and the ideas they debate. In *Soldiers' Pay* we see people trying to deal with the conditions created by war. By contrast, *Mosquitoes* seems populated by characters who suffer from self-inflicted wounds, yet who seem to enjoy talking about them, as if talk could make the wounds heal.

The action in *Soldiers' Pay* is developed over several months. In *Mosquitoes*, time is more compressed; everything that happens occurs in a little more than four days during August. There is a prologue that sets the stage, an epilogue that tries to make some sense of what has happened, and in between there are four chapters, one for each day the characters spend on board a yacht in Lake Ponchartrain, just north of New Orleans. The prologue and epilogue are set in New Orleans.

The first scene of the prologue is in the dingy studio of a sculptor named Gordon, perhaps the only true artist in the novel and a man far more dedicated to the practice of his craft than to talking about it. In the studio is a statue that establishes Gordon's credibility as an artist. The work has a quality about it, a vitality that creates the illusion of arrested motion:

> when you tore your eyes away and turned your back on it at last, you got again untarnished and high and clean that sense of swiftness, of space encompassed; but on looking again it was as before: motionless and passionately eternal—the virginal breastless torso of a girl, headless, armless, legless, in marble temporarily caught and hushed yet passionate still for escape, passionate and simple and eternal in the equivocal derisive darkness of the world. Nothing to trouble your youth or lack of it: rather something to trouble the very fibrous integrity of your being.[2]

Also in the studio, though much less impressive than the statue, is another of the novel's characters, Ernest Talliaferro. Talliaferro is no artist but rather a hanger-on among artists. Without any cause he fancies himself to be a patron and supporter of the arts. His overriding concern in life is sex; and, since he evidently believes that artists are more sexually charged than other people, he believes that by cultivating friendships with them he can learn how to dominate women. At the beginning of the novel, Talliaferro is confiding in Gordon, who is trying to work, telling him that "The sex instinct . . . is quite strong in me," that it is in fact "my most dominating compulsion" (p. 9). Gordon is not impressed by Talliaferro's confession nor by learning from Talliaferro that he has been invited, along with several other artists, aboard a yacht belonging to Mrs. Maurier, a wealthy widow who likes to surround herself with artists.

Added to the themes of sex and art in the opening scene is

that of talk. As it is developed in the novel, one of the key differences between artists and nonartists is that artists create, while nonartists talk about creating. Talliaferro, we learn, believes in conversation and that "Conversation—with an intellectual equal consisted of admitting as many so-called unpublishable facts as possible about oneself. Mr. Talliaferro often mused with regret on the degree of intimacy he might have established with his artistic acquaintances had he but acquired the habit of masturbation in his youth. But he had not even done this" (pp. 9-10).

Punctuating the world of art represented by Gordon and the world of fastidious (and imaginary) eroticism represented by Talliaferro are representatives of the larger outside world, the mosquitoes who are happy to feed on artists and sycophants alike. The word *mosquitoes* is never used in the text of the novel. The insects are known only by their effect, as when Talliaferro slaps "vainly at the back of his hand" (p. 10), makes a savage slap at his neck (p. 11), and "standing on one leg like a crane," slaps "at his ankle, viciously and vainly" (p. 13). Here as elsewhere the mosquitoes serve as a subtle but constant reminder that there is a larger world surrounding the one in which the novel's characters move, and that artificial constructs—for example, art, criticism, education, and religion—cannot fence out the larger reality that is indifferent to the fates of individual men and women.

Gordon refuses the invitation for a cruise on board Mrs. Maurier's yacht, and, to get rid of Talliaferro, asks him to get a bottle of milk at a nearby store. While running his errand Talliaferro unexpectedly encounters Mrs. Maurier and her eighteen-year-old niece, Patricia Robyn, who is visiting her aunt. Thinking that Talliaferro has not invited Gordon to go on the cruise, Mrs. Maurier decides that the three of them should return to the studio so she can extend the invitation personally, thinking that it will be interesting for "Patricia to see how genius looks at home" (p. 21). In Gordon's studio,

Mrs. Maurier behaves with a combination of stupidity and rudeness. She blandly tells her niece that "Artists don't require privacy as we do; it means nothing whatever to them" (p. 30); and she makes no aesthetic response to Gordon's statue at all, only acknowledges that it is beautiful and asks "what does it signify" (p. 26). When Talliaferro suggests that the statue is "untrammeled by any relation to a familiar or utilitarian object" (p. 26), Mrs. Maurier responds enthusiastically, not to the statue but to Talliaferro's words; "Oh yes, untrammeled. . . . The untrammeled spirit, freedom like the eagle's" (p. 26).

Much of Faulkner's characterization in *Mosquitoes* is achieved through the revelation of basic similarities and differences between people in groups. This method is established from the outset. In the prologue, Mrs. Maurier and Talliaferro show themselves to be similar: nonartists who seek to enhance their own self-images by association with real artists, or people whom they at least consider to be real artists. Though Patricia Robyn is not an artist herself she and Gordon share a similar aesthetic response to the statue and, as the narrative develops, there is sexual attraction as well, though it is not equally shared. Patricia is like many of Faulkner's young female characters. She is slim, almost boyish, yet possesses a compelling physical attraction. When Gordon first notices her he examines "with growing interest her flat breast and belly, her boy's body which the poise of it and the thinness of her arms belied. Sexless, yet somehow vaguely troubling. Perhaps just young, like a calf or a colt" (p. 24). Patricia physically resembles the statue Gordon has carved, and she responds very strongly to it. Her response to Gordon is somewhat ambivalent, but she is intrigued by him. While examining the statue she asks, "Why are you so black. . . . Not your hair and beard. I like your red hair and beard. But you. You are black" (p. 25). Interestingly, Gordon uses dark imagery to describe the statue, which by the end of the novel he associates with

Patricia. "She is dark, darker than fire," he says, "more terrible and beautiful than fire" (p. 329).

The remainder of the prologue serves to introduce some of the other characters: Patricia's brother, whom she usually refers to as Josh; Dawson Fairchild—generally assumed to be based on novelist Sherwood Anderson, whom Faulkner met in New Orleans and whose influence he later acknowledged; a poet named Mark Frost; and a critic of the arts whose first name is Julius, whose last name is probably Kauffman (see p. 327), and who is usually referred to as the Semitic man. Julius points to a profound difference between Fairchild and Gordon, the two characters in the novel with the most legitimate claims for being artists, claims strengthened by the fact that they do not spend time trying to convince others that they are artists. Responding to Fairchild's assertion that it is impossible for someone consciously to be an artist all the time, Julius claims ironically that Fairchild is not an artist. "There is somewhere within you," he says, "a bewildered stenographer with a gift for people. . . . You are an artist only when you are telling about people . . ." (p. 51). By contrast he asserts that "Gordon is not an artist only when he is cutting at a piece of wood or stone" (p. 51). Thus, Julius suggests that Gordon, who views the world constantly as an artist, never as anything else, has an intensity that Fairchild lacks.

It is in the fifth section of the prologue that Fairchild makes his first appearance. The scene is set in a French Quarter restaurant where Fairchild is being a host of sorts to a visiting Rotarian named Mr. Hooper. With him are Julius and Mark Frost, and they are soon joined by Talliaferro. Mr. Hooper is an exponent of twentieth-century American materialism and he views Christianity as part of the country's material culture, to be promoted just like any other business. Having been led to believe by Fairchild that Talliaferro is a Rotarian, he congratulates him on the New Orleans Rotary organization, saying that New Orleans is a worthy place, "Except for this southern laziness of yours. You folks need more northern blood, to bring out all your possibilities" (p. 35). He has what he thinks is an ingenious plan for getting people to attend church regularly: "by keeping them afraid they'd miss something good by staying away" (p. 36). Hooper represents another aspect of the world, the macrocosm that encompasses the smaller world of artists, dilettantes, and hangers-on who go sailing on Mrs. Maurier's yacht, and his pronouncements give rise to criticisms about American culture, particularly the institutions of religion and education. Fairchild remarks that "God must look about our American scene with a good deal of consternation, watching the antics of those volunteers who are trying to help him" (p. 40), and he muses that only Americans would have to conceive of God as "a Rotarian or an Elk or a Boy Scout" (p. 40); Julius suggests that the church should never have tried to Christianize Jesus, that the old ideal of humility was better than the modern concept of "willynilly Service" (p. 41). Education is linked to religion on the ground that the primary benefit of each is to get the children out of the house. Julius elaborates on modern education: "to take an education by the modern process is like marrying in haste and spending the rest of your life making the best of it. But . . . I have no quarrel with education. I don't think it hurts you much, except to make you unhappy and unfit for work, for which man was cursed by the gods before they had learned about education" (pp. 41-42). It is Fairchild who states the principle that applies not only to the themes of education and religion, but to most of the other ideas that are discussed in the novel:

> When you are young, you join things because they profess high ideals. You believe in ideals at that age, you know. Which is all right, as long as you just believe in them as ideals and not as criterions of conduct. But after a while you join more things, you are getting older and more sedate and sensible; and believing in ideals is too much trouble so you begin to live up to them with your

outward life, in your contacts with other people. And
when you've made a form of behavior out of an ideal, it's
not an ideal any longer, and you become a public nuisance
(pp. 38-39).

The last sentence of that quotation is one of the keys to understanding the characters in *Mosquitoes*. Those who spend the
most time trying to verbalize concepts of an ideal—whether it
be of art, sex, economics, or life in general—are usually those
who are farthest removed from it.

Faulkner injects some stylistic diversity into the narrative as
the prologue comes to an end. He breaks the movement of
linear time by using a stream-of-consciousness style to take the
reader inside Gordon's mind. This technique also hints at a
theme to be developed later in the novel, that it is one of the
functions of art to create artificially an ordered picture of life
and thereby help us to better understand something about the
nature of human existence, which in itself tends to be disor-
derly, illogical, and chaotic. We get our first glimpse of this
turmoil in Gordon's thoughts:

fool fool you have work to do o cursed of god cursed
and forgotten form shapes cunningly sweated cunning to
simplicity shapes out of chaos more satisfactory than
bread to the belly form by a madmans dream gat on the
body of chaos le garcon vierge of the soul horned by
utility o cuckold of derision (p. 47).

As the prologue began by introducing the themes of art and
sex—albeit comically in light of Talliaferro's posturings—so it
ends; but by now the tension between the two themes has
become much more serious and is centered in just one man,
Gordon. His sense of discipline, his commitment to his art,
tells him to stay in his studio; the sexual attraction he feels for
Patricia Robyn compels him to go on the yachting party, a
meaningless social activity he would otherwise avoid. Com-

paring himself to the angel Israfel,[3] and thinking at the same time of Patricia, the tension between sex and art becomes painfully acute: "what will you say to her bitter and new as a sunburned flame bitter and new those two little silken snails somewhere under her dress horned pinkly yet reluctant o israfel ay wax your wings with the thin odorless moisture of her thighs strangle your heart with hair . . ." (p. 48).

The chapter that covers the first day of the voyage on board Mrs. Maurier's yacht, the *Nausikaa*, introduces the rest of the main characters: Eva Wiseman (a poet), Julius's sister Dorothy Jameson (a painter), Major Ayers (a British businessman), David West (a steward who has gotten his job with the help of Dawson Fairchild), and Jenny Steinbauer and her boyfriend Pete (two young people whom Patricia meets and asks to come along). Very little actually happens. There is lunch, an attempt at a bridge game, an impromptu swimming party, and we see Mrs. Maurier becoming increasingly upset over her inability to control the men, most of whom are with Fairchild who has come aboard liberally supplied with liquor. The ship's steering mechanism is damaged when Josh, Patricia's brother, takes a rod from it to use in boring out a pipe he is making.

By the beginning of the second day the crew has discovered that the helm of the yacht does not operate properly, but they do not know why. The result is that the vessel drifts toward the shore and runs aground on a sandbar. The characters continue to talk. On the third day Patricia Robyn persuades David West to leave the yacht with her and to walk into Mandeville, a resort town on the lake. While David and Patricia have their adventure, which turns into a fiasco, Fairchild organizes an ineffectual attempt to free the *Nausikaa* from the sandbar. Gordon leaves the yacht's company and, since no one sees him go, is feared drowned. On the fourth day a tugboat comes to free the yacht. The day is filled with more talk of art, sex, and the meaninglessness of words. The epilogue sets the novel's characters back out into the larger world they left four days ago, but it does not attempt to resolve in any absolute way the various themes that have been explored during the course of the voyage.

The structure of *Mosquitoes* reveals one of Faulkner's abiding interests, the influence of time on the human condition and the question of what time actually is. Framed by a prologue and epilogue, the structure of *Mosquitoes* is best described as circular. Whereas in *Soldiers' Pay* the actions of the various characters were portrayed through a linear progression of the events (March through May) the characters in *Mosquitoes* end up in the same places and conditions from which they had started, and with the original basic tension between art and sex unresolved. Thus, novelistic structure seems to support one of the novel's major themes, voiced by Julius: "Life everywhere is the same. . . . Manners of living it may be different . . . but man's old compulsions, duty and inclination: the axis and the circumference of his squirrel cage, they do not change" (p. 243).[4] Responding to Fairchild's assertion that the function of art is to help people "remember grief and forget time," Julius counters: "Something, if all a man has to do is forget time. . . . But one who spends his days trying to forget time is like one who spends his time forgetting death or digestion" (p. 319). Time, in a sense, is an invention of man and therefore he cannot escape from it. The world of nature, of the cosmos with its "remote chill stars" and "decaying . . . moon" looking down on an "empty world" (p. 162), exists independently of man's world of finite time and by implication is indifferent to the condition of man. The impression of linear time in the novel—the four successive days of the voyage—is deceptive. By breaking the days of the voyage into hourly units Faulkner shows the fragmented nature of "real" time and achieves an effect of simultaneity, a method that also enhances the counterpointing of characters and events within the novel. Though not particularly complex in this novel, Faulkner's handling of time and his growing thematic concerns with the concept of time—especially as this would lead to a deep interest in the past—is of paramount importance in such novels as *The Sound and the Fury*, *Absalom, Absalom!*, and *Go Down, Moses*.

Summarizing the reception of the novel at the time it was published, Joseph Blotner points out that while it was praised by Conrad Aiken and Lillian Hellman, it was far from a critical success. Popular critics generally found the novel imitative and undistinguished,[5] an opinion borne out by more recent criticism. Cleanth Brooks observes that "Faulkner is not always careful of the rules, but he is never careless"; and of *Mosquitoes* he concedes that though the young writer may be "sometimes shaky on the spelling of certain words and not always aware of their exact meanings," the novel nevertheless reveals Faulkner's fascination with words and "what one could do with them."[6] Michael Millgate evaluates the novel as a satiric roman a clef—a novel in which one of the "keys" to understanding the work is being able to identify the real people represented by the fictional characters—and believes that it represents a deliberate turning away from the influence of Sherwood Anderson who, in the character of Dawson Fairchild, is treated in a not too flattering manner.[7]

Like *Soldiers' Pay*, however, *Mosquitoes* has been the subject of a number of thoughtful and useful scholarly essays. Because of the liberal sprinkling of literary allusions throughout the work, *Mosquitoes* has held a special attraction for those interested in the literary sources that may have influenced Faulkner's early career. Sometimes the impulse for source hunting has been taken to extreme ends; but there have been some very sound studies on relationships between *Mosquitoes* and the works of T. S. Eliot, James Joyce, and Joseph Hergesheimer.[8] By far the most exhaustive and useful study of possible sources and influences for *Mosquitoes* is Edwin T. Arnold's previously cited dissertation, "William Faulkner's *Mosquitoes*: An Introduction and Annotations to the Novel."

With *Mosquitoes*, Faulkner's apprenticeship as a novelist came to an end. And if this second novel was not quite as impressive as his first attempt had been, that only serves to heighten the achievement of *Flags in the Dust*, the first of Faulkner's novels to be set in his fictional Jefferson, and the first novel in which he begins to grapple with the problem of the past in some of its more complex aspects.

---

[1]Mary Dunlap, "Sex and the Artist in *Mosquitoes*," *Mississippi Quarterly*, 22 (Summer 1969): 190.

[2]*Mosquitoes* (New York: Boni & Liveright, 1927), p. 11. Subsequent references are placed within text.

[3]The name Israfel may be a particular reference to Edgar Allan Poe's poem "Israfel," and/or a more general reference to the angel of Arabic literature who is to blow his trumpet on Judgment Day. In his typescript, Faulkner used the name of Araphel who appears in the apocryphal book of Enoch. These various sources are all discussed by Edwin T. Arnold III in his "William Faulkner's *Mosquitoes*: An Introduction and Annotations to the Novel," Ph.D. dissertation, University of South Carolina, 1978, pp. 59-60.

[4]See also Faulkner's 1925 essay, "Verse Old and Nascent": "Life is not different from what it was when Shelley drove like a swallow southward from the unbearable English winter; living may be different, but not life. Time changes us, but Time's self does not change" (*Early Prose and Poetry*, p. 118).

[5]See Blotner, pp. 548-549.

[6]Brooks, *Toward Yoknapatawpha and Beyond*, pp. 132-133.

[7]See Millgate, pp. 68, 72.

[8]See, respectively, Gwynn, "Faulkner's Prufrock—And Other Observations," *Journal of English and Germanic Philology*, 52 (January 1953): 63-70; Joyce W. Warren, "Faulkner's 'Portrait of the Artist,' " *Mississippi Quarterly*, 19 (Summer 1966): 121-131; and Phyllis Franklin, "The Influence of Joseph Hergesheimer upon *Mosquitoes*," *Mississippi Quarterly*, 22 (Summer 1969): 207-213.

Flags in the Dust (Sartoris)

The severely cut and edited version of *Flags in the Dust* that was published as *Sartoris* in 1929 begins with the scene in which Will Falls gives Bayard Sartoris (known as "old Bayard") a pipe that had belonged to Bayard's father, John Sartoris. *Flags in the Dust*, the novel that Faulkner reluctantly allowed Ben Wasson to edit as a condition for getting it published, moves the opening scene back a little bit so that we first see Will Falls telling Bayard Sartoris a story about his father that he has told him many times before: how during the Civil War Col. John Sartoris managed to fool a detail of Yankee cavalry that had come looking for him. The difference is an important one. The uncut version establishes at the outset not just the importance of the past as a key to understanding human behavior, but also the primacy of point of view in interpreting the past. Neither the past nor time itself has any concrete reality beyond an individual's perception of them. As in *Soldiers' Pay*, the seasonal cycles of nature establish the existence of time; but it is the interpretation of human events within time that invests the dimension with meaning. In its cyclical movement through time, nature does not make moral choices. Men do; and in *Flags in the Dust* the choices that men make derive in part from a welter of differing views on the meaning of time and of the past.

In this sense the novel begins on an ironic note. Will Falls, from whose point of view the reminiscence is told, was not himself a witness to the scene he describes. But Bayard Sartoris was, a salient fact that does not in the least affect the way that Falls tells the story:

> Cunnel was settin' thar in a cheer, his sock feet propped
> on the po'ch railin', smokin' this hyer very pipe. Old

Louvinia was settin' on the steps, shellin' a bowl of peas
fer supper. . . . And you was settin' back agin' the post.
They wa'nt nobody else thar 'cep' yo' aunt, the one 'fo'
Miss Jenny come. . . . You was 'bout half-grown, I
reckon.[1]

Blandly, Falls pauses to ask Bayard just how old he was at the
time. Bayard says that he was fourteen, and then adds, "Do I
have to tell you that every time you tell me this damn story?"
(p. 3). Thus it appears that Falls's story is in itself a kind of
ritual, part of a body of reminiscences by which he remembers
and ascribes certain values to the life of Bayard's father. Apparently the effect of Falls's storytelling is the same each time: "As
usual old man Falls had brought John Sartoris into the room
with him. Freed as he was of time, he was a far more definite
presence in the room than the two of them [Falls and Bayard]
cemented by deafness to a dead time and drawn thin by the
slow attenuation of days" (p. 5).

    The first chapter of the novel is filled with references to time
and to the past. The Sartoris house is itself a reminder of the
family's past; within the house there are various objects associated with specific aspects of the past. For example, a "narrow window set with leaded vari-colored panes . . . which
John Sartoris' youngest sister [Virginia Du Pre] had brought
from Carolina in a straw-filled hamper in '69" (p. 11) is associated in Bayard's mind with the way in which Miss Jenny
recounts the death of her brother and Bayard's uncle, also
named Bayard, in Virginia during the Civil War. The story—of
how Jeb Stuart, Bayard Sartoris, and a detail of Confederate
cavalry raided a Yankee headquarters for coffee, and of how
Bayard was shot by a cook when he returned to the commis-
sary tent in search of anchovies—is one that Miss Jenny, like
Will Falls, has told many times:

    and as she grew older the tale itself grew richer and richer,
    taking on a mellow splendor like wine; until what had

been a hair-brained prank of two heedless and reckless boys wild with their own youth, was become a gallant and finely tragical focal-point to which the history of the race had been raised from out the old miasmic swamps of spiritual sloth by two angels valiantly and glamorously fallen and strayed, altering the course of human events and purging the souls of men (p. 12).

In a sense, old man Falls and Miss Jenny do not just remember the past. They create it, and create it in such a way that the past becomes consistent with, and is used to support, their comprehension of reality. This is not altogether bad inasmuch as their views are based on positive values: a sense of right and wrong and a belief in the integrity of community and family. However, some of the other characters in the novel do not interpret the past from such a healthy point of view.

Problems posed by the past are sometimes not far removed from the present. In this case the present is the spring of 1919, and the problem of the immediate past is posed in the character of young Bayard Sartoris (grandson of old Bayard). He and his twin brother John were both fliers in World War I. Bayard survived the war but John was shot down and killed in July of the previous year, a few months before the signing of the Armistice in November 1918. Though physically sound, young Bayard is badly wounded in a psychological sense. His brother's death is something he cannot get over; and when he arrives home unexpectedly he launches immediately into a disjointed, almost hysterical account of John's death. Unlike the stories told by Miss Jenny or old man Falls, Bayard's accounts and memories yield no meaning or conclusion to his brother's death. He is oppressed by "the dark and stubborn struggling of his heart" (p. 39); and the fate of his brother looms larger in his mind than does the memory of his wife, who died in childbirth while he was away. At home now, and in the room that he and his brother had shared growing up, and that he had shared briefly with his wife, he thinks not of her but of his brother: "the spirit of their violent complementing days lay like a dust everywhere in the room, obliterating the scent of that other presence" (p. 42).

Time is also bound to processes of change, of which there are a number of indicators in the first chapter of the novel. Simon Strother, an old retainer of the Sartoris family, transports Miss Jenny and old Bayard in a horse-drawn carriage and is contemptuous of those blacks who carry their employers about in automobiles. Arriving in Jefferson to pick up Miss Jenny from a party, he tells one such chauffeur, "Dont block off no Sartoris ca'iage, black boy. . . . Block off de commonality, ef you wants, but dont intervoke no equipage waitin' on Cunnel er Miss Jenny" (p. 22). Another symbol of change and modernity is the railroad, which old Bayard's father, the Colonel Sartoris of Will Falls's memory, built during the years following the Civil War. What had been one man's dream and the creation of one man's enterprise and sacrifice has been altered from its original conception so that the railroad now "belonged to a syndicate and there were more than two trains on it, and they ran from Chicago to the Gulf, completing his dream, though John Sartoris himself slept these many years . . . lapped in the useless vainglory of that Lord which his forefathers had imagined themselves in the rare periods of their metaphysical speculations" (p. 37). Change is not ultimately shaped or controlled by the dreams and values of those who set it in motion. Whether ordained by God or Mammon, change generates its own momentum, and there is only one thing that is certain about it: in time it will occur.

The second chapter begins on a comic note. Simon's son Caspey has served in a Negro labor battalion in France during the war, and the experience seems to have left him unfit for life back home. Caspey arrives home the same day that Bayard does; and Miss Jenny, on learning that he is sleeping late the morning after his arrival remarks, "Well, let him sleep this morning. Give him a day to get over the war. But if it made a fool out of him like it did Bayard, he'd better . . . go back to it. I'll declare, men cant seem to stand anything" (p. 45). The war may not have made a fool of Caspey, but it did give him some unsettling ideas. He feels himself somehow to have been liberated by the war, and at one point he boasts, "I got my white in France, and I'm gwine git it here, too" (p. 56). To Simon, his sister Elnora, and his nephew Isom he announces, "I dont take nothin' f'um no white folks no mo'. . . . War done changed all that. If us colored folks is good enough to save France f'um de Germans, den us is good enough to have de same rights de Germans has. . . . Yes, suh, it wuz de colored soldier saved France and America bofe" (p. 53). Asked by Isom how many Germans he killed during the war, Caspey replies, "I aint never bothered to count 'um up. Been times I kilt mo' in one mawnin' dan dey's folks on dis whole place" (p. 53). Caspey's accounts of adventure and personal heroism fall into the category of humorous tall tales, but their function is not altogether different from the reminiscences of Will Falls and Miss Jenny. Caspey, like them, is interpreting the past as he wishes it to have been.

In contrast to Caspey and his temporary disillusionment, young Bayard sinks deeper and deeper into his personal despair. No longer having an airplane to fly, he continues to seek speed, violence, and possibly death by going to Memphis to purchase a fast automobile. He succeeds in giving himself a concussion by trying, while drunk, to ride a temperamental horse. In the second chapter we are also given more information about the twinship of Bayard and John Sartoris. Narcissa Benbow, who will marry Bayard, correctly senses a basic difference between the two brothers. In her memory she sees John as someone "who had not waited for Time and its furniture to teach him that the end of wisdom is to dream high enough not to lose the dream in the seeking of it" (p. 63). She remembers both brothers as having an "air of smoldering abrupt violence"; in Bayard this was "a cold, arrogant sort of leashed violence, while in John it was a warmer thing, spontaneous and merry and wild" (p. 64). John, it would seem, did not pursue violence for the sake of violence alone. Bayard does; and ultimately his pursuit of violence becomes an escape from time and memory, and from the responsibility of coping with grief. These distinctions, though observed by Narcissa, are pretty much lost on her. Narcissa insulates herself from time by adopting an air of "grave tranquility like a visible presence or an odor or a sound" (p. 94), an "aura of grave on serene repose" (p. 26). Concerning the Sartoris twins, "it was not in her nature to differentiate between motives whose results were the same," and she reacts to both with "that shrinking, fascinated distaste, that blending of curiosity and dread, as if a raw wind had blown into that garden wherein she dwelt" (p. 65).

The interlocking themes of time and the past, of fate and mortality, are further advanced in the second chapter when old Bayard climbs into the attic and opens a chest filled with family memorabilia, including the family Bible. The chest has not been opened since 1901, when Bayard's son John died, and so "each opening was in a way ceremonial, commemorating the violent finis to some phase of his family's history, and while he struggled with the stiff lock it seemed to him that a legion of ghosts breathed quietly at his shoulder" (p. 80). Bayard is extracting the Bible now to record the deaths of John Sartoris (his grandson) in July of 1918 and of young Bayard's wife and son in October of the same year. As he does so, he shows a depth of understanding of the complexity of time that is not matched by any other character in the novel:

> Yes, it was a good gesture, and Bayard sat and mused quietly on the tense he had unwittingly used. Was. Fatality again: the augury of a man's destiny peeping out at him from the roadside hedge, if he but recognise it. . . .
>   The unturned corners of man's destiny. Well, heaven, that crowded place, lay just beyond one of them,

they claimed; heaven, filled with every man's illusion of himself and with the conflicting illusions of him that parade through the minds of other illusions . . . (pp. 82-83).

Recalling that day when at the age of fourteen he helped his father escape the Yankee cavalry, Bayard remembers hiding in the undergrowth and later, after the patrol had passed, going to a spring, "and as he leaned his mouth to it the final light of day was reflected onto his face, bringing into sharp relief forehead and nose above the cavernous sockets of his eyes and the panting animal snarl of his teeth, and from the still water there stared back at him for a sudden moment, a skull" (p. 82). Unlike Miss Jenny, Bayard does not need to create myths in order to reach an understanding of his fellow Sartorises. To his credit, Bayard possesses a sober and unsentimental realization that time's ultimate fate for man, be he Sartoris or not, is death, and that the dividing line between life and death is always a narrow one.

One of the major character pairings in *Flags in the Dust* derives from the contrast drawn by Faulkner between Bayard Sartoris and Horace Benbow, though the two characters appear only once in a scene together. Horace's homecoming occurs in the third chapter of the novel, and that chapter is largely given over to the relationship between him and his sister Narcissa and the affair that leads to his marriage to Belle Mitchell. As Horace moves closer to Belle, Narcissa moves closer to Bayard, who, after occupying himself for a season with the business of the farm, injures himself seriously by running his automobile off a bridge. One obvious contrast between Horace and Bayard is their relationship to Narcissa. In neither case—that of brother-sister or husband-wife—is there a healthy or completely natural relationship. Both men, in different ways, are too weak and selfish to give anything of themselves.

Other equally obvious contrasts between Horace and Bay-

ard—their wartime service and their postwar courtships—
tend to make the same point. They are both isolated by their
self-centeredness from the community in which they live. As
Cleanth Brooks has observed, Bayard Sartoris and Horace
Benbow are different kinds of romantic personalities.[2]
Horace's brand of romanticism—intellectual, sensitive, and
aesthetic—is as destructive and antisocial as Bayard's violent,
Byronic gestures.

There is also a comparison established between old Bayard
and young Bayard in the third chapter. Following his automobile accident, young Bayard returns to his room and takes
from a chest several objects that had belonged to his brother: a
New Testament, a jacket, a shotgun shell, and a bear's paw. He
takes these painful reminders of his brother, along with a
photograph of John's eating club group at Princeton, outside,
where he burns them. This scene contrasts with old Bayard's
opening of the attic chest; while Bayard shows a mature sense
of reverence for the past, his grandson seeks to destroy it, as if
he were attempting to purge his soul with fire and by so doing
relieve himself of his burden of remorse and guilt.

The novel reaches its denouement in the fourth chapter,
during which the action is advanced from October to Christmas of 1919. Narcissa is now married to Bayard and pregnant
with his child. Another automobile accident, which forces
Bayard off the road and sends him crashing through forest
undergrowth before he can regain control of his car, proves to
be too much of a stress for his grandfather, who is riding with
him, and old Bayard dies of a heart attack. Young Bayard
cannot bring himself to return home after he has caused his
grandfather's death. He seeks temporary escape by going to
visit with the MacCallums, a country family that embodies
many of the virtues—honesty, self-reliance, pride, courtesy—that Faulkner admired in the rural people of Mississippi.
Bayard and John had been in the habit of hunting with the
MacCallums before the war; and it was Rafe MacCallum who,

in the second chapter, pressed Bayard to come for a visit, sensing that Bayard was deeply disturbed and needed to reestablish contact with fundamental things. The MacCallum clan is not altogether idealized. MacCallum and his six sons live in a womanless world; and even though there is a Negro cook, it is Henry MacCallum—about whom there is "something domestic, womanish" (p. 308)—who looks after the kitchen and supervises the various household chores. Only Buddy, the youngest, offers any hope that the family name might be perpetuated.

It is while he is visiting the MacCallums that some of Bayard's inmost thoughts about his brother's death are revealed. He told Narcissa earlier that after John jumped from his burning plane, he disappeared in the clouds, and Bayard was unable to get sight of him again. This aspect of John's death is particularly tormenting to Bayard and the first night at the MacCallum place he relives the moment, thinking:

> Perhaps he was dead, and he recalled that morning, relived it again with strained and intense attention from the time he had seen the first tracer smoke. . . ; relived it again, as you might run over a printed tale, trying to remember, feel, a bullet going into his body or head that might have slain him at the same instant. That would account for it, would explain so much: that he too was dead and this was hell, through which he moved forever and ever with an illusion of quickness, seeking his brother who in turn was somewhere seeking him, never the two to meet (p. 315).

Not only may death be an escape for Bayard; it may also be that on some subconscious level Bayard feels that in death he might find the twin he has lost in life. Bayard leaves the MacCallums on Christmas Eve, before they learn of old Bayard's death. Bayard spends that night in a Negro's barn, and on Christmas Day he has himself driven to a train depot so he can leave the country.

From that point the novel moves quickly to a conclusion. The fifth chapter briefly chronicles Horace Benbow's unhappiness in his marriage to Belle Mitchell. It also plots, in erratic fashion, Bayard's progress from place to place until he dies in an airplane crash on the fifth of June, the day Narcissa gives birth to their son. As though to deny the fate Miss Jenny seems to predict for the child by wanting to name it John, Narcissa decides that his name shall be Benbow Sartoris.

Though *Flags in the Dust* is set in Yocona rather than Yoknapatawpha County, the book clearly has its place among Faulkner's Yoknapatawpha novels. The town of Jefferson is the same as in later works and *Flags in the Dust* introduces a number of family names that figure significantly in Faulkner's fictional county and town: Sartoris, Benbow, and Snopes. The character V. K. Suratt later appears as V. K. Ratliff in *The Hamlet*. The novel is quite different from Faulkner's first two productions. Unlike *Soldiers' Pay* and *Mosquitoes*, there is no preamble, no setting of the stage. The work is in motion from the outset, and in its array of characters and multiplicity of story lines it is a far more ambitious undertaking than its predecessors. *Flags in the Dust* is the first of Faulkner's works that has any detailed development of black characters, who are generally presented as having a greater sense of fidelity and reverence for family and community values than their white counterparts. As Cleanth Brooks points out, the novel "is not an argument about what the relation between the two races ought to be, but a rendering of the actuality of its time."[3] Just as complex as Faulkner's treatment of black characters is his treatment of poor whites. The largest clan of poor whites in the Yoknapatawpha fiction is the Snopeses. Byron Snopes gets detailed treatment in *Flags in the Dust* and there are references to other members of the family who reappear in later novels. Though Snopeses are generally associated with the baser qualities of human nature—lust, greed, acquisitiveness, rapacity— Faulkner is very careful to make it clear that greed and rapacity, in all their guises, are endemic to the race of man and are much larger than any individual exponent of them.

The theme of material greed, and the willingness of men to desecrate the land in exchange for personal gain and wealth, receives a brief but powerful treatment in a later part of the novel describing the town to which Horace and Belle move after their marriage:

> Ten years ago the town was a hamlet, twelve miles from the railroad. Then a hardwood lumber concern had bought up the cypress swamps nearby and established a factory in the town. It was financed by eastern capital and operated by as plausible and affable a set of brigands as ever stole a county. They robbed the stockholders and the timber owners and one another and spent the money among the local merchants, who promptly caught the enthusiasm. . . . People in neighboring counties learned of all this and moved there and chopped all the trees down and built themselves mile after mile of identical frame houses with garage to match. . . . Yes, there was money there, how much, no two estimates ever agreed; whose, at any one given time, God Himself could not have said. But it was there, like that afflatus of rank fecundity above a foul and stagnant pool on which bugs dart spawning, die, are replaced in mid-darting . . . (pp. 341-342).

When published as *Sartoris* on 31 January 1929, Faulkner's third novel was not highly praised. In some cases it was simply misread, as in the case of the *New York Times* reviewer who declared the theme of the novel to be the struggle of the Old South against modern industrialism.[4] This is a variety of criticism that has been perpetuated in scholarly treatments as well. Walter Brylowski, for example, agrees that "the novel focuses primarily on two contrasting societies—the bucolic, backward-looking society symbolized by the horse, and the new machine society symbolized by the airplane and Bayard's automobile."[5]

Cleanth Brooks disagrees with those who argue a narrow Old South/New South approach to the novel. Concerning the character of Bayard Sartoris, he writes that "we must be careful not to misconstrue his Southern heritage. It is not . . . his sense of an ancestral responsibility for slavery that is gnawing at him. He is restless and disturbed, but his plight reflects the stunning effect of the war rather than the decadence of the Southern aristocratic tradition or the burden of a family curse."[6] Brooks concentrates on an understanding of the characters of the novel, stressing also Faulkner's development of tension between the male and female worlds of the novel: "Except for *Sanctuary*, no Faulkner novel brings the war between the sexes more clearly into the open or stresses more sharply what Faulkner conceives of as the basically different attitudes of men and women."[7] Michael Millgate focuses his comments on relations between the manuscript and typescript of *Flags in the Dust* and the published text of *Sartoris*. He also praises the technical advances achieved by Faulkner. Seasonal motifs are much better blended into the fabric of the work than they were in the first two novels, so that "in *Sartoris* the land, the weather, the seasons, and all aspects of the natural world function as essential elements in the conditioning environment of the characters."[8]

The differences between *Flags in the Dust* and the 1929 text of *Sartoris* are significant; Ben Wasson, acting with Faulkner's assent but not with his approval, cut about one quarter of *Flags in the Dust* in order to satisfy the demands of the publisher. The question of how good *Flags in the Dust* is still occupies critics. Most criticism that exists is of *Sartoris*, which is not the novel Faulkner wrote. Millgate reasons that "although *Flags in the Dust* was an imperfect novel, with a number of episodes treated at unnecessary length, it was in many ways a more satisfying book than *Sartoris*."[9] What its own merits or weaknesses may be is another question. We know that Faulkner thought highly of the work, and that he told Horace Liveright it would make his name for him as a writer.[10] Wasson's criticism, as reported by Douglas Day, that *Flags in the Dust* "was not one novel, but six, all struggling along simultaneously," was taken by Faulkner as corroborating "evidence of fecundity and fullness of vision."[11]

Faulkner said that *Sartoris* was the book that "has the germ of my apocrypha in it."[12] The statement is even more true of *Flags in the Dust* because it is a more complete work. In some ways, the germ that it contains begins to come to fruition immediately, in *The Sound and the Fury* with its intense examination of a single family, while the development of the broader themes of economics and social class does not occur until later works, such as *The Hamlet*.

---

[1]*Flags in the Dust* (New York: Random House, 1973), p. 3. Subsequent references are placed within text.

[2]See Brooks, *William Faulkner: The Yoknapatawpha Country* (New Haven: Yale University Press, 1963), p. 103.

[3]Brooks, *The Yoknapatawpha Country*, pp. 113-114.

[4]"A Southern Family," *New York Times Book Review*, 3 March 1929, p. 8.

[5]Walter Brylowski, *Faulkner's Olympian Laugh: Myth in the Novels* (Detroit: Wayne State University Press, 1968), p. 52.

[6]Brooks, *The Yoknapatawpha Country*, p. 104.

[7]Brooks, *The Yoknapatawpha Country*, p. 107.

[8]Millgate, p. 77.

[9]Millgate, p. 84.

[10]See *Letters*, p. 39.

[11]"Introduction," *Flags in the Dust*, p. viii.

[12]*Faulkner in the University*, p. 285.

The Sound and the Fury

When he was asked what he considered his best work, William Faulkner was not inclined to give a direct answer, though he consistently identified *The Sound and the Fury*, his fourth novel, published on 7 October 1929 by Jonathan Cape and Harrison Smith, as the book he worked at the hardest. It was, he said, "The one that failed the most tragically and the most splendidly. . . . the one that I worked at the longest, the hardest, that was to me the most passionate and moving idea, and made the most splendid failure."[1] Explaining to a questioner at the University of Virginia in 1957 how the novel grew, Faulkner said:

> It began with the picture of the little girl's [Caddy's] muddy drawers, climbing that tree to look in the parlor window with her brothers that didn't have the courage to climb the tree waiting to see what she saw. And I tried first to tell it with one brother, and that wasn't enough. That was Section One. I tried with another brother, and that wasn't enough. That was Section Two. I tried the third brother, because Caddy was still to me too beautiful and too moving to reduce her to telling what was going on, that it would be more passionate to see her through somebody else's eyes, I thought. And that failed and I tried myself—the fourth section—to tell what happened, and I still failed.[2]

This explanation is consistent with that given in an introduction written for *The Sound and the Fury* in 1933 (but which was not published until 1973), in which Faulkner stated that the novel was essentially the story of Caddy Compson. "When I began the book," he wrote, "I had no plan at all. I wasn't even writing a book. . . . The story is all there, in the first section as Benjy told it. I did not try deliberately to make it obscure;

when I realized that the story might be printed, I took three more sections, all longer than Benjy's, to try to clarify it."[3] Faulkner also indicates in the introduction that the writing of *The Sound and the Fury* represented a turning point in his career, one that had personal as well as professional significance. He claimed that the writing of the novel taught him about reading and writing, and that since the writing of the book he had discovered

> that the emotion definite and physical and yet nebulous to describe which the writing of Benjy's section . . . gave me—that ecstasy, that eager and joyous faith and anticipation of surprise which the yet unmarred sheets beneath my hand held inviolate and unfailing—will not return. The unreluctance to begin, the cold satisfaction in work well and arduously done, is there and will continue to be there as long as I can do it well. But that other will not return. I shall never know it again.[4]

The Compson family itself held great interest for Faulkner, and some of his short stories dealt with events involving Compson children. However, the earliest known version of *The Sound and the Fury* is a manuscript of 148 pages entitled "Twilight." Michael Millgate suggests that this title, if applied to the first section of the manuscript, might "refer to the half-world of Benjy himself, held in a state of timeless suspension between the light and the dark, comprehension and incomprehension, between the human and the animal"; whereas, applied to the book as a whole, "the word immediately suggests the decay of the Compson family caught at the moment when the dimmed glory of its eminent past is about to fade into ultimate extinction."[5] The book's final title is taken from *Macbeth* (act 5, scene 5): "Life's but a walking shadow, a poor player / That struts and frets his hour upon the stage / And then is heard no more: it is a tale / Told by an idiot, full of sound and fury, / Signifying nothing." Cleanth Brooks feels that the title is an appropriate one, "for the novel has to do with the discovery that life has no meaning."[6] Certainly, *The Sound and the Fury* does not present a rosy picture of the condition of man, but the title has broader implications. Taken in context with Macbeth's speech, it implies many of the things the original title did, and more: especially the concept of time, man's mortality—his "hour upon the stage"—as a backdrop that helps to dramatize the smallness and the greatness of human actions.

The Sound and the Fury may be, as Faulkner claimed, the story of Caddy Compson. But in telling her story from the first-person points of view of her three brothers, and from a final third-person point of view, Faulkner is also telling the story of the disintegration of the Compson family. Brooks emphasizes this point, and in so doing provides a useful counterweight against those critics who have viewed the novel as an allegory depicting the decline and fall of the Old South.

The four chapters of the novel are structured as units of time. Three are narrated by Caddy's brothers, Benjy, Quentin, and Jason. The final chapter focuses on Dilsey, the Compson family maid, who embodies qualities of endurance and loyalty that Faulkner frequently associates with his black characters. Together, the Benjy and Jason sections along with the final chapter render the events that take place on 6, 7, and 8 April 1928 (Friday, Saturday, and Easter Sunday). Quentin's section takes place on 2 June 1910, the day of his suicide. In the chronology of the book, however, the sequence of events is 7 April (Benjy's section), 2 June (Quentin's section), 6 April (Jason's section), and 8 April, which, though narrated in third person, is essentially Dilsey's section. Within Benjy's and Quentin's sections in particular there are many shifts in time. Thus, both in terms of external and internal structure, Faulkner—as he had done in different ways in his previous novels—shows time to be disjointed and fragmented, not a smooth chain of logically linked events. The way in which individual characters view or react to time is an important key to understanding their actions and motivations.

At the first reading of *The Sound and the Fury*, Benjy's section is the most difficult, both because of the stream-of-consciousness style used by Faulkner and because it is a first-person narration by an idiot. Some critics have argued that Benjy is the moral center of the novel and have based their interpretations of other characters on the way they react to Benjy; others have viewed him as a Christ figure since the time of the year is Easter and the day that his narration is given is his thirty-third birthday.[7] These views were never endorsed by Faulkner. Concerning the Christian symbolism in the novel (or in any of his novels, for that matter), Faulkner stated that it had the "Same advantage the carpenter finds in building square corners in order to build a square house"; and his own interpretation of Benjy was on an emotional, not a moral, basis: "You can't feel anything for Benjy because he doesn't feel anything. The only thing I can feel about him personally is concern as to whether he is believable as I created him. He was a prologue like the gravedigger in the Elizabethan dramas. He serves his purpose and is gone."[8]

At the beginning of Benjy's section, he and Luster, the young Negro who has charge of him, are watching some golfers. But because Benjy does not know what golf is, this information—as is true elsewhere in the section—must be gained by inference:

> Through the fence . . . I could see them hitting. They were coming toward where the flag was and I went along the fence. Luster was hunting in the grass by the flower tree. They took the flag out, and they were hitting. Then they put the flag back and they went to the table, and he hit and the other hit.[9]

The "hitting" refers to the action that is taking place, the "flag" to the flag on the green, and the "table" to the flat tee where the golfers start play on the next hole. Since Benjy is not capable of complex thought, his experiences are reported precisely as he perceives them and conversations just as he hears them. It is in keeping with his character that these should be transmitted to the reader in the form of simple declarative statements, without explanatory transitions. Sometimes Benjy's statements are elliptical, as when he says "They were hitting little, across the pasture" (p. 2), omitting the word "balls." Benjy's perceptions are related in sensory terms; thus, he smells the cold of winter, and he associates his memories of Caddy most often with the smell of trees (see p. 5). Benjy's section introduces, at one time or another, all of the novel's major characters. It establishes very clearly the importance of Caddy to Benjy and to the novel as a whole, and it contains the scene in which Caddy climbs the tree to look in on her grandmother's funeral—which Faulkner said was the central image for the work.

In a letter to his agent, Ben Wasson, written in the summer of 1929 before the novel was published, Faulkner identified seven different time sequences in Benjy's section: "Damuddy [the grandmother] dies. Benjy is 3. (2) His name is changed. He is 5. (3) Caddy's wedding. He is 14. (4) He tries to rape a young girl and is castrated. 15. (5) Quentin's death. (6) His father's death. (7) A visit to the cemetery at 18."[10] Time shifts in the section are indicated through a change in typefaces, and it is only by references to Benjy's birthday, the cake Dilsey is baking for him, and Luster's search for a quarter so he can go to the circus that the reader can tell when the action is in the present time (7 April 1928). For example, at the beginning of Benjy's section (p. 3), the difficulty of crawling through a fence takes him back in time (for two italicized paragraphs) to a Christmas season when Caddy helped him through the fence. Then there is a lengthier narrative from the same time period (set in roman type) involving Benjy, Caddy, Mrs. Compson, Maury (her brother), and Versh (oldest of Roskus and Dilsey's children), who had charge of Benjy when he was a child. This five-page narration, broken by a brief italicized paragraph in present time, ends with another italicized one-paragraph shift to the present (p. 8), which in turn serves as a bridge to another narration from the past—T. P., another of Roskus and Dilsey's children, is driving Mrs. Compson and Benjy into town so that Mrs. Compson can visit the graveyard where Mr. Compson and her son Quentin are buried.

It is not surprising that Benjy's recollections do not follow a chronological sequence. Time has no meaning for him: past and present are all part of a single continuum; only his perceptions of people and events have meaning. This is not to say that his narration is random or illogical. As Faulkner intended, the stream-of-consciousness style dramatizes "that unbroken-surfaced confusion of an idiot which is outwardly a dynamic and logical coherence."[11] A good example of this "logical coherence" is when Benjy finds Caddy's bastard daughter (named Quentin, after Caddy's dead brother) in the porch swing with a man wearing a red tie (p. 56)—he is from the circus and is the same man that Quentin later runs off with; Benjy remembers here an event that took place on 6 April 1928 and is treated in detail in Jason's section—and this leads to his recollection of finding Caddy in the same situation with a man named Charlie. Another time shift brings the action back to the present and there is a longer scene with Quentin and the man with the red tie. For Benjy, the connection between the two episodes is one of event, not of time. For the reader the scenes help to establish both the relationship between Caddy and her daughter and the different motivations for their promiscuity.

Though Benjy is oblivious to time, his brother Quentin is obsessed with it, as is indicated at the beginning of his section: "When the shadow of the sash appeared on the curtains it was between seven and eight oclock and then I was in time again" (p. 93). When this narration is delivered, on the day of his suicide, Quentin is quite deranged and the flashbacks to earlier times show the course his madness has followed. As Millgate has pointed out, "Whenever Quentin acts, his concern is for the act's significance as a gesture rather than for its practical efficacy,"[12] an inclination that is well illustrated by his fights with Gerald Bland, a fellow student at Harvard, and Dalton Ames, Caddy's lover. Quentin's acts are also based on his obsession with Caddy and her loss of innocence, which he is still unwilling or unable to accept.

The progression of events is much clearer in Quentin's section than in Benjy's. Quentin is consistent in his madness, and from the moment he leaves his dormitory room at Harvard, events lead logically and inexorably to the moment he commits suicide by jumping into the Charles River, his body weighted by flatirons. Interspersed throughout the section are references to Caddy's loss of virginity, her marriage to Herbert Head, and her affair with Dalton Ames. Conversations with Mr. Compson about these various matters are remembered, giving a particular insight into Mr. Compson's character—his alcoholism, the bleakness of his outlook, and his rationalization of misery and suffering. It is revealed that Mr. Compson sold Benjy's lot—which is turned into the golf course mentioned in the first section—to make it possible for Quentin to attend Harvard for one year. Quentin's thought processes are naturally more complex than Benjy's and this is reflected in the style of his section. At the same time his associations are more difficult to follow since different images relating to the same fixation tend to crowd one another, as in the following: *"Did you ever have a sister? One minute she was. Bitches. Not bitch one minute she stood in the door* Dalton Ames. Dalton Ames. Dalton Shirts. I thought all the time they were khaki. . . . until I saw they were of heavy Chinese silk or finest flannel . . ." (p. 113). In this passage are references to Quentin's obsession with Caddy, to her marriage, and to his perception of Dalton Ames. As in Benjy's section, typeface changes indicate time shifts, but here they reveal the frenetic nature of Quentin's personality underlying his surface calm and deliberateness.

Time is Quentin's great enemy because time brings change. Thus, once the premise of his madness is accepted, Quentin's actions are understandable. The way to defeat change is to defeat time, and the ultimate way to defeat time is through death. Quentin's other efforts to change reality, to somehow negate Caddy's loss of virginity, are to no avail. He tries to convince his father that he and Caddy have committed incest, hoping that through some ultimate sin he might have Caddy to himself: "Because if it were just to hell; if that were all of it. Finished. If things just finished themselves. Nobody else there but her and me. If we could just have done something so dreadful that they would have fled hell except us" (p. 97). At every turn, however, Mr. Compson denies Quentin his illusions. He tells him that "time is your misfortune" (p. 129), that "people . . . cannot do anything very dreadful at all they cannot even remember tomorrow what seemed dreadful today" (p. 98), and that "men invented virginity not women" (p. 96). At other places Mr. Compson tells his son that "Purity is a negative state and therefore contrary to nature" (p. 143), that man is simply the "sum of his climatic experiences. . . . the sum of what have you. A problem in impure properties carried tediously to an unvarying nil: stalemate of dust and desire" (p. 153), and that womanhood is a "Delicate equilibrium of periodical filth between two moons balanced" (p. 159). But as he strips away illusion, Mr. Compson gives nothing in its place, and the result is that Quentin, as we see him, is living in a twilight state that calls to mind the original title of the novel: "twilight . . . that quality of light as if time really had stopped for a while" (pp. 209-210).

Jason's section is rendered in traditional first-person narration. There are no italicized breaks to indicate time shifts because Jason is not at all confused—in his own mind, at least—about the past, the present, or the future. For him, time is a linear progression of seconds and minutes and hours. His goals and motivations are entirely materialistic, and he views himself as the victim of circumstances that have militated against him. His obsession with Caddy is quite different from Quentin's, but it is still very strong. He blames Caddy for the fact that he is only a store clerk; for when it was discovered that Caddy was pregnant by another man and she was cast off by her husband, Jason lost his opportunity at the bank job he had been promised. He freely takes his frustrations out on Caddy's daughter Quentin, now seventeen, who is living with Jason, Mrs. Compson, Benjy, and Dilsey. Jason feels justified in taking for himself the $200 a month that Caddy sends for Quentin's support—as he as been doing for fifteen years—and at the same time he lets his mother believe, in high-minded fashion, that they accept nothing from Caddy at all. Quentin may be a bastard by birth, but Jason is one by temperament. He systematically blackmails his sister, robs his niece, and hoodwinks his mother. At one point, when Caddy slips into town just to get a glimpse of her daughter, Jason takes $100 to arrange it; and later, when she sends Quentin $50 to spend for herself, Jason sees that Quentin gets only $10 of it.

All of Jason's efforts are ultimately fruitless, and seem to have self-defeat built into them. He gambles on the cotton market while berating "those eastern jews" who control it, and complains that "any damn foreigner that cant make a living in the country where God put him, can come to this one and take money right out of an American's pockets" (p. 239). Yet he persists in playing the market. The consistency of Jason's illogic is further revealed when he states his reason for not betting on the New York Yankees to win the World Series: "You think a team can be that lucky forever?" (p. 314). Jason resents Quentin's promiscuity as an affront to his own self-esteem. The latter portion of his section—which has some fine touches of comedy—involves his pursuit of Quentin and the circus man wearing the red tie. It turns out to be a futile chase that leaves Jason stranded in the country, five miles from town, with a flat tire. Not until the fourth section of the novel does

Jason find out how complete his comeuppance has been, when he discovers that Quentin has broken into his room and taken the money—sent by Caddy for her support—that he has been hoarding for the past fifteen years.

The fourth section of *The Sound and the Fury* is narrated from the third-person point of view and takes place on Easter Sunday. The chief character in this section is Dilsey, whose qualities of self-assurance, faith, and courage make her the most admirable character in the novel. Her sense of time is different from Benjy's and Quentin's and Jason's. When she hears a defective cabinet clock in the Compson house strike five times, she knows it is really eight o'clock. She does not need mechanical contrivances, which are often unreliable, to tell her what the time is. She knows. The quality of her faith, and the degree to which she is moved by it are shown by Faulkner's description of the scene at Dilsey's church during the Easter sermon.

Jason's pattern of frustration and self-defeat continues. Discovering Quentin's theft, he cannot report the true amount that has been taken because that would reveal his own thievery. He gets little sympathy from the sheriff, and his attempt to track Quentin down is unsuccessful. The novel ends with Benjy being driven around the town square by Luster: "his eyes were empty and blue and serene . . . as cornice and façade flowed smoothly once more from left to right; post and tree, window and doorway, and signboard, each in its ordered place" (p. 401). Both the images and the rhythm of the scene are suggestive of the passage in *Macbeth* from which the novel takes its title. The scene suggests a single smooth continuum to the characters' lives, without destination or meaning.

Late in 1945, sixteen years after *The Sound and the Fury* was first published, Faulkner prepared a genealogy of the Compson family from 1699 to 1945 to be published in Malcolm Cowley's *Portable Faulkner* (1946). "Appendix: Compson" was intended to provide background material for Cowley's selections from *The Sound and the Fury*, but it was considered by Faulkner to be a separate work from the novel; indeed, when Faulkner wrote the appendix, he did not have a copy of the novel at hand and there were factual discrepancies. When these seeming inconsistencies were pointed out by Cowley, Faulkner was cooperative about making minor changes, but he was unconcerned about making the appendix completely consistent with the facts of his novel. The only significance that Faulkner attached to the appendix was that it indicated to him that the Compson family and their story were still alive and growing.

Contemporary reviews of *The Sound and the Fury* were encouraging. "I believe simply and sincerely that this is a great book," Lyle Saxon wrote in the *New York Herald Tribune*. Most major reviewers concurred, but perhaps, as Joseph Blotner argues, because of the nation's financial decline, good notices did not translate into book sales. The initial printing of 1,789 copies was enough to satisfy customers for almost eighteen months.

Despite its modest sales at the time of its first publication, *The Sound and the Fury* has become one of Faulkner's most respected and most studied works; many critics maintain that it is his best novel. It has attracted far more critical attention than any other of his books. Among the most useful critical studies are Millgate's account of the novel's composition, with his cogent critical discussion, and Brooks's chapter in *The Yoknapatawpha Country* emphasizing the decline of the Compson family, and especially the role of Mrs. Compson in that decline. Eileen Gregory presents a helpful discussion of the composite picture that is given of Caddy in "Caddy Compson's World," and John W. Hunt finds a source of thematic suspense in the juxtaposed themes of loss and absence (Quentin and Caddy), and presence and endurance (Benjy and Dilsey).[13] Olga Vickery offers a well-reasoned discussion of Faulkner's handling of time in the novel: "Though man's measurement of time is logical, his comprehension of it depends not only on reason but on memory and hope. . . . Whereas memory confines the individual to the past, imagination can free him or, conversely, confirm his bondage."[14] Seen from this perspective, the message of *The Sound and the Fury* is not necessarily a negative or pessimistic one, that the world simply has no meaning. It says rather that as long as man is in time he has the ability to make choices, and must take responsibility for those choices.

---

[1]*Faulkner in the University*, p. 77.

[2]*Faulkner in the University*, p. 1.

[3]Meriwether, ed., "An Introduction to *The Sound and the Fury*," pp. 412, 414.

[4]Meriwether, ed., "An Introduction to *The Sound and the Fury*," pp. 414-415.

[5]Millgate, p. 86.

[6]Brooks, *The Yoknapatawpha Country*, p. 347.

[7]This kind of approach received an early impetus in Evelyn Scott, *On William Faulkner's The Sound and the Fury* (New York: Cape & Smith, 1929).

[8]*Lion*, pp. 245, 246.

[9]*The Sound and the Fury* (New York: Cape & Smith, 1929), p. 1. Subsequent references are placed within text.

[10]*Letters*, p. 44.

[11]*Letters*, p. 44.

[12]Millgate, p. 96.

[13]See Meriwether, ed., *The Merrill Studies in The Sound and the Fury* (Columbus, Ohio: Merrill, 1970), pp. 89-101; and John W. Hunt, *William Faulkner: Art in Theological Tension* (Syracuse, N.Y.: Syracuse University Press, 1965), pp. 35-99.

[14]Olga Vickery, *The Novels of William Faulkner: A Critical Interpretation* (revised edition, Baton Rouge: Louisiana State University Press, 1964), p. 257.

As I Lay Dying

William Faulkner most frequently spoke of *As I Lay Dying* as a tour de force—a display of great technical skill—and, by Faulkner's definition, a work that was conceived whole:

> Sometimes technique charges in and takes command of the dream before the writer himself can get his hands on it. That is *tour de force* and the finished work is simply a matter of fitting bricks neatly together, since the writer knows probably every single word right to the end before he puts the first one down. This happened with *As I Lay Dying*. It was not easy. No honest work is. It was simple in that all of the material was already at hand. It took me just about six weeks in the spare time from a 12 hour a day job at manual labor. I simply imagined a group of people and subjected them to the simple universal natural catastrophes which are flood and fire with a simple natural motive to give direction to their progress.[1]

Actually, the manuscript of the novel was written between 25 October and 11 December 1929, and the typescript is dated 12 January 1930. Still, *As I Lay Dying* was written in a remarkably short period of time for so complex a novel.[2] Though Faulkner often said it was written "without changing a word,"[3] there were numerous manuscript and typescript revisions.[4] Publication came on 6 October 1930, with an initial printing of just over 2,500 copies.

While *The Sound and the Fury* is the story of a town family, *As I Lay Dying* is the story of a country family, the Bundrens. Together, the two novels represent Faulkner's most extended use of the stream-of-consciousness technique in his writing. Each novel has the effect of taking the reader inside the minds of the individual characters so it is possible to see and understand their thought processes; but in *As I Lay Dying* the technique is used for a different purpose. The chapters in *As I Lay Dying* are, for the most part, quite short. They are narrated in the first person and are usually identified by the first name of the person who is speaking. Whenever there is dialogue involving other characters in a chapter, it is reported by that chapter's first-person voice. And, with the exception of the narrations of Cora, Tull, Peabody, Samson, Whitfield, Armstid, Moseley, and MacGowan (fourteen chapters), the remainder of the fifty-nine chapters are narrated by members of the Bundren family: Darl, Cash, Jewel, and Vardaman (the sons); Dewey Dell (the daughter); Addie and Anse (the mother and father). Portions of Darl's monologues differ significantly from those of other characters. His madness makes him appear to be something of a mystic; and, as his thoughts project into the future, he seems actually to be prescient. It is he, for example, who imagines Addie's death while he and Jewel are on their way to pick up a load of lumber (pp. 46-51). Addie's one monologue has also presented some problems to readers because it occurs while the family is on its way to Jefferson to bury her. It is not a supernatural passage in which Addie speaks from the casket. Rather it is a flashback—without the use of italics—in which Addie is thinking about her life shortly before she died.

Essentially, the story this novel tells is of Addie Bundren's death and the difficulties experienced by the rest of the family in getting her buried. The journey to Jefferson—where Addie has insisted she be buried, alongside members of her own family—is impeded and complicated by a number of natural obstacles and human problems. In turn, Faulkner uses these difficulties to reveal the character traits of individual family members.

Throughout the novel the stream-of-consciousness technique is used to indicate the difference between what the characters say in their own words and the complex thoughts and feelings that lie behind those words. Consider, for example, Darl's description of Jewel mounting his horse: "They stand in rigid terrific hiatus, the horse trembling and groaning. Then Jewel is on the horse's back. He flows upward in a stooping swirl like the lash of a whip, his body in midair shaped to the horse."[5] If asked to describe this scene verbally, in his own natural language, Darl would not use these words and images; he would not be able to. Thus Darl, as well as other characters in the novel, is given verbal abilities he does not actually possess to express his inner thoughts and perceptions. In other places, complex thought processes are rendered in simple, declarative terms, as in Vardaman's statement—which is the shortest chapter in the novel—"My mother is a fish" (p. 79). Vardaman is the youngest child in the family. Earlier, he has caught a fish which his father has directed him to clean. The child, trying to understand a very difficult abstract concept (death) laden with emotional overtones (it is his mother who is dead) has only one concrete representation, a dead fish, by which to understand death. The only way he can express what he is trying to understand is to say, "My mother is a fish."

Changes in typeface are used to indicate time shifts, but not in quite the same way as they are in *The Sound and the Fury*; and they also indicate shifts in thinking, as in Dewey Dell's association between distance and time. Riding in the wagon on the way to Jefferson, she sees a sign indicating that the New Hope church—which, because Dewey Dell is pregnant, has an ironic connotation—is three miles away. She thinks to herself: "Now it [the sign] begins to say it. New Hope three miles. New Hope three miles. *That's what they mean by the womb of time: the agony and the despair of spreading bones, the hard girdle in which lie the outraged entrails of events* (pp. 114-115). The passage refers in part to Addie, whose corpse by this time has begun to smell; but it also refers to Dewey Dell and her hopes to have her pregnancy aborted. The wish is associated in her mind with the name of the church; and then the shift to a higher level of abstraction takes place in which her pregnancy is identified with the source of human agony and despair. In Dewey Dell's mind, her physical condition comes to represent her view on the human condition itself. In other places, italicized passages are used to indicate flashbacks that help explain the story.

On the level of surface action, *As I Lay Dying* is the story of the Bundren family's struggle to get Addie buried in Jefferson. And in this sense the work is a familiar literary type: it is a quest novel in which all of the action is pointed toward the achievement of a particular goal. Despite the flashbacks and the stream-of-consciousness passages, the events of the novel are arranged chronologically, plotting the course of the Bundren family from the country to the town. At the beginning of the novel Addie is on her deathbed, and from the time of her death to the time of her burial in Jefferson the family must overcome many obstacles. First, Addie dies before Cash has finished making her coffin. And Darl and Jewel have taken the wagon to pick up and transport a load of wood, for which they will be paid three dollars. But the first time they set out to do this job a wheel breaks on the wagon and they have to return home. The trip to Jefferson does not begin until two days after Addie has died, and the grimness of the journey is made more emphatic by the fact that it takes ten days, during the course of which Addie's body is steadily decomposing. Heavy rains have made the roads difficult to travel, and the nearest bridge has been washed out. That makes it necessary to travel away from Jefferson to get to the next nearest bridge and by the time the Bundrens arrive there that bridge has been washed out, too. They then backtrack and in an attempt to ford the flooded river the wagon and mules are lost and Cash is almost drowned. As he tries to get out of the river, he is kicked by Jewel's horse and suffers a broken leg. Later, in place of a cast, the leg is encased in concrete. To continue the journey, the family borrows the wagon of a neighbor named Tull and hires a team of mules from one of the Snopes clan. In the course of this transaction, Anse swaps Jewel's horse as part of the payment for the mules. Further on, at Gillespie's farm, they suffer their ordeal by fire. To bring an end to the whole agonizing experience, Darl sets fire to the barn in which Addie's coffin is being kept overnight. The attempt does not work. Gillespie's barn is destroyed but Jewel—suffering severe burns on his back—manages to get the coffin out. To avoid legal action by Gillespie, the family agrees to send Darl to the state mental institution at Jackson. Once the family arrives in Jefferson, Addie is buried. Anse finds himself another wife to take back home, and Darl is sent to Jackson. Dewey Dell, hoping that she will be able to have her pregnancy aborted in Jefferson, encounters Skeet MacGowan, a pharmacist's assistant who takes advantage of her ignorance to seduce her, telling her that he has a "treatment" that will solve her problem.

In most quest novels, the achievement of the ultimate goal is a positive accomplishment. This is not the case in *As I Lay Dying*. Faulkner uses a traditional form for ironic purposes. With Addie buried, the object of the journey accomplished, the family is no closer together. There is nothing uplifting about the accomplishment of their task. Anse gets a new wife, a gramophone, and a set of false teeth he has wanted for a long time. Dewey Dell is still pregnant, Darl is sent to the state asylum, and the rest of the family continues to lead their own isolated lives. This isolation is reinforced by the technique of the novel itself. The short individual monologues serve to emphasize the essential isolation of the characters, and nowhere do the lives of people touch one another in any kind of intimate or significant way. In her monologue, Addie gives voice to the kind of isolation and emptiness that is part of the human condition. She remembers that her father used to tell her "that the reason for living was to get ready to stay dead a long time" (p. 161), and she comments on the ineffectiveness of words as a means of personal communication: "words don't ever fit even what they are trying to say at. . . . I would think how words go straight up in a thin line . . . and how terribly doing goes along the earth, clinging to it, so that after a while the two lines are too far apart for the same person to straddle from one to the other" (pp. 163, 165). Aloneness in itself is not a negative condition; some degree of aloneness is necessary to preserve a sense of self. It becomes a negative condition when it is used as a means of isolation or alienation, which is how Darl frequently uses his intuitiveness. The person who is most visibly destroyed in the novel—who "lays dying"—is Darl. The development of his character shows the growth of his madness. But in a broader sense the title refers effectively to the entire family. The Bundren's journey is one that is marked by increasing tension and fragmentation within the family.

As with *The Sound and the Fury*, Faulkner was disappointed with the sales and the reception of *As I Lay Dying*. The initial critical response to the novel was mixed. Most reviewers agreed with Clifton Fadiman, who wrote in the *Nation* that Faulkner had created "a psychological jig-saw puzzle." Psychological interpretations of the novel have persisted, though Faulkner's responses to such readings of his work were always consistent: he did not view himself as a psychological novelist. Thus, when he was asked at one of the classroom conferences at the University of Virginia if Jewel's purchase of a horse was a substitute for his mother, Faulkner replied, "now that's something for the psychologist. He bought that horse because he wanted that horse. Now there was the need to use symbolism which I dug around, scratched around in my lumber room, and dragged out."[6] Faulkner is saying here what he always said under such circumstances. As a novelist his function was to write interestingly, dramatically, and truthfully about people, not ideas.

For additional study, Olga Vickery offers a good general discussion of *As I Lay Dying*,[7] and André Bleikasten has written a book-length study which serves as a good introduction to critical scrutiny of the novel. [8] A useful discussion of

Darl's importance is provided by John K. Simon's " 'What Are You Laughing At, Darl?': Madness and Humor in *As I Lay Dying.*"[9]

---

[1]*Lion*, p. 244.

[2]See Millgate, p. 108.

[3]*Faulkner in the University*, p. 87.

[4]See George P. Garrett, "Some Revisions in *As I Lay Dying*," *Modern Language Notes*, 73 (June 1958): 414-417.

[5]*As I Lay Dying* (New York: Cape & Smith, 1929). Quote is from the 1964 Vintage edition, p. 12. Subsequent references to this edition are placed within text.

[6]*Faulkner in the University*, p. 109.

[7]Vickery, *The Novels of William Faulkner*, pp. 50-65.

[8]André Bleikasten, *Faulkner's As I Lay Dying*, translated by Roger Little (Bloomington: Indiana University Press, 1973).

[9]John K. Simon, " 'What Are You Laughing At, Darl?': Madness and Humor in *As I Lay Dying*," *College English*, 25 (November 1963): 104-110.

Sanctuary

The first version of *Sanctuary* was written by Faulkner in 1929, though the novel was extensively revised before it was first published on 9 February 1931. In his introduction to the 1932 Modern Library edition of the novel, Faulkner explained:

> This book was written three years ago. To me it is a cheap idea, because it was deliberately conceived to make money. . . . I took a little time out, and speculated what a person in Mississippi would believe to be current trends, chose what I thought was the right answer and invented the most horrific tale I could imagine and wrote it in about three weeks and sent it to Smith,[1] who had done *The Sound and the Fury* and who wrote me immediately, "Good God, I can't publish this. We'd both be in jail."[2]

Later, on being sent the galley proofs of the first version, Faulkner realized "that it was so terrible that there were but two things to do: tear it up or rewrite it."[3] He chose the latter and, paying out of his own pocket part of the expense of resetting the novel in type, attempted "to make out of it something which would not shame *The Sound and the Fury* and *As I Lay Dying* too much."[4]

This introduction has been the source of some confusion about *Sanctuary*, especially among those critics who have been too willing to take Faulkner literally. *Sanctuary* was not written in three weeks. Both the manuscript and the typescript texts of the first version were dated by Faulkner as having been started in January 1929 and completed in May of the same year.[5] As Michael Millgate has pointed out, Faulkner, in his 1932 introduction to the novel, is referring to the first version of *Sanctuary*, not the published novel; he also suggests that "When Faulkner spoke of a cheap idea the abruptness and forcefulness of his condemnation was an index of the imperiousness of his artistic integrity rather than of the actual value of his original intentions in writing *Sanctuary*."[6] Faulkner worked very hard to make a good novel out of what he considered to be a poor one. In his study of Faulkner's revisions, Millgate demonstrates that the problem with the first version of the novel was structural, not topical. "There was," Millgate writes, "a large element of deliberate sensationalism in the original conception of *Sanctuary* . . . but the crucial fault may have lain in the combination of these sensational intentions with a too casual conception of the overall structure of the novel, an ill-considered assumption on Faulkner's part that the Temple Drake material could be readily wedded to a development of the Horace Benbow material with which he had already worked in *Sartoris*."[7] In fact, the revised version of *Sanctuary* is in some ways more violent than the first; for example, the vivid description of Lee Goodwin's lynching in the published version does not appear in the unpublished version.[8] The ultimate result of Faulkner's revisions was to make *Sanctuary* the story of Temple Drake, who after being victimized by evil commits the most evil act in the novel; and, though he does not figure as prominently as in the first version, it is also the story of Horace Benbow, a man who recognizes evil and tries to fight it, but who is too weak to do so effectively.

Temple Drake is a University of Mississippi coed who, through a misadventure with her boyfriend Gowan Stevens, finds herself at the hideaway of a bootlegger named Lee Goodwin. Fearful of the attention she receives from the men at the place, Temple hides herself in a corn crib. She is sought out by Popeye, a Memphis gangster connected with Goodwin's bootlegging business. Popeye first murders Tommy, the man who has set himself the task of guarding Temple, and then rapes her with a corn cob. After the rape Popeye abducts Temple, taking her to a Memphis whorehouse, and Goodwin is arrested for Tommy's murder. At the end of the novel, at Goodwin's trial, it is Temple's perjured testimony—she tells the court it was Goodwin who raped her and who killed Tommy—that leads to Goodwin's conviction and his subsequent lynching. Horace Benbow serves as Goodwin's lawyer. He has run away from his wife, Belle, and by defending Goodwin—if he can do so successfully—Horace hopes to win some measure of self-respect and also to strike a blow for the principle of justice. However, the forces of evil in this novel, which take many forms, are overpowering; and by the end of the work Horace is a defeated man. Quite simply, the world presented in *Sanctuary* offers no place of safety or refuge for anyone.

Horace is one of the first characters to be presented. For the past ten years he and Belle and Little Belle, her daughter by a previous marriage, have been living in Kinston. Belle is a willful, dominant woman, and Horace is trying to assert some measure of independence by running away from her. Ironically, in running from Kinston to Jefferson he is running from one obstinate woman to another, from his wife to his sister, Narcissa. Walking from Kinston to Jefferson, Horace leaves the road to get a drink of water from a spring. There he encounters Popeye, who functions in the novel not so much as a complex, three-dimensional character but as a symbol of unthinking and emotionless violence. Faulkner's description of him emphasizes his lack of humanness. He wears black suits and his face has a "queer, bloodless color, as though seen by electric light" and displays a "vicious depthless quality of stamped tin."[9] His eyes resemble "two knobs of soft black rubber" and "His skin had a dead, dark pallor. His nose was faintly aquiline, and he had no chin at all. His face just went away, like the face of a wax doll set too near a hot fire and forgotten" (pp. 4, 5). To make sure Horace represents no threat to the bootlegging operation, Popeye takes him back to the house as night begins to fall.

Chapter 2 is set at the Old Frenchman place, the location of Goodwin's hideout. It introduces other characters and gives additional information about Horace Benbow which helps explain his reason for leaving home. After Ruby Lamar—Lee Goodwin's common-law wife and the only woman living at the Old Frenchman place—has served supper, Horace and the other men move out to the porch where Horace talks about his life at Kinston. Horace shows himself to be the same kind of person he was in *Flags in the Dust*; he is, as Millgate notes, "the intellectual of generous impulses but inadequate courage or will to action, tending always to dissipate his energies in talk."[10] Ruby expresses this judgment succinctly when, after listening to Horace talk, she concludes, "He better get on to where he's going, where his women folks can take care of him" (p. 13).

Belle's dominance over Horace is symbolized by his weekly trips to the railroad station to pick up packages of shrimp. Though Horace considers the chore demeaning, he continues to perform it. Disturbed by his relationship with Belle, Horace is even more concerned about the nature of his relationship with his stepdaughter, Little Belle. For him, Little Belle is identified with nature in ways that are both attractive and repellent, desirable and base. Describing the hammock in the grape arbor at Kinston where Little Belle sometimes goes with her boyfriends, Horace claims "That's why we know nature is a she; because of that conspiracy between female flesh and female season. So each spring I could watch the reaffirmation of the old ferment hiding the hammock; the green-snared promise of unease" (p. 13). Horace's feelings about sexuality and women in general and Little Belle in particular are ambivalent. In this respect his character is consistent; for just as in *Flags in the Dust*, where his relationship with Narcissa had definite sexual overtones, so in *Sanctuary* his emotional involvement with Little Belle goes far beyond a wish for her acceptance or respect. How far it is not possible to say; but as

Horace is drawn deeper and deeper into the world of violence and evil—grim realities with which he has not formerly had to contend—his thoughts and feelings about Little Belle are bound up inextricably with his reactions to the unfolding story of Temple Drake.

The essential story of *Sanctuary* is a story of evil: the corruption of Temple Drake by evil and the defeat of Horace Benbow's idealism by evil. As such it is considered by many critics to be Faulkner's most pessimistic novel. The action is set in the spring of the year, traditionally a time of renewal and rebirth. The conclusion of the action—after Temple has perjured herself and Lee Goodwin has been found guilty of murder—suggests the opposite. Driving home with Narcissa after the trial, Horace remarks, "It does last. . . . Spring does. You'd almost think there was some purpose to it" (p. 285). This comment is very much in the twentieth-century wasteland tradition which views modern civilization as devoid of traditional values and hence of moral focus. The seasonal motif is carried through to the end of the novel, where Temple, sitting in the Luxembourg Gardens in Paris, her face "sullen and discontented and sad," listens to music in a "season of rain and death" (p. 309). The promise of renewal is false and the only values that an individual may hold to are existential in nature, values that come from within the individual and enable him to cope with a world in which evil is a living force. This is precisely the nature of Ruby Lamar's values. Her privately fashioned code of conduct gives her a strength that is not matched by any other character in the novel.

Evil in *Sanctuary* takes many forms. At first it is associated, especially by Horace Benbow, with a female principle, but this concept is gradually expanded. When Ruby, in chapter 19, tells Horace her version of what happened to Temple at the Old Frenchman place, he begins to associate Temple with Little Belle. Back in his house in Jefferson, he looks at a photograph of his stepdaughter that he has placed on his dresser: "The image blurred . . . like something familiar seen beneath disturbed though clear water; he looked at the familiar image with a kind of quiet horror and despair, at a face suddenly older in sin than he would ever be, a face more blurred than sweet, at eyes more secret than soft" (pp. 162-163). Faulkner does not attempt in this work to force the simplistic proposition that all females are evil. The female principle—applied to men or women—is a metaphor, and it is qualified at various places in the novel. In chapter 22, when Ruby and her child, who have come to Jefferson to be near Lee Goodwin after his arrest, are forced out of the hotel, an act undoubtedly engineered by Narcissa Benbow, and Horace is trying to find another place for them to stay, he tries to convince Ruby he does not care what the womenfolk of Jefferson might think of his actions in her behalf. Ruby is skeptical, and Horace realizes that her skepticism issues from a "feminine reserve of unflagging suspicion of all people's actions which seems at first to be mere affinity for evil but which is in reality practical wisdom" (p. 194). Respectability is one of the forms that evil takes in the novel. After her rape, while Popeye is taking her to Memphis and they pass through the town of Dumfries, Temple's fear of being recognized by someone she knows—possibly she does not realize Popeye's intentions at this point and believes that he is taking her someplace where he can let her out of the car, having no further use for her—brings her out of her state of shock: "Temple began to look about, like one waking from sleep. 'Not here!' she said. 'I can't—' " (p. 135). She is too proud to escape. Later Temple leaves Popeye's car to hide behind a barrel so a boy from her school will not recognize her (p. 136). Narcissa is motivated almost entirely by her concern for respectability to the degree that she betrays her brother for it, and this betrayal directly influences the outcome of Goodwin's trial. Horace's defense of Goodwin and the solicitude he shows for Ruby and her child is an embarrassment to Narcissa. She tells her brother "this is my home, where I must spend the rest of my life. Where I was born. I dont care where else you go nor what you do. I dont care how many women you have nor who they are. But I cannot have my brother mixed up with a woman people are talking about" (p. 178). In the face of this concern, issues of truth and justice have no impact on Narcissa. Respectability has also been suggested as one of Temple's motives for perjuring herself at Goodwin's trial.

One of the most chillingly dramatic changes that takes place in the novel is the change in Temple after Popeye takes her to Miss Reba's whorehouse. Through Clarence Snopes, a conniving state senator who visits Miss Reba's, Horace learns of Temple's whereabouts and manages to get an interview with her. When last seen, Temple was disheveled, fearful, bleeding from the effects of her rape, and in a state of shock. Less than a month has passed when Horace enters her room. At first Temple hides herself beneath the covers, but when she emerges the effect is startling: "Temple flung the covers back and sat up. Her head was tousled, her face puffed, two spots of rouge on her cheekbones and her mouth painted into a savage Cupid's bow. She stared for an instant at Horace with black antagonism" (p. 207). As she tells Horace her story he is reminded of "one of those bright, chatty monologues which women can carry on when they realise that they have the center of the stage; suddenly Horace realised that she was recounting the experience with actual pride, a sort of naive and impersonal vanity, as though she were making it up" (pp. 208-209). After hearing Temple's story, Horace thinks to himself, "Perhaps it is upon the instant that we realise, admit, that there is a logical pattern to evil, that we die" (p. 214). With the possible exception of the lynching of Lee Goodwin, Popeye's rape of Temple is the most violent act of physical brutality in the novel; but Temple's perjured testimony against Goodwin is the most evil act. Regardless of what her specific motives are—family respectability, hatred of men, moral lassitude—they all issue from her corruption and the eventual willful embracing of the principle of evil.

With the publication of *Sanctuary* Faulkner found a wider

readership than he had ever reached before. In the first two months, the novel sold more than 7,000 copies, and the critical reception, though mixed, served to enhance his popular reputation. The reviewers who found fault with *Sanctuary* were disturbed by the subject matter. In the *Saturday Review of Literature*, editor Henry Seidel Canby argued that with *Sanctuary* sadism in American literature had reached its peak. Joseph Blotner reports that early reviews of the novel expressed "horror," "distaste," and even "disgust," all sentiments which would have the effect of enhancing sales. Other critics recognized Faulkner's merits as an author. Clifton Fadiman placed him in the first rank of young American novelists; playwright Robert Sherwood wrote that Faulkner was possessed of "prodigious genius"; and Alexander Woollcott called *Sanctuary* a novel of "grandeur."

Recent critics have disagreed about the merits of the novel. Some, including Michael Millgate, have argued that while it is not a "cheap idea" as Faulkner maintained, neither is *Sanctuary* among his greatest works. Millgate agrees with Faulkner's own comment in 1955 that he had "made a fair job" of the novel. Albert Camus, on the other hand, believed that with *Pylon*, *Sanctuary* represented the height of Faulkner's literary achievement. Cleanth Brooks agrees, calling *Sanctuary* in some respects Faulkner's most pessimistic novel and "certainly one of his most brilliant."

Many of Faulkner's novels have been explored for their mythological aspects, and *Sanctuary* is one of these. A useful interpretation of the novel in this context is offered by Thomas L. McHaney, who suggests in a reference to Faulkner's 1932 introduction that the " 'cheap idea' behind *Sanctuary* . . . is a brilliantly successful adaptation of Eliot's idea in *The Waste Land*, a subtle and fully articulated suffusion of primitive myth and ritual into a modern fiction."[11] Faulkner's source for the telling of the myth is James Frazer's *The Golden Bough*, specifically Frazer's treatment of various fertility rituals. Of course, Faulkner's intended effect is ironic and the use of myth adds "deeper levels of significance to a modern story with wasteland implications."[12] Useful discussions of the theme of evil in *Sanctuary* are offered by Brooks and by Aubrey Williams.[13] And in "What Really Happens in *Sanctuary*," Tamotsu Nishiyama examines the motives for Temple's perjury.[14] An edition of the original version of *Sanctuary* has been prepared by Noel Polk, who in an afterword discusses the nature of Faulkner's revisions.[15]

[1]Harrison Smith, Faulkner's publisher.

[2]*Essays, Speeches & Public Letters*, pp. 176, 177.

[3]*Essays, Speeches & Public Letters*, p. 178.

[4]*Essays, Speeches & Public Letters*, p. 178.

[5]See Millgate, p. 114.

[6]Millgate, p. 117.

[7]Millgate, p. 117.

[8]Millgate, p. 115.

[9]*Sanctuary* (New York: Cape & Smith, 1931). Quote is from the 1967 Vintage edition, p. 4. Subsequent references to this edition are placed within text.

[10]Millgate, p. 117.

[11]McHaney, "*Sanctuary* and Frazer's Slain Kings," *Mississippi Quarterly*, 24 (Summer 1971): 224.

[12]McHaney, "*Sanctuary* and Frazer's Slain Kings," p. 242.

[13]Brooks, *The Yoknapatawpha Country*, pp. 116-138; Aubrey Williams, "William Faulkner's 'Temple' of Innocence," *Rice Institute Pamphlet*, 47 (1960): 51-67.

[14]Tamotsu Nishiyama, "What Really Happens in *Sanctuary*," *Studies in English Literature*, 42 (March 1966): 235-243.

[15]Polk, *Sanctuary: The Original Text* (New York: Random House, 1981): see pp. 293-306.

Light in August

Within six months after *Sanctuary* was published, Faulkner was working on the manuscript of his next novel. In August 1931 he began a manuscript tentatively called "Dark House," which seems to have been a false start on the novel that became *Light in August* (though it may also have been an early attempt to organize the material for *Absalom, Absalom!*). By November he had a complete manuscript for his seventh novel and had settled on the title. After careful revision "measuring each choice by the scale of the Jameses and Conrads and Balzacs,"[1] *Light in August* was published on 6 October 1932.

Light in August is Faulkner's longest novel and its cast of characters is large. The major characters are developed gradually and their backgrounds are revealed in bits and pieces. For example, Gail Hightower's background is not fully revealed until the next to the last chapter of the novel, and the identity of the man who watched over Joe Christmas at the orphanage (Doc Hines, who first appears in chapter 6) is not revealed until chapter 16. The treatment of Joe Christmas begins with his arrival in Jefferson (chapter 2), is followed intermittently by developing action that takes him to the moment when he goes to kill Joanna Burden (chapter 5), then shifts abruptly to an extended flashback beginning with Christmas's life at the orphanage (chapters 6-9). It is understandable that this kind of fictional technique might give the appearance of a fragmented structure. But it also gives Faulkner greater latitude to compare and contrast his characters, to show their impact on community life, and to reveal and analyze community reactions to their deeds.

As with *The Sound and the Fury*, Faulkner's idea for *Light in August* began with a central idea, in this case "with Lena Grove, the idea of the young girl with nothing, pregnant, determined to find her sweetheart. It was—that was out of my admiration for women, for the courage and endurance of women."[2] The early chapters of the novel serve not only to introduce some of the major characters—Lena Grove, Byron Bunch, Gail Hightower—but also to establish the concept of community. As she nears Jefferson, Lena Grove has been on the road for four weeks looking for Joe Brown—known to her as Lucas Burch—the man who has gotten her pregnant and who promised to marry her. She has been looked after by various people along the way. "Folks have been kind," she remarks. "They have been right kind."[3] Lena's condition brings out the best instincts of the people with whom she has contact. Before Lena's arrival in Jefferson, Byron Bunch has lived apart from the community, and the townspeople know very little about him. So quiet and unassuming that he is almost a nonentity, he is described as "that small man who will not see thirty again, who has spent six days of every week for seven years at the planing mill, feeding boards into the machinery" (p. 42). The town neither knows nor cares why Byron chooses to work all day on Saturday: "The other workmen, the town itself or that part of it which remembers or thinks about him, believe that he does it for the overtime which he receives. Perhaps this is the reason. Man knows so little about his fellows. In his eyes all men or women act upon what he believes would motivate him if he were mad enough to do what that other man or woman is doing" (p. 43). The only person with whom Byron has any social intercourse in Jefferson is Gail Hightower, the disgraced minister who was turned out of his church as a result of community outrage, but who refused to leave Jefferson and has been living alone there for the past twenty-five years. In the first two chapters there are also references to an event that will loom large later in the novel, and that helps to establish the time of the opening scenes: the murder of Joanna Burden, the maiden daughter of an abolitionist who moved into Jefferson after the Civil War. Joanna has spent her time promoting social causes for the benefit of the Negro race. The driver of the wagon taking Lena into Jefferson sees smoke from the burning house in chapter 1, and in chapter 2 the workmen at the planing mill can see the smoke and they speculate about its origin. One man asks, "What can it be? I dont remember anything out that way big enough to make all that smoke except that Burden house" (p. 44). Another workman responds, "Maybe that's what it is. My pappy says how he can remember fifty years ago folks said it ought to be burned, and with a little human fat meat to start it good" (p. 44). Ironically, that is almost exactly what has happened; for at the time the house starts burning Joanna Burden lies dead in her bedroom, her throat slashed by Joe Christmas.

Chapter 3 of the novel is devoted almost entirely to Gail Hightower, though the details of his life are not revealed until much later. Hightower has a fixation on the past and is in a sense captured by it. He is obsessed by his grandfather's exploits in the Civil War, especially by a particular action—a cavalry raid on General Grant's stores in Jefferson—in which his grandfather was killed. The town's view is that Hightower had been "born about thirty years after the only day he seemed to have ever lived in" (p. 57). From the time that he is in seminary, Hightower is determined that he must go to Jefferson to carry out his ministry. Hightower's fixation is hardest on his wife, and it eventually drives her to madness and suicide. The townspeople read in their Sunday papers that "she had jumped or fallen from a hotel window in Memphis . . . and was dead. There had been a man in the room with her. . . . He was drunk. They were registered as man and wife, under a fictitious name" (pp. 61-62). This is too much for the people of Jefferson. Though Hightower at first refuses to resign, he finally acquiesces when his congregation locks him out of the church. He refuses to leave Jefferson, however, and consequently every action—or implied action—on Hightower's part becomes the subject of rumor. When he keeps in his employ the Negro woman who had cooked for him and his wife, it is rumored that Hightower had deliberately "made his wife go bad and commit suicide because he was not a natural husband, a natural man, and that the negro woman was the reason" (p. 65). In all of the business with Hightower, the community acts and reacts according to the precepts of an unwritten code. Hightower is punished severely for violating the terms of the community code, but he is also protected by it. When Hightower's refusal to leave town results in his being tied to a tree and beaten unconscious, the townspeople realize that matters have gotten out of hand, and they even offer to prosecute the men responsible for the beating. After this incident, the town recognizes that Hightower "would be a part of its life until he died, and that they might as well become reconciled" (p. 67). The ex-minister takes his own self-selected place, isolated, cut off from the mainstream of community life, finding meaning only in his obsession with the past.

Joe Christmas is first introduced in chapter 2 of the novel; and the day of his arrival in Jefferson is three years before the time of present action in the novel. His own isolation from any kind of community and his indifference to those around him is established at the outset. To the other men at the planing mill where he goes to work he presents an "air of cold and quiet contempt" (p. 28). To Christmas's apparent contemptuousness, the workers at the planing mill respond with "baffled outrage" (p. 28). The foreman suggests, "We ought to run him through the planer. . . . Maybe that will take that look off his face" (p. 28), and another remarks, "that's a pretty risky look for a man to wear on his face in public. . . . He might forget and use it somewhere where somebody wont like it" (p. 28). Christmas's bootlegging activities and the arrival of Joe Brown—some six months before the time of the present action—are accounted for in chapter 2, and in chapter 4 more details are given on the events that are taking place. The burning of Joanna Burden's house takes place on Saturday, and on

Sunday Byron Bunch tells Hightower about the arrival of Lena Grove and reports gradually what he has heard of events at the Burden place: (1) that Joanna Burden's body was removed from the burning house by a countryman who was passing the house and saw the fire; (2) that her nephew has offered $1,000 for the capture of the murderer; (3) that Brown and Christmas are somehow involved; and (4) that Christmas is part Negro. Chapter 5 provides additional details about the relationship between Christmas and Brown, who share the cabin behind the Burden house, and ends at midnight on Friday with Joe on his way to murder Joanna Burden, though his motive for doing so has not yet been revealed. The chapter seems to end prophetically, with Christmas thinking to himself: *"Something is going to happen. Something is going to happen to me"* (p. 110).

Chapter 6 begins with the statement, "Memory believes before knowing remembers" (p. 111), and suggests that there is something about the nature of memory that defies logic and reason; that the past will shape character and influence future action in ways the individual may not realize. A major aspect of Christmas's character is his uncertainty about his identity. He presumes himself to be of mixed white and Negro blood, though at times he does not appear to be absolutely certain that this is the case. At the end of the novel Gavin Stevens uses the mixed blood hypothesis to rationalize Christmas's behavior on the day he is killed. However, there is no direct evidence—save the assertions of the fanatical Doc Hines—that Christmas's Mexican father had any Negro blood. When questioned on this point in 1957, Faulkner responded:

> I think that was his tragedy—he didn't know what he was, and so he was nothing. He deliberately evicted himself from the human race because he didn't know which he was. . . . that to me was the tragic, central idea of the story—that he didn't know what he was, and there was no

way possible in life for him to find out. Which to me is the most tragic condition a man could find himself in—not to know what he is and to know that he will never know.[4]

It is, in part, Christmas's attitude toward women, sex, and religion that makes it possible for him to murder Joanna Burden. Thus, his early experiences in these areas, beginning at the age of five, are important for an understanding of his character. Joe gets his name from having been left on the doorstep of an orphanage at Christmas. In the habit of sneaking into the dietitian's room to eat small amounts of toothpaste, Joe on one occasion is forced to hide in a closet when the dietitian returns unexpectedly to her room with a young doctor. Joe continues to eat toothpaste while the couple make love, and though the five-year-old boy does not fully comprehend the nature of the sexual encounter that takes place, the experience makes a lasting impression on him. The toothpaste eventually makes him sick; he vomits and is discovered. Thinking that Joe is spying on her, the dietitian berates him: "you little rat! Spying on me! You little nigger bastard!" (p. 114). Later, at the age of eighteen, when he is living with the McEacherns, Joe has his first direct sexual experience with a young Negro girl. He is with a group of other boys, and when his turn comes, Joe is overcome by a sense of "terrible haste. There was something in him trying to get out, like when he had used to think of toothpaste" (p. 146). Unable to complete the sex act, he reacts violently and begins to hit the girl. Later still, Joe learns about menstruation from Bobbie Allen, a prostitute he wants to marry. Though the biological reality of menstruation has been described to him by another boy, he does not really understand it. The first night he is alone with Bobbie, and she explains to him that she cannot have sex with him because she is having her period, Joe's reaction is again violent. He strikes her, then he runs from the road into a recently plowed field where "as though in a cave he seemed to see a diminishing row of suavely shaped urns in moonlight, blanched. And not one was perfect. Each one was cracked and from each crack there issued something liquid, deathcolored, and foul. He touched a tree, leaning his propped arms against it, seeing the ranked and moonlit urns. He vomited" (pp. 177-178).

All of Christmas's formative experiences teach him to be distrustful of women; and his experiences in the McEachern home, which is dominated by Mr. McEachern, are almost totally negative. Mr. McEachern is humorless, loveless, and his moral precepts are based on a strict fundamentalist religion. Thus, Joanna Burden's relationship with Christmas takes place on a level where his defense mechanisms are most important to him and, when she threatens to breach them he becomes dangerous. She uses him first to satisfy her own newly discovered and long repressed sexuality. Later, overcome by guilt as a result of her strict religious upbringing, she presents herself as an instrument of God and insists that they both pray for forgiveness. He refuses. She then tries to force him to kneel and pray at gunpoint; he still refuses. When she pulls the trigger, the weapon misfires. At this point Christmas kills Joanna and sets fire to her house.

Several days after the murder, Joe Christmas is arrested and endures the exhortation to the townspeople of his grandfather, Doc Hines, to lynch him. Joe escapes and seeks sanctuary with Reverend Hightower. He is pursued by Percy Grimm and a contingent of volunteer guards. Cornered in Hightower's kitchen, Christmas is shot by Grimm who then castrates the body.

Though Christmas's fate is tragic, Faulkner rejected the notion that the novel itself was intended to present a tragic view of life: "the only person in that book that accepted a tragic view of life was Christmas because he didn't know what he was and so he deliberately repudiated man. . . . The others seemed to me to have had a very fine belief in life, in the basic possibility for happiness and goodness."[5] At the same time, neither

Christmas's fate nor the fates of any other characters in *Light in August* are predetermined. Though time and circumstance influence the outcome of any human event, the individual must still make choices. When he offers Joe Christmas protection, Hightower makes a very difficult choice to enter once more the mainstream of human events, though he withdraws into the past again at the end of the novel. Christmas makes a choice, a desperate one, when he decides to seek sanctuary in Hightower's house rather than accept the legal punishment for Joanna Burden's murder. And Byron Bunch makes a choice at the end of the novel.

After Joanna Burden's murder, Lena Grove, convinced from the description of him by Byron Bunch that Christmas's roommate, Joe Brown, is really Lucas Burch, the father of her about-to-be-born child, insists that Bunch take her to the cabin behind the Burden house where Brown has been living. Her baby is born there. When Brown claims the $1,000 reward for providing information leading to Joe Christmas's arrest, a deputy takes him to the cabin. When Brown enters and sees Lena and her newborn child, he runs away and hops a freight train. The novel ends as, three weeks later, Lena resumes her search, accompanied by Bunch, who desires to marry her. While she accepts his help, she stubbornly refuses his advances and single-mindedly pursues the father of her child. Bunch chooses to accompany her and to assist her in the search: "I done come too far now. . . . I be dog if I'm going to quit now" (p. 479), he tells her.

In part because of the way the novel is "framed"—the first chapter on Lena Grove, the last chapter on Lena and Byron Bunch—the overall meaning of *Light in August* offers a positive view on human existence. Distinguishing between tragic and comic modes of fiction, Cleanth Brooks writes, "Tragedy always concerns itself with the individual, his values, his tragic encounter with the reality about him, and the waste which is suffered in his defeat. Comedy involves . . . the author's basic alignment with society and with the community."[6] The central story of *Light in August* is tragic; but by framing the work as he does, Faulkner says that life itself is not tragic, at least not necessarily tragic. Lena is the vital "link in the eternal progression from mother to daughter who provides the final norm for our judgment";[7] and Byron Bunch, by forsaking his isolation and assuming responsibility for Lena and her child when none is expected or demanded of him, makes a strong and positive commitment to life.

By the time *Light in August* was published, Faulkner was regarded as a major literary figure and his work was reviewed respectfully, if not always comprehendingly. Some reviewers found the novel obscure and carelessly constructed, but there was a consensus on the force of his characterization and the power of his story. Sales were dampened by the Depression economy and the fact that the novel was published by the new firm of Smith and Haas, itself struggling to survive in a time of financial uncertainty.

Recent scholars have found *Light in August* a rewarding object for critical speculation. The meaning of Faulkner's title for the novel has been the subject of considerable discussion. Faulkner himself offered various explanations, of which the most consistent seems to have been his response to a question posed by a student at the University of Virginia in 1957: "in August in Mississippi there's a few days somewhere about the middle of the month when suddenly there's a foretaste of fall, it's cool, there's a lambence, a luminous quality to the light, as though it came not from just today but from back in the old classic times. It might have fawns and satyrs and the gods and—from Greece, from Olympus in it somewhere. It lasts just for a day or two, then it's gone, but every year in August that occurs in my country, and that's all that title meant, it was just to me a pleasant evocative title because it reminded me of that time, of a luminosity older than our Christian civilization."[8] Michael Millgate has discussed Faulkner's use of light imagery in the novel, observing that the kind of light described in Faulkner's explanation of the title is the same as that "which shines on the day of Christmas's death and at the moment when Hightower finally recognizes the truth about himself and the extent of his responsibility both for his own suffering and for that of his dead wife."[9] Millgate also suggests that:

> Faulkner seems to hint at some wider meaning in his references to "the old classic times . . . fawns and satyrs and the gods" and the "pagan quality" of Lena Grove. The "earth-mother" qualities in Lena Grove are clearly hinted at in her name, and have long been recognised. But given Faulkner's undoubted familiarity with the stories of classical mythology and with the works of Joyce and Eliot,[10] and his probable acquaintance with Frazer's *The Golden Bough*, it would not be surprising if he had further analogies in mind.[11]

Among these are analogies between Joe Christmas and Jesus Christ, Lena Grove and the Virgin Mary, Byron Bunch and Joseph, Mary's husband.[12] Further, in the relationship between Joanna Burden and Lena Grove, "there are reasons for thinking that Faulkner may have intended a series of allusions to the goddess Diana and to the sacred groves where she was worshipped. . . . It seems probable that Faulkner had some kind of deliberate time scheme in mind as he wrote the book, and since the ancient festival of Diana used to be celebrated in August it is conceivable that he intended some allusion to it."[13] In this respect, *Light in August* may represent a direct continuation from *Sanctuary* of Faulkner's interest in classical myths and their relevance to human nature in the twentieth century.

In addition to the general estimates of Brooks and Millgate, the reader may wish to consult Robert M. Slabey's "Myth and Ritual in *Light in August*" for its discussion of Christian symbolism as well as other mystic aspects.[14] For a discussion of narrative technique in the novel, see Sister Kristin Morrison,

"Faulkner's Joe Christmas: Character Through Voice."[15]
Francois Pitavy's *Faulkner's Light in August* is a book-length
study that examines a variety of technical and thematic aspects
in the work.[16]

---

[1]Blotner, p. 704.
[2]*Faulkner in the University*, p. 74.
[3]*Light in August* (New York: Smith & Haas, 1932), p. 10. Subsequent
references are placed within text.
[4]*Faulkner in the University*, p. 72.
[5]*Faulkner in the University*, p. 97.
[6]Brooks, *The Yoknapatawpha Country*, p. 72.
[7]Brooks, *The Yoknapatawpha Country*, p. 72.
[8]*Faulkner in the University*, p. 199.
[9]Millgate, p. 133.
[10]James Joyce and T. S. Eliot.
[11]Millgate, p. 133.
[12]See Millgate, p. 133.
[13]Millgate, pp. 134, 136.
[14]Robert M. Slabey, "Myth and Ritual in *Light in August*," *Texas Studies
in Literature and Language*, 2 (Autumn 1960): 328-349.
[15]Sister Kristin Morrison, "Faulkner's Joe Christmas: Character
Through Voice," *Texas Studies in Literature and Language*, 2 (Winter 1961):
419-443.
[16]*Faulkner's Light in August*, translated by Gillian E. Cook and Francois
Pitavy (Bloomington: Indiana University Press, 1973).

Pylon

In mid-October 1934 Faulkner wrote to his agent, Morton Goldman, requesting the return of his "air story, 'Courage' " because he was planning to write a novel out of it. On 25 November Faulkner finished a manuscript of *Pylon* and by 15 December he had typed it, revising as he went, and sent it to Smith and Haas. Publication day was 25 March 1935. "I wrote that book because I'd got in trouble with *Absalom, Absalom!*," he said in 1957. "I had to get away from it for a while so I thought a good way to get away from it was to write another book, so I wrote *Pylon*."[1]

Compared with some of Faulkner's major works, the story line in *Pylon* appears remarkably simple. He tells the story of a group of barnstorming aviators—in the process describing an entertainment phenomenon, the air show, that enjoyed a brief popularity in the period between the two world wars—and of a nameless newspaper reporter's fascination with them. Concerning the people who participated in these air shows, Faulkner said:

> They were ephemera and phenomena on the face of a contemporary scene. That is, there was really no place for them in the culture, in the economy, yet they were there, at that time, and everyone knew that they wouldn't last very long, which they didn't. That time of those frantic little aeroplanes which dashed around the country and people wanted just enough money to live, to get to the next place to race again. Something frenetic and in a way almost immoral about it. . . . That they had escaped the compulsion of accepting a past and a future . . . they had no past. They were as ephemeral as the butterfly that's born this morning with no stomach and will be gone tomorrow.[2]

Though *Pylon* is not set in Yoknapatawpha County, it nonetheless has some interesting relationships to Faulkner's earlier Yoknapatawpha fiction. The barnstorming pilots of *Pylon* are, as Cleanth Brooks points out, "prefigured in *Flags in the Dust* in the account of the twin brothers, John and Bayard Sartoris"; and the deaths of Bayard and Roger Shumann—the chief pilot in the novel, and the leader of the group that occupies the reporter's imagination—are similar in nature.[3] Further, "*Pylon* repeats with variations the pattern discerned in *Flags*: the unreflective man of action played off against the inactive man of words. Like Bayard and John Sartoris in *Flags* . . . [Roger] Shumann and [Jack] Holmes are reckless of life and limb. . . . Like Horace Benbow in *Flags*, the Reporter is the dreamer and would-be writer, who participates only vicariously in what he sees as heroic action."[4] The role that the reporter attempts, unsuccessfully, to play in the novel—"patron (even if no guardian) saint of all waifs, all the homeless the desperate and the starved"[5]—is "precisely the role that Horace [Benbow] tries to assume in *Sanctuary*."[6]

The first of the novel's seven chapters describes the event around which the novel is organized, the dedication of Feinman Airport during the Mardi Gras festivities. To publicize the new airport, an air show has been organized featuring races, parachute jumps, and other special events. The prize money being offered has drawn a large number of aviators to New Valois (New Orleans), among them the group of Roger and Laverne Shumann, Jack Holmes, six-year-old Jack Shumann, and Jiggs, the mechanic. The beginning of the novel raises the issue of material values, as Jiggs goes into a store to put a down payment on a pair of boots that he has seen in the store window "in unblemished and inviolate implication of horse and spur, of the posed countrylife photographs in the magazine advertisements" (p. 7). Jiggs has no place in this world; but the owning of the boots helps him to maintain an illusion about himself, as though his life and circumstances were better than they are. When he is unable to sustain such illusions, he sinks into the despair of alcoholism. Later, on the way to the airport, he tells the bus driver the basic problem the group faces: "Ship's obsolete. It was fast two years ago, but that's two years ago. We'd be O.K. now if they had just quit building racers when they finished the one we got. There aint another pilot out there except Shumann that could have even qualified it" (pp. 13-14). Once at the airport, Jiggs teases the six-year-old Jack by asking him, "Who's your old man today, kid?" (p. 20), though the reason for the boy's violent reaction to the question is not revealed until later.

The reporter, who is at the airport to cover the race for his newspaper, is introduced and great emphasis is placed on his bizarre appearance. He resembles "something which had apparently crept from a doctor's cupboard and, in the snatched garments of an etherised patient in a charity ward, escaped into the living world" (p. 20). He is tall and gangly, wearing a suit of "no age or color, as though made of air and doped like an aeroplane wing with the incrusted excretion of all articulate life's contact with the passing earth," and he evinces "the leashed, eager loosejointed air of a halfgrown highbred setter puppy" (p. 21). His imagination is immediately captivated by the group of Roger, Laverne, Jack, Jiggs, and the boy; he is especially attracted to Laverne. Toward the end of the chapter, Roger, through superior flying skills and a willingness to take chances by flying close to the pylons that mark the course for the air race, takes second place in a Thursday race, though he will not be paid until Saturday. Thus, with no money and no place to stay, the group has to accept the hospitality the reporter eagerly thrusts upon them.

The second chapter gives additional information about the group, reveals the reporter's obsession with them, and establishes the relationship between the reporter and his editor, Hagood. The reporter is a romantic who consistently tries to make the aviators more heroic, adventurous, and daring than they are; and he tries to ascribe their involvement in the world of air racing to idealistic rather than practical motives. He honestly believes that the fliers are a superhuman breed. He tells Hagood that "they aint human like us; they couldn't turn those pylons like they do if they had human blood and senses and they wouldn't want to or dare to if they just had human brains. Burn them . . . and they dont even holler in the fire; crash one and it aint even blood when you haul him out: it's cylinder oil the same as in the crankcase" (p. 45). The reporter tells Hagood that Laverne lives with both Roger and Jack; that when the boy Jack was born in a hangar in California they did not know which of the two was the father, so they rolled dice to determine who would marry Laverne. And it was Laverne who taught Jack to fight whenever someone asks him who his father is. The reporter is also absorbed with the group's lack of a past, or at least of any sense of the past. Again he tells Hagood, "They aint human, you see. No ties; no place where you were born and have to go back to it now and then even if it's just only to hate the damn place good and comfortable for a day or two" (p. 46). This is the only point at which the reporter occupies common ground with the aviators; for in his namelessness and rootlessness he appears to be as bereft of a past as they.

In the third chapter, "Night in the Vieux Carré" (New Orleans's French Quarter), the reporter becomes more deeply involved with the group, and Holmes is outraged over the reporter's obvious infatuation with Laverne. A number of important concepts are introduced in this chapter. The hollowness of a materialistic, mechanized society is implied in Faulkner's description of the automobile: "a machine expensive, complex, delicate and intrinsically useless, created for some obscure psychic need of the species if not the race, from the virgin resources of a continent, to be the individual muscles bones and flesh of a new and legless kind" (p. 87), a description that might be applied to airplanes as well. The relativity of time and reality is a theme that runs throughout the novel, but in this chapter it receives a pointed treatment. The elevator in the newspaper building always has a stack of newspapers in it, and the operator keeps his watch on top of the stack. Leaving the building Thursday night, Hagood looks at the watch and then puts it back on the top newspaper, "placing it without apparent pause or calculation in the finicking exact center of the line of caps, so that now, in the shape of a cheap metal disc, the cryptic stripe was parted neatly in the exact center by the blank backside of the greatest and most inescapable enigma of all" (p. 85). The two symbols, the clock and the newspaper, represent man's attempt to shape and order time and reality to his own liking. Particularly in its dramatization of the reporter's beliefs and fantasies, *Pylon* somberly shows the futility of such attempts.

After the group has spent the evening in the reporter's apartment, the events that will culminate in the death of Roger Shumann begin to fall rapidly into place. Roger has a narrow escape when his airplane crashes on Friday. At the reporter's suggestion they go to see Matt Ord, a flier and racer who has enjoyed economic success and is now set up in business. Among fliers, Ord is the exception to the rule; and he appears to be perfectly content with a profitable, middle-class style of life. While the reporter and Shumann are together, the reporter reveals his desire for Laverne very explicitly: "maybe if I was to even sleep with her, it would be the same. Sometimes I think about how it's you and him [Holmes] and how maybe sometimes she dont even know the difference, one from another, and I would think how maybe if it was me too she wouldn't even know I was there at all" (p. 175).

The reporter knows that Ord has been working on an experimental airplane, and he hopes Ord will let Shumann fly it. Ord, however, knows that the airplane is unsafe and refuses. Later, the reporter prepares a false bill of sale that he and Shumann sign and thus, through subterfuge, they manage to get the use of the airplane. The reporter assumes, incorrectly, that he is helping Shumann to do what he must do—fly in the race because of some unwritten code of honor. Actually, Shumann's true motive is hinted at in the fifth chapter. The night before the race, Roger tries to explain to Laverne his reason for flying in it. She responds by saying, "But it's seven months yet" (p. 192), to which Roger answers, "Yair. Just seven months. And one more meet, and the only ship we have with a shot engine and two wrenched longerons" (p. 193). The fact is that Laverne is pregnant—though this time they know it is by Jack. The prospect of winning $2,000 has made the risk of flying Ord's airplane acceptable to Shumann because the group is going to become larger and will require additional income. Thus, Shumann's decision to fly in the race is not based on some abstract principle of the reporter's imagining; it is utterly practical.

The gamble does not pay off. The airplane comes apart during the race, crashing into the lake and killing Shumann. In his description of the crash site, Faulkner once more focuses attention on the clutter of twentieth-century society. Near the place where Shumann crashes, there is a dredged-out slip that is kept clear of silt by "a sunken mole composed of refuse from the city itself—shards of condemned paving and masses of fallen walls and even discarded automobile bodies—any and all the refuse of man's twentieth century clotting into com-munities large enough to pay a mayor's salary—dumped into the lake" (pp. 236-237). Attempts to recover Shumann's body are unsuccessful, and because he is partially responsible for Roger's death the reporter never sees Laverne again. Jack Holmes offers the reporter some realistic advice: "stick to the kind of people you are used to after this" (p. 261). Still, the reporter does not seem to understand what has happened; another reporter, in the last chapter, offers the most accurate analysis. After listening to one of his colleagues argue that Shumann would not have risked his life if it was just money he was after, he retorts: "It was the money. Those guys like money as well as you and me" (p. 292). He argues further that Laverne is doing the right thing in leaving town as soon as possible:

> when a game blows up in your face you dont sit down on the pocketbook that used to make a bump on your ass and cry about it, you get out and hustle up another roll and go on and find another game that maybe you can beat. Yes. They want money, all right. . . . So I don't know any-more than you guys do but if somebody told me that Shumann had some folks somewhere and then they told me the name of the town she bought hers and the kid's tickets to, I would tell you where Shumann used to live. And then I would bet a quarter maybe that the next time you see them [Laverne and Holmes], the kid wont be there (pp. 292-293).

Though the speaker cannot know all the motives involved, he has the facts absolutely correct. That such a chain of events could take place has never occurred to the reporter; but this is exactly what Jiggs later confirms to the reporter. Knowing that another child is on the way, Laverne leaves Jack with Roger Shumann's parents.

Pylon is a wasteland novel in which Faulkner attempts to show a particular segment of modern American society to be spiritually barren, destitute of enduring values, and populated primarily by people who have no sense of the past and no hope for the future. Brooks is correct in his judgment that "the world of *Pylon* is presented as a strange and even nightmarish place in which the fabric of humanity is put to its hardest test."[7] In this novel the test is failed. Even in terms of style and structure, in his frequent use of run together words and in the absence of type breaks to indicate shifts in time and location, it is as if Faulkner were trying to issue an indictment against contemporary materialistic culture in a single, remorseless breath.

With the notable exception of Ernest Hemingway, who declared his admiration for *Pylon* in *Esquire*, reviewers were very critical of the novel. As was often the case, charges were leveled of "deliberate obfuscation," as John Chamberlain put it, and John Crowe Ransom went so far as to declare that "William Faulkner is spent."

Since its initial reception, the consensus of the relatively few critics who have written about *Pylon* has been that it is clearly a minor work, though in theme and technique it displays similarities with Faulkner's more significant achievements. Among the studies the reader may wish to consult are two articles by Donald T. Torchiana that deal, respectively, with theme and character: "Faulkner's *Pylon* and the Structure of Modernity" and "The Reporter in Faulkner's *Pylon*."[8] A general estimate worth the reader's attention is novelist Reynolds Price's "*Pylon*: The Posture of Worship."[9] Finally, Joseph R. McElrath, Jr., offers a useful discussion of the character of Laverne in "*Pylon*: The Portrait of a Lady."[10]

---

[1]*Faulkner in the University*, p. 36.

[2]*Faulkner in the University*, p. 36.

[3]Brooks, *Toward Yoknapatawpha and Beyond*, p. 180.

[4]Brooks, *Toward Yoknapatawpha and Beyond*, p. 182.

[5]*Pylon* (New York: Smith & Haas, 1935), p. 183. Subsequent references are placed within text.

[6]Brooks, *Toward Yoknapatawpha and Beyond*, p. 190.

[7]Brooks, *Toward Yoknapatawpha and Beyond*, p. 182.

[8]Donald T. Torchiana, "Faulkner's *Pylon* and the Structure of Modernity," *Modern Fiction Studies*, 3 (Winter 1957-1958): 291-308; Torchiana, "The Reporter in Faulkner's *Pylon*," *History of Ideas Newsletters*, 4 (Spring 1958): 33-39.

[9]Reynolds Price, "*Pylon*: The Posture of Worship," *Shenandoah*, 19 (Spring 1968): 49-61.

[10]Joseph R. McElrath, Jr., "*Pylon*: The Portrait of a Lady," *Mississippi Quarterly*, 27 (Summer 1974): 277-290.

Absalom, Absalom!

It is unclear exactly when Faulkner began work on his eighth novel, but as early as February 1934 he began a manuscript he called "A Dark House," which was clearly an early attempt at the work that became *Absalom, Absalom!* The manuscript carrying the novel's final title was written between 30 March 1935 and 31 January 1936, and there was substantial revision of that version before publication on 26 October 1936.

"Dark House" has been presented as a working title for *Light in August* as well as *Absalom, Absalom!*[1] There is a plenitude of darkness in both novels. *Absalom, Absalom!* begins in the dark "office" of Miss Rosa Coldfield's home, which is described as "a dim hot airless room with the blinds all closed and fastened for forty-three summers because when she was a girl someone had believed that light and moving air carried heat and that dark was always cooler"; and Miss Rosa is dressed in "the eternal black which she had worn for forty-three years."[2] Appearing in many different forms, this bleak imagery pervades the entire novel. Thomas Sutpen's plantation ends up as a dark house, and the Harvard dormitory room shared by Quentin Compson—who first appeared in *The Sound and the Fury*—and his roommate, Shreve McCannon, is frequently described in terms of a mausoleum. Moreover, the story that is told in *Absalom, Absalom!* is certainly a dark and mystifying tale.

On the surface, *Absalom, Absalom!* appears to be a remarkably simple story: the destruction of Thomas Sutpen and the failure of his dream to create an empire. Yet it is one of the most complex novels Faulkner wrote, for the story is told and retold from the points of view of several different characters; and at the end Thomas Sutpen—as well as his children, Judith and Henry, and their half brother, Charles Bon—remains as elusive and shadowy as he was at the beginning of the novel. The source for the title is biblical, invoking the story of David and his son Absalom. Faulkner obviously saw both Christian and classical parallels to the course of events that eventually causes Sutpen's downfall: "the Greeks destroyed him, the old Greek concept of tragedy," Faulkner later said. "He wanted a son which symbolized this ideal [of immortality], and he got too many sons—his sons destroyed one another and then him."[3] But *Absalom, Absalom!* is more than just the story of Thomas Sutpen and his family. It is also the story of the people who relate, interpret, and even try to create the meaning of the Sutpen story. This is especially true of Quentin and Shreve. Neither Sutpen nor his wife, Ellen, nor his daughter, Judith, ever speaks for himself. There is one letter from Charles Bon to Judith; all else is reported and interpreted by witnesses—not always reliable—or is interpreted by others on the testimony of witnesses. In some cases, as with Miss Rosa, the roles of witness and interpreter are intertwined. Nowhere is the story of Sutpen summarized or presented whole; in retrospect we see bits and pieces of the same story being told many times and from different points of view. This intricate layering of points of view was quite deliberate on Faulkner's part. As he said:

> I think that no one individual can look at truth. It blinds you. You look at it and you see one phase of it. Someone else looks at it and sees a slightly awry phase of it. But taken all together, the truth is in what they saw though nobody saw the truth intact. So these [viewpoints] are true as far as Miss Rosa and as Quentin saw it. Quentin's father saw what he believed was truth, that was all he saw. But the old man was himself a little too big for people no greater in stature than Quentin and Miss Rosa and Mr. Compson to see all at once. It would have taken perhaps a wiser or more tolerant or more sensitive or more thoughtful person to see him as he was. It was . . . thirteen ways of looking at a blackbird.[4] But the truth, I

would like to think, comes out, that when the reader has read all these thirteen different ways of looking at the blackbird, the reader has his own fourteenth image of that blackbird which I would like to think is the truth.[5]

The novel begins with an "awry" look at Thomas Sutpen, from the bitterly antagonistic viewpoint of Miss Rosa Coldfield. The time is September 1909, just before Quentin Compson leaves Jefferson to attend Harvard, and Miss Rosa is telling Quentin her version of the Sutpen story.[6] Though there are some hard facts in this chapter, the emphasis is upon Miss Rosa's highly subjective interpretation of Sutpen, whom she describes as a "man-horse-demon," a symbol of evil and destructiveness who seems to burst suddenly upon the town of Jefferson with the "faint sulphur-reek still in hair clothes and beard, with grouped behind him his band of wild niggers like beasts half tamed to walk upright like men" (p. 8). Indeed, Miss Rosa's whole attitude is one of "impotent and static rage" and "indomitable frustration" (p. 7). But there is more to the chapter than Miss Rosa's fury. One of the primary themes of the novel resides in the question of the past, and particularly Quentin Compson's attempt to understand and reconcile himself to the past. For Quentin the past is a heavy burden, and as he listens to Miss Rosa he imagines himself to be two separate people, one of whom is a part of the "deep South dead since 1865 and peopled with garrulous outraged baffled ghosts," and the other "who was still too young to deserve yet to be a ghost, but nevertheless having to be one for all that, since he was born and bred in the deep South" (p. 9).

The first chapter also contains pieces of specific information that bear importantly on the remainder of the story, and there are implications that there is additional information not yet revealed. For example, while we do not yet know precisely why Miss Rosa has sent for Quentin, we do know that Quentin, over time, has heard a good deal about Thomas Sutpen from his father; thus Sutpen's history already occupies a prominent place in Quentin's fertile imagination. The bare facts of Sutpen's story are revealed: he arrived in Jefferson in 1833, twelve years before Miss Rosa was born, with some slaves and a French architect; he built a ten-square-mile plantation ("Sutpen's Hundred") out of a virgin swamp; he married Miss Rosa's sister Ellen and had two children, Henry and Judith, respectively six and four years older than their aunt Rosa; and Rosa had herself, at some time, been engaged to Thomas Sutpen. Ironically, most of the events that Miss Rosa describes took place before her birth, and all of her assertions about Sutpen's motives are purely conjectural. They are also, for the most part, inaccurate.

The chapter ends with Miss Rosa's description of something else she has not actually observed: one of the Negro fights Sutpen was in the habit of staging and in which he sometimes participated. As reported, this scene implies an important difference between Henry and Judith, and one that is insisted upon by Miss Rosa throughout; namely, that in terms of temperament Judith is much more like her father than her mother. Further, Miss Rosa maintains that Judith and a Negro girl sneaked into the barn to watch the fight and that looking down from the loft that night there were "two Sutpen faces" (p. 30). The Negro girl is Clytemnestra (called Clytie), Sutpen's daughter by one of his slaves; and Miss Rosa's reference to her at the end of the chapter subtly introduces the theme of miscegenation which will later occupy a prominent place in the novel.

The second chapter focuses on Quentin and Mr. Compson. It takes place after Quentin has talked with Miss Rosa, but before he has returned with the wagon to drive her out to the plantation house that Sutpen built, and that now (1909) is all that is left of Sutpen's Hundred. Both Mr. Compson's description and perception of Thomas Sutpen—his knowledge of the man is based on what he has learned from his own father—

are quite different from Miss Rosa's. More reflective and dispassionate in his analysis, Mr. Compson describes Sutpen at the time of his arrival in Jefferson as "a man of about twenty-five. . . . with a big frame but gaunt now almost to emaciation, with a short reddish beard which resembled a disguise and above which his pale eyes had a quality at once visionary and alert, ruthless and reposed in a face whose flesh had the appearance of pottery . . ." (pp. 32-33). Perceptually, Sutpen is compared to a man who has recently been ill: "Not like a man who had been peacefully ill in bed and had recovered . . . but like a man who had been through some solitary furnace experience which was more than just fever, like an explorer say, who . . . was overtaken by the added and unforeseen handicap of the fever also and fought through it at enormous cost not so much physical as mental" (p. 32). Mr. Compson does not have the strong emotional bias that Miss Rosa has, and as a result the bits and pieces of the Sutpen story that he supplies—some of which are repetitious and represent expansions on Miss Rosa's narration—are more orderly. It is still, however, not a complete picture.

As Miss Rosa's chapter served to introduce the concept of the past and the burden of history, so Mr. Compson's chapter introduces the concept of community and communal reactions to Sutpen. The source of Sutpen's wealth is a mystery to the town, and the townspeople are not inclined to give him the benefit of any doubts. Mr. Compson remarks that this suspicion made Sutpen "in a sense a public enemy" because the town realized that "he was getting it involved with himself" (p. 43). Sutpen is placed in jail on the basis of nothing stronger than vague suspicions of unspecified illdoing; and it is only because Quentin's grandfather and Mr. Coldfield, a man of unquestioned probity, sign a bond for his release that Sutpen is set free. Shortly thereafter, Sutpen marries Coldfield's daughter, thus gaining social respectability. Respectability is one of the key ingredients in the formula for success and empire that

Sutpen has deduced from his experiences in life. Reviewing what he knows of the events surrounding Sutpen's life, Mr. Compson judges that even at the age of fourteen Sutpen had "a fixed goal in his mind which most men do not set up until the blood begins to slow at thirty or more," and that he pursued this dream (it is not named yet) with the knowledge that there was virtually no margin for error, that he must ever maintain "that alertness for measuring and weighing event against eventuality, circumstance against human nature" (p. 53).

The third chapter shifts back to Miss Rosa and carries her and Quentin's story forward. The character of Charles Bon is first referred to in this chapter, as is the character of Wash Jones. The stage is beginning to fill up and, using a kind of imagery that he had employed before, especially in *Flags in the Dust* and *Light in August*, we are told that just at the time when Sutpen's plans seem to be falling into place (his plantation is established; he has two children, one of whom is a male heir to perpetuate his dream; and his wife seems content with the life she is leading), "while he was still playing the scene to the audience, behind him Fate, destiny, retribution, irony—the stage manager, call him what you will—was already striking the set and dragging on the synthetic and spurious shadows and shapes of the next one" (pp. 72-73). This concept is a familiar one in Faulkner's work. Fate does not determine the outcome of human events; it establishes a particular context in which human events occur. Always, within any given context, there are many individual choices to be made. The "scenery" that Fate is dragging onto the stage is, of course, the Civil War, and thus the dimension of history and the past is reintroduced into the chapter. Among the more important details in this chapter is that there was a row of some sort at Sutpen's Hundred at Christmas, "whether something between Henry and Bon on one hand and Judith on the other, or between the three young people on one hand and the parents on the other. But anyway, when Christmas day came, Henry and Bon were gone" (p. 79).

This is all Miss Rosa knew at the time; and following this partial revelation of a reported event, the narrator suggests the existence of a relationship between Henry and Judith that is similar in some respects to the relationship between Quentin and Caddy in *The Sound and the Fury*: "the town knew that between Henry and Judith there had been a relationship closer than the traditional loyalty of brother and sister even; a curious relationship" (p. 79). For this reason the town concludes incorrectly that the argument could not have been between Henry and his father, because after Henry and Bon leave there is no apparent strain in the relationship between Judith and her father. We are also told in this chapter that Bon first visits Sutpen's Hundred as Henry's guest during the Christmas of 1859, while the two are on vacation from the University of Mississippi. Bon returns with Henry the following spring on his way home to New Orleans, and it is learned that Sutpen is himself in New Orleans when the second visit takes place. The chapter ends with Miss Rosa's recollection of Wash Jones coming into town for her, though at this point the reason for his coming is not revealed.

The narrative centers of chapters 4 and 5 alternate, respectively, between Mr. Compson and Miss Rosa. It is in Mr. Compson's chapter that one of the few pieces of hard evidence in the novel is presented: the letter that Charles Bon writes to Judith Sutpen near the end of the Civil War stating that they have waited long enough, implying that at his return they will marry. In his chapter, Mr. Compson is primarily concerned with the relationships between Bon and Henry and Judith, and with the events he thinks took place just after Christmas of 1860 when Bon and Henry left Sutpen's Hundred, where they had gone to spend their Christmas vacation. The chief question that Mr. Compson raises and then tries to answer is why Henry eventually kills Bon. Regardless of how he interprets the few facts he has to work with, he tells his son that "It's just incredible. It just does not explain" (p. 100). In the whole

relationship between Bon and Sutpen and Henry and Judith
there seems to Mr. Compson to be an unreconcilable paradox:

> there they are: this girl, this young countrybred girl who
> sees a man for an average of one hour a day for twelve days
> during his life and that over a period of a year and a half,
> yet is bent on marrying him to the extent of forcing her
> brother to the last resort of homicide . . . this father who
> had seen that man once, yet had reason to make a six
> hundred mile journey to investigate him and either dis-
> cover what he already and apparently by clairvoyance
> suspected . . . this brother in whose eyes that sister's and
> daughter's honor and happiness . . . should have been
> more jealous and precious than to the father even, yet
> who must champion the marriage to the extent of re-
> pudiating father and blood and home to become a fol-
> lower and dependent of the rejected suitor for four years
> before killing him apparently for the very identical reason
> which four years ago he quitted home to champion . . .
> (pp. 99-100).

In Mr. Compson's view, Bon's New Orleans background
makes him experienced beyond his years and gives him an aura
of sophistication that seduces Henry and Judith alike. He
further presumes that what Sutpen discovers in New Orleans is
that Bon already has a wife of sorts, an octoroon mistress by
whom he has had a son. The postulated obstacle, then, that
Henry must overcome is one of bigamy, and Mr. Compson
imagines how carefully Bon must have introduced him to New
Orleans culture in the hopes that Henry would be able to
understand his relationship to the octoroon. However, Henry
is unable to reconcile himself to what he regards as an already
existing marriage, and throughout the time that they serve
together in the war he is giving Bon the opportunity to renounce that marriage or—as Bon indicates in his letter to
Judith—to let Fate settle the question by taking either or both
of their lives. Presumably, based on the available evidence at

this point in the novel, when Bon does not renounce his octoroon "wife," Henry, at the last possible moment, kills him.

In contrast to Mr. Compson's narration, Miss Rosa's chapter focuses on her version of the actions that take place after
Henry kills Bon. It is during this period, after Ellen Sutpen has
died, that Miss Rosa goes to live at Sutpen's Hundred and, after
Sutpen's return from the war, becomes engaged briefly to him.
Sutpen, trying to supply himself with another male heir, pro-
poses marriage to Miss Rosa, but he makes the marriage conditional. According to Miss Rosa, Sutpen suggests that they mate
first; if Miss Rosa produces a male child Sutpen will then marry
her. Outraged, Miss Rosa breaks off the engagement and returns to Jefferson. There is also a glancing reference at this
point to Sutpen's ultimate end. Driving out to Sutpen's
Hundred with Wash Jones, Miss Rosa refers to him as *"that
brute progenitor of brutes whose granddaughter was to
supplant me, if not in my sister's house at least in my sister's
bed . . . that brute who . . . overrides both weakly just and
unjust strong"* (p. 134). Miss Rosa is saying that Sutpen later
tries the same experiment he proposed to her with Milly Jones,
Wash Jones's granddaughter. Milly gives birth to a female
child, and when Wash realizes that the man whom he idolizes
does not intend to meet what Wash had understood to be his
part of the unspoken bargain he kills Sutpen.

The chief event of the chapter, though, is Henry's killing of
Bon. Miss Rosa never actually sees the body; it has already
been taken into Judith's bedroom by the time she arrives, and
Henry has fled. The only evidence she has that a crime has been
committed is that she helps put Bon's coffin into the ground.
She tells Quentin that she remembers *"that afternoon when we
carried the coffin from the house. . . . I tried to take the full
weight of the coffin to prove to myself he was really in it"* (pp.
150-151). By the end of the chapter Quentin's imagination is
wholly caught up in Sutpen's story; and he is particularly
obsessed by the image of what he himself imagines to have been

the scene of confrontation between Judith and Henry: "that door [Judith's], the running feet on the stairs beyond it almost a continuation of the faint shot . . . as the door crashed in and the brother stood there . . . the pistol still hanging against his flank" (p. 172). Quentin even imagines the brief conversation that takes place between Henry and Judith. It is immediately after this imagined conversation that Miss Rosa tells Quentin why she wants him to go with her out to the old Sutpen place where, it is thought, Clytie has been living alone since Judith's death in 1884. It is because there is something hidden in the house: "It has been out there for four years, living hidden in that house" (p. 172).

The sixth chapter shifts the focus of the narrative to Quentin and Shreve's Harvard dormitory room. The time is now January 1910 and Quentin has been at Harvard since sometime in September. He is still obsessed with Henry and Judith:

he had something which he still was unable to pass: that door, that gaunt tragic dramatic self-hypnotized youthful face like the tragedian in a college play, an academic Hamlet waked from some trancement of the curtain's falling and blundering across the dusty stage from which the rest of the cast had departed last Commencement, the sister facing him across the wedding dress which she was not to use . . . the two of them slashing at one another with twelve or fourteen words and most of these the same words repeated two or three times so that when you boiled it down they did it with eight or ten (p. 174).

All of this is purely a product of Quentin's imagination; and through the terms in which the scene is rendered Faulkner manages to evoke once more the "stage" imagery that he had used earlier in the novel (see pp. 72-73); now, however, it becomes all the more apparent that it is not just historical events but also the creative and fallible imaginations of the novel's characters that set the stage on which human actions are played out.

Primarily on the basis of evidence supplied originally by Quentin's grandfather and told to him by his father, additional details are given about Sutpen's life following his return from the war. Bon's New Orleans son, Charles Etienne Saint-Valery Bon, is brought to Sutpen's Hundred, or what remains of it, by Judith, and before he dies he produces a son named Jim Bond who is evidently retarded. Aside from the flashbacks, there are three narrative voices that predominate from chapter 6 to the end of the novel: Quentin's, Shreve's—which gradually assumes a more and more dominant role—and that of a third-person narrator who comments on the combined imaginings of Shreve and Quentin.

Chapter 7, again based on the testimony of Quentin's grandfather, gives the most detailed treatment of Sutpen's past life, from the time he left the mountains of western Virginia through his sojourn in Haiti to his arrival in Jefferson. It is also made clear that Sutpen produced a son while he was in Haiti, and that neither Quentin's father nor his grandfather were aware that this person might have been Charles Bon. Quentin himself learns it (or deduces it) as a result of his nighttime visit with Rosa Coldfield to the Sutpen plantation house. While Quentin is restating Sutpen's reason for repudiating his first wife, Shreve interrupts him: "Your old man. . . . When your grandfather was telling this to him, he didn't know any more what your grandfather was talking about than your grandfather knew what the demon [Sutpen] was talking about when the demon told it to him, did he? And when your old man told it to you, you wouldn't have known what anybody was talking about if you hadn't been out there and seen Clytie" (p. 274). This raises another possibility for Shreve's and Quentin's imaginations in the Judith/Bon relationship to work on; that the barrier which Henry could not overcome was not bigamy but incest, and perhaps, based on Shreve's speculations, miscegenation.

The turning point in Sutpen's life was when his family was living in the tidewater area of Virginia. Sent by his father to a plantation house to deliver a message, Sutpen is turned away from the front door by a Negro slave. He is at first more baffled than hurt. He finally concludes that "to combat them [the system that allowed him to be turned away before he could state his business] you have got to have what they have that made them do what the man did. You got to have land and niggers and a fine house to combat them with" (p. 238). This is the object of Sutpen's design: to prove himself superior within the system that has shamed him. But because he is not part of a traditional system he can never really be a part of the class upon which he models his design. As Cleanth Brooks has pointed out, for Sutpen "tradition is not a way of life 'handed down' or 'transmitted' from the community. . . . It is an assortment of things to be possessed, not a manner of living that embodies certain values and determines men's conduct."[7] Thus, when his dream begins to fall apart Sutpen cannot attribute the cause as having anything to do with human nature. He can only conclude that the flaw lies in the design itself, and if he can only discover what it is, his dream might yet be realized.

However, the real center of dramatic attention in the latter portion of the novel is Quentin Compson, and *Absalom, Absalom!* is as much Quentin's story as it is Thomas Sutpen's. Flights of imaginative fancy reach their highest altitude in the novel's final two chapters. Quentin and Shreve know that Sutpen, while in Haiti, was married, produced a son, and later repudiated his family. All else concerning that aspect of Sutpen's life is pure speculation. It is never revealed what Sutpen learned when he made his trip to New Orleans in the spring of 1860 or what he said to Henry the following Christmas; and there is no other evidence to prove conclusively that Bon is Sutpen's son. Consider, then, the speculations that are built on this flimsy evidence, especially by Shreve. It is he who invents Bon's childhood; who invents the New Orleans lawyer hired by Bon's mother to find her husband; who postulates the plans of the lawyer to blackmail Sutpen—inventing even the letter of introduction the lawyer writes to Henry before Bon's arrival at the University of Mississippi; who imagines Bon, after the Christmas of 1860, taking Henry to New Orleans to meet his Haitian mother; who speculates that Henry might have been able to reconcile himself to Bon's incest with Judith. But Bon's fate is sealed when Sutpen seeks Henry out during the late stages of the war and tells him that Bon is part Negro. That would imply the reason Sutpen had for repudiating his first family, and would mean that the ultimate barrier Henry was unable to overcome was neither bigamy nor incest but miscegenation. Though Quentin does not make any of these claims himself, he evidently agrees with Shreve's version.

If true, Shreve's version would have the satisfying symmetry of a logical sequence of cause and effect, ironically coming full circle to destroy the man who set it in motion. But it is necessary to consider the relationship of Quentin and Shreve to the Compson story. Shreve is entertained by it. At the beginning of chapter 7 he comments to Quentin, "Jesus, the South is fine, isn't it. It's better than the theatre, isn't it. It's better than Ben Hur, isn't it" (p. 217). And later he interrupts Quentin's version of the story, telling him, "you wait. Let me play a while now" (p. 280). Quentin, however, is not playing. He is tormented; and it is not necessary to go back to *The Sound and the Fury* and to consider his relationship with his sister Caddy to discover the source of that torment. Quentin's imagination is absorbed by the relationship between Henry and Judith and the imagined confrontation that occurs between them after Henry has shot Bon. He is, moreover, identified with Henry as Shreve is with Bon (see p. 334). He has two sources of evidence from which he feeds his imagination: Miss Rosa's assertion that Judith was engaged to Bon and Bon's letter to

Judith in which he does not actually propose marriage but says, "*We have waited long enough*," and concludes by saying, "*I now believe that you and I are, strangely enough, included among those who are doomed to live*" (pp. 131, 132). What, then, makes Quentin conclude, after his visit to the Sutpen place with Miss Rosa, that Bon is Sutpen's son?[8] Does Henry Sutpen tell him, or does he infer it through some other piece of evidence? Consider the evidence. Quentin encounters Clytie in the house, and it is known that Clytie is Sutpen's daughter. When Quentin discovers that Henry Sutpen is in the house, having come home to die, he is presented with a bizarre picture indeed; not Henry and Judith reunited and living together at last as brother and sister, but Henry and his Negro half sister and the ubiquitous, retarded Jim Bond hovering in the background. In Quentin's mind, this is a compounding of evils, incest and miscegenation, come together at last beneath the roof of the dark house. If this is the case, then Shreve's speculations about Henry Sutpen are quite ironic because they describe, unknowingly, Quentin's own tortured state of mind. Thus, when Shreve pauses at the end of his narrative account of the Henry/Bon story and demands of Quentin, "Aint that right? Aint it? By God, aint it?" (p. 359), Quentin's "Yes" is as much in reference to himself as it is to what he believes to have been true about Henry Sutpen.

Absalom, Absalom! is many stories that all ensue from one source. In it Faulkner raises difficult questions about how human events and motions can be judged and evaluated. Physical evidence is seldom as complete as we would like and is not always trustworthy. *Absalom, Absalom!* is certainly the story of Henry Sutpen, and in his treatment of him Faulkner illustrates beautifully the futility of attempting to lead one's life according to some abstract master plan that is divorced from tradition and community. But it is also the story of Quentin Compson, and in some respects his is the most tragic story in the novel. Quentin has sources of tradition and community to draw on, but cannot do so in a positive or meaningful way. His story becomes the story of a personality in the process of self-destruction.

Although *Absalom, Absalom!* is widely regarded now as one of Faulkner's masterpieces, many contemporary reviewers, including Clifton Fadiman in the *New Yorker*, Mary Colum in *Forum*, and an anonymous reviewer in *Time*, were baffled or unimpressed by the novel. Qualified praise was offered in the *Nation* by William Troy, in the *New York Times* by Harold Straus, in the *New Republic* by Malcolm Cowley (who gave his liberal's stamp to the novel for its social concerns), and in the *Review of Reviews* by Hershel Brickell. The book sold well, going through three printings totaling 10,000 copies in the first three months of publication, but Faulkner's royalties were still slim, amounting to between $2,000 and $3,000 on initial sales.

As James B. Meriwether has pointed out, "Critical controversy concerning *Absalom, Absalom!* . . . has abounded since its first publication." [9] It has prompted more critical articles than any other novel by Faulkner except *The Sound and the Fury*. Among the welter of interpretations and perspectives that have been published about *Absalom, Absalom!*, the most balanced and useful general estimates remain those of Brooks and Millgate, who have already been cited in this chapter. Additional studies dealing with three important aspects of the novel are: Floyd C. Watkins, "What Happens in *Absalom, Absalom!*"; M. E. Bradford, "Brother, Son, and Heir: The Structural Focus of Faulkner's *Absalom, Absalom!*," an article which deals with several of the issues surrounding the life of Charles Bon; and Elisabeth S. Muhlenfeld, "Shadows with Substance and Ghosts Exhumed: The Women in *Absalom, Absalom!*" [10]

---

[1]See introduction, p. 42. The manuscript title page of *Light in August* shows the canceled title of "Dark House," which is not in itself conclusive

evidence that this was the novel's original title. See Blotner, pp. 701-702.

[2]*Absalom, Absalom!* (New York: Random House, 1936). Passage quoted is from the 1966 Modern Library edition, p. 7. Subsequent references to this edition are placed within text.

[3]*Faulkner in the University*, p. 35.

[4]This is a reference to a poem by Wallace Stevens, "Thirteen Ways of Looking at a Blackbird."

[5]*Faulkner in the University*, pp. 273-274.

[6]The chronology to the Modern Library edition (p. 380) incorrectly identifies the time as September 1910.

[7]Brooks, *The Yoknapatawpha Country*, p. 298.

[8]This is not to argue that Bon is not Sutpen's son, but to underline the nature of inferred evidence in the novel. In *The Yoknapatawpha Country* (pp. 436-438) Brooks makes it quite clear that Quentin possesses more information—whether true or false—about the Sutpen story than his father did, and that this information was based on his nocturnal trip to the Sutpen home with Miss Rosa.

[9]Meriwether, "William Faulkner," *Sixteen Modern American Authors*, ed. Jackson R. Bryer (New York: Horton, 1973), p. 247.

[10]Floyd C. Watkins, "What Happens in *Absalom, Absalom!*," *Modern Fiction Studies*, 13 (Spring 1967): 79-87; M. E. Bradford, "Brother, Son, and Heir: The Structural Focus of Faulkner's *Absalom, Absalom!*," *Sewanee Review*, 78 (Winter 1970): 76-98; Elisabeth S. Muhlenfeld, "Shadows with Substance and Ghosts Exhumed: The Women in *Absalom, Absalom!*," *Mississippi Quarterly*, 25 (Summer 1972): 289-304.

The Unvanquished

To make *The Unvanquished*, Faulkner used six short stories that had been published previously between 1934 and 1936. The seventh and final chapter, "An Odor of Verbena," was written to complete the novel,[1] which was published 15 February 1938. The material for the first six stories was originally conceived "as a long series. . . . I realized that they would be too episodic to be what I considered a novel, so I thought of them as a series of stories . . . but by the time I'd finished the first one I saw that it was going further than that, and then when I'd finished the fourth one, I had postulated too many questions that I had to answer for my own satisfaction."[2] Though the finished work remains episodic in nature, Faulkner's revisions (some stylistic changes were made, and in a few instances new material was added) were minor and simply helped to achieve the effect of novelistic unity.[3] There is unity of time and place, and the action advances in such a way that there is consistent character development throughout the novel.

The central character and narrator of *The Unvanquished* is Bayard Sartoris, who appeared as a much older man in *Flags in the Dust*; and the primary story line of the novel is Bayard's growth to maturity. Bayard has a black companion named Ringo. The two boys are the same age, and Faulkner uses this pairing for purposes of contrast and to mark stages in the development of Bayard's character. In the first chapter of the novel, Bayard and Ringo are twelve years old.

The novel begins in the summer of 1863, and the two boys amuse themselves by acting out the battle of Vicksburg, which is then taking place. From the perspective of the two twelve-year-olds, the Civil War has no immediate reality, and they clothe it imaginatively in an aura of adventure. In their daily lives, slavery and freedom have no meaning. Yankees are enemies because they are outsiders who threaten to disrupt the pattern of daily life. The person who most exemplifies the quality of Bayard's and Ringo's world, and who sets the moral standards by which it operates, is Rosa Millard, known as Granny to both boys. Bayard's father, Col. John Sartoris, assumes bigger-than-life proportions in the eyes of the boys. When Colonel Sartoris returns to the plantation for a brief visit, Bayard remarks that "He was not big; it was just the things he did, that we knew he was doing, had been doing in Virginia and Tennessee, that made him seem big to us"; and that he "was as big as he needed to look and—to twelve years old—bigger than most folks could hope to look."[4] Despite the almost idyllic tone and good humor of the first chapter, there are intimations that the harsher realities of the war and the outside world are about to make themselves known. Neither Bayard nor Ringo is ready yet to assume the responsibilities of manhood, a point that is emphatically made when they fire at a Yankee soldier and then hide behind Granny's skirts for protection.

In the second chapter the boys are one year older. The chief events that occur are Granny's attempt to take the family to Memphis and the burning of the Sartoris home by Yankee soldiers. The characters Buck and Buddy McCaslin are introduced, and considerable attention is given to their attitudes about people and land. Bayard remembers his father saying that "they were ahead of their time," that they "not only possessed, but put into practice, ideas about social relationship that maybe fifty years after they were both dead people would have a name for" (p. 54). The basis of their social attitude lies in their belief that "people belonged to land," (p. 54), not vice versa; and though they own slaves, Buck and Buddy have devised a system by which blacks are not simply given but earn their freedom through the work they do for the plantation. Further, Buck and Buddy have persuaded the " 'white trash'—men who had owned no slaves and some of whom even lived worse than the slaves on big plantations . . . to pool their little patches of poor hill land along with the niggers and the McCaslin plantation, promising them in return nobody knew exactly what, except that their women and children did have shoes, which not all of them had had before, and a lot of them even went to school" (p. 55). In this way the themes of social order, progress, and justice are first presented. The McCaslins' intuitive concepts about these matters are at variance with many of the assumptions of the society in which they live; yet they are of that society and not against it. Experience will lead Bayard to a similar position. He will reject certain traditional concepts of justice and codes of behavior, but he will not repudiate his society or his family.

In the next two chapters Granny and the boys go in search of the silver the Yankees have taken from the Sartoris plantation, and in the process they stumble on the idea of using forged requisitions to get mules from the Northern army. In partnership with Ab Snopes Granny resells the mules, a business arrangement that eventually leads to her death. In the course of looking for the family silver, Granny and the boys travel to Hawkhurst plantation, where Bayard's cousin Drusilla Hawk is introduced. In describing the journey and in introducing Drusilla, considerable emphasis is placed on the nature of experience. Bayard and Ringo make comparisons between themselves on the basis of what each has seen and done. As Bayard puts it, "What counted was, what one of us had done or seen that the other had not, and ever since that Christmas I had been ahead of Ringo because I had seen a railroad, a locomotive" (p. 91). Experience of this kind is innocent and harmless; but for Drusilla, whose fiance was killed at the battle of Shiloh, experience has been a bitter teacher, and what she desires more than anything is revenge on those who have disrupted her life.

Granny's dealings with Ab Snopes lead to the first major turning point in Bayard's life, at the age of fifteen. At first glance, the partnership between Granny and Ab Snopes seems an unlikely one. To take property that is not rightfully hers is not consistent with Granny's character. Her motives, however, have nothing to do with self-gain. With the help of a Methodist minister named Fortinbride, the profits from the enterprise—as well as some of the mules she and Ab are unable to sell—are distributed to the needy people of the neighborhood, black and white alike. A strict accounting is kept: "Each time Granny would make them tell what they intended to do with the money, and now she would make them tell her how they had spent it, and she would look at the book to see whether they had lied or not. And the ones that she had loaned the . . . mules that Ab Snopes was afraid to try to sell would have to tell her how the mule was getting along and how much work it had done" (p. 157). Only when, as a final transaction, Granny attempts to deal with the marauder Grumby does she violate the principles by which she had previously conducted her business. Her motives are not base but they are personal. Formerly, "she had made independent and secure almost everyone in the county save herself and her own blood . . . soon Father would return home to his ruined plantation and most of his slaves vanished; and how it would be if, when he came home and looked about at his desolate future, she could take fifteen hundred dollars in cash out of her pocket and say, 'Here. Start over with this' " (p. 172). Though understandable, her decision is a mistaken one and Grumby kills her. With the help of Buck McCaslin, Bayard and Ringo set out to avenge Granny's murder. Toward the end of the lengthy pursuit, Buck is wounded and forced to return home. Thus the boys are alone when they finally encounter Grumby. Though he is helped by Ringo, it is Bayard who actually shoots and kills his grandmother's murderer. The boys then take Grumby's body back to the cotton compress where Granny was murdered and peg it to the door. As a final symbolic act they sever Grumby's right hand and attach it to the marker above Granny's grave.

Bayard's entry into manhood, at the age of fifteen, is through bloody violence and revenge.

The final chapters of *The Unvanquished* are concerned with the postwar period. Here the "unvanquished" characters of the novel are presented. In one sense Faulkner seems to imply that the unvanquished are the womenfolk for whom the present "is just one continuous monotonous thing full of the repeated follies of their menfolks" (p. 223), and whose primary concerns are for appearance and respectability. For example, the concern for appearance makes it imperative—in her mother's eyes—that Drusilla and John Sartoris be married since, at the end of the war, Drusilla was serving as a soldier— and, she says, "not much of one at that" (p. 233)—in Sartoris's troop of cavalry. But in a more enduring sense the chief unvanquished character in the novel is Bayard, who has the ability to change as the times change, and the courage to rise above tradition when he has to.

John Sartoris's method of restoring social order is rooted in the way he had previously tried to preserve it, through violence and by taking the law into his own hands. When the Burdens—whose story was first told in *Light in August*—are organizing the Negro vote and it appears that a Negro might be elected sheriff of Jefferson, Sartoris deals with the Burdens by killing them, though in accordance with his code of behavior he lets them have the first shot. He appoints Drusilla voting commissioner, directs that the ballot box be taken to his plantation, and then insists on making bond before returning home. His reasoning is ironic: "Don't you see we are working for peace through law and order?" (p. 239). When, a number of years later, his fortunes largely restored, he is shot and killed by his business partner, Ben Redmond, it is expected generally by family and friends that Bayard will exact an eye-for-an-eye revenge. This expectation reaches an extreme in the character of Drusilla—now John Sartoris's widow—who is described as

"the Greek amphora priestess of a succinct and formal violence" (p. 252), and who wears sprigs of verbena in her hair
because "she said verbena was the only scent you could smell
above the smell of horses and courage" (p. 253). Bayard, who
is now twenty-four and who is studying law at the University
of Mississippi, accepts the responsibility of maintaining family
honor but rejects violence.

Shortly before his death, John Sartoris seems to realize that
his methods have become outmoded. He tells his son, "now
the land and the time too are changing; what will follow will be
a matter of consolidation, of pettifogging and doubtless
chicanery in which I would be a babe in arms but in which you,
trained in the law, can hold your own—our own" (p. 266). But
Bayard also responds to an injunction of biblical law, realizing
that "if there was anything at all in the Book, anything of hope
and peace for His blind and bewildered spawn which He had
chosen above all others to offer immortality, *Thou shalt not kill*
must be it" (p. 249). Thus, when Bayard goes to confront Ben
Redmond he goes unarmed, and this act of bravery shames
Redmond into leaving town. Though he rejects violence,
Bayard maintains the highest standards of personal courage;
and though he arrived at manhood through violence, it is
through forebearance that he achieves maturity.

Because it is less complex than his major works—less baf-
fling, as the reviewers would say—the reception of *The Unvanquished* was more favorable than usual for one of Faulkner's novels. Complimentary reviews far outnumbered fault-
finding ones, and most reviewers agreed that Faulkner had
conceded agreeably to popular tastes. The most significant
indication of the general appeal of the novel was the purchase
of movie rights by MGM for $25,000.

While it pleased reviewers, *The Unvanquished* has not attracted the attention of literary critics. Along with *Pylon*, it is
one of the least studied of Faulkner's novels. Though Faulkner

suggested that readers unfamiliar with his work might begin with *The Unvanquished*,[5] Michael Millgate, while not derogating the merits of the work, points out that "the discriminating reader . . . is likely to find within its covers little incentive to read further in Faulkner's work and few indications of those qualities which make him a major writer."[6] Useful interpretive insights, focusing respectively on "An Odor of Verbena" and "Skirmish at Sartoris," are William E. Walker's "*The Unvanquished*: The Restoration of Tradition" and James B. Meriwether's "Faulkner and the South."[7]

---

[1]See introduction, p. 49.

[2]*Faulkner in the University*, p. 252.

[3]For a description of these revisions, see Millgate, pp. 165-166.

[4]*The Unvanquished* (New York: Random House, 1938), pp. 10, 14. Subsequent references are placed within text.

[5]See *Faulkner in the University*, p. 2.

[6]Millgate, p. 170.

[7]William E. Walker, "*The Unvanquished*: The Restoration of Tradition," *Reality and Myth: Essays in American Literature in Memory of Richard Croom Beatty*, edited by Walker and Robert L. Welker (Nashville: Vanderbilt University Press, 1964), pp. 275-297; Meriwether, "Faulkner and the South," *Southern Writers: Appraisals in Our Time*, edited by R. C. Simonini, Jr. (Charlottesville: University of Virginia Press, 1964), pp. 142-161.

The Wild Palms

Faulkner's *The Wild Palms* has been a frequently misread and misunderstood novel. Olga Vickery, in one of the earlier book-length estimates of Faulkner's work, recognized the integral nature of the alternating "Wild Palms" and "Old Man" chapters:

> The interlocking narratives of *The Wild Palms* . . . reveal yet another facet of Faulkner's interest in formal and technical experimentation. For the total meaning of the book is derived from a recognition of the three possible ways in which the stories are related. Regarded as parallel, each is concerned with the relationship between the individual, society, and nature, and between freedom and order. In both, the same pattern of confinement, flight, and capture is developed though in different contexts. Juxtaposed, the two narratives obviously modify and influence the reader's interpretation of either one. . . . together, the two stories transcend the peculiarities of a specific time and place as described in each and depict that cyclic movement of culture which Faulkner has explored from various points of view in all his major works. The emphasis is shifted from the individual and his personal history to man and history in general.[1]

Faulkner's feelings about the unity of *The Wild Palms* were never in doubt. In a 1955 interview he stated emphatically, "I did not know it would be two separate stories until after I had started the book. When I reached the end of what is now the first section of *The Wild Palms*, I realized suddenly that something was missing, it needed emphasis, something to lift it like counterpoint in music. So I wrote on the 'Old Man' story until 'The Wild Palms' story rose back to pitch."[2] Faulkner's statement not only clarifies his intent, it also establishes "Wild Palms"—the love story of Harry Wilbourne and Charlotte Rittenmeyer—as the dominant story of the novel.

The Wild Palms was begun in November 1937 as a novel about Harry Wilbourne and Charlotte Rittenmeyer called "If I Forget Thee, Jerusalem," and it was early in 1938 when Faulkner added the "Old Man" section to his conception of the book. He finished his revised typescript late in June and sent the novel to Random House, who published the book on 19 January 1939. Faulkner's arguments for retaining his original title were unavailing.

Thomas L. McHaney, in the most exhaustive study of the novel to date, discusses in detail the meaning of the original title in relation to the work as a whole. It comes, McHaney writes, "from a psalm about the Babylonian captivity; it is an admonition to remember freedom and the past. The whole psalm provides a rich context of imagery and theme, underscoring the importance of hands and cunning and the preciousness of memory; emphasizing captivity; and explicitly bridging the two disparate tales which make up the novel. Unlike the substituted title, which refers to the main plot alone, the original title announces the unity of the book."[3]

McHaney also identifies and discusses three strata of allusion in the novel: biographical, literary, and philosophical. This discussion is particularly useful in clarifying what Michael Millgate earlier perceived as "some kind of autobiographical or purely personal significance" in *The Wild Palms*.[4] In the area of philosophical allusions, McHaney finds close parallels with the works of Nietzsche and, particularly, Schopenhauer; the connection helps to validate Vickery's insight about the "cyclic movement of culture." According to McHaney, "The cyclic adventures of both convict and lovers underscore Schopenhauer's view that life is an endless cycle of pain and boredom to be escaped only by contemplation of the ideal, through art, or by retreat into the oblivion of will-lessness."[5]

The picture presented to us by these few comments is a challenging one. It shows *The Wild Palms* to be an intricate novel that contains richness of meaning on many different levels and that demands great concentration on the reader's part.

The Wild Palms begins, as do many of Faulkner's works, with a partial insight into a particular human condition; in this case Harry, an intern, and his married lover, Charlotte, are in a beach house in Pascagoula, Mississippi, at a point near the end of their love affair. They are renting the house from an older couple, a doctor and his wife, who live close by. How Harry and Charlotte got there, and the precise reason for their being where they are, is not explained. That explanation is left to the remaining "Wild Palms" chapters, which backtrack to tell their story. The novel begins with the "knocking of an unseen hand upon an unknown door" and events are "gradually revealed as filtered through the wakening and reflecting consciousness of a middle-aged doctor."[6] Indeed, there is more initial emphasis placed on the character of the older doctor than on Harry Wilbourne, and what we learn of Harry and Charlotte comes through a series of fragmentary impressions and insights, filtered through the consciousness of the older doctor and through a third-person narrator.

There is a subtle ironic contrast drawn by Faulkner between the doctor and his wife and Harry and Charlotte. The older couple has lived a conventional, dull life together, and "though they had slept in the same bed for twenty-three years now they still had no children."[7] Charlotte and Harry have gone to extreme ends to avoid conventionality and respectability, which they feel would cheapen and ultimately destroy the intensity of their passion. Yet the relationship between each couple has been unproductive. The doctor and his wife are childless and—though the fact is not revealed to the reader in the first chapter—Charlotte is dying as the result of an abortion that Harry has performed on her.

From behind a hedge of oleander bushes that separates his

bungalow from the one he rents to the couple, the doctor observes Harry and Charlotte (especially Charlotte), and wonders what her malady might be. "It seemed to him that he saw the truth already, the shadowy indefinite shape of truth, as though he were separated from the truth only by a veil just as he was separated from the living woman by the screen of oleander leaves" (p. 6). But mortal man is not capable of seeing, or cannot bear to see, the truth whole. Thus the doctor's trepidation increases as the "veil" parts further and further. When Harry tells the doctor that Charlotte is bleeding, the doctor assumes that she is coughing or spitting blood. When he understands that this is not the case, he asks Harry, "Where is she bleeding?"; to which Harry replies with a question of his own, "Where do women bleed?" (p. 17). The doctor still does not know all the facts but he knows enough to realize that he wishes he were not involved at all:

> *Because I am at the wrong age for this. . . . If I were twenty-five I could say, Thank God I am not him because I would know it was only my luck today and that maybe tomorrow or next year it will be me and so I will not need to envy him. And if I were sixty-five I could say, Thank God, I am not him because then I would know I was too old for it to be possible and so it would not do me any good to envy him because he has proof on the body of love and of passion and of life that he is not dead. But now I am forty-eight and I did not think that I deserved this* (p. 17).

The doctor is beginning to perceive that Harry Wilbourne has experienced a passion more intense than anything he himself has ever imagined, and the realization fills him with an overwhelming sense of loss. Having sublimated his passion with a veneer of conventionality and respectability, the doctor feels that he has earned a measure of peace and should not be reminded of what he has missed. In a sense this feeling establishes yet another parallel with Harry Wilbourne, who throughout the course of his adolescence, through his medical training, and up to the point of his internship has abjured all forms of passion and emotional involvement. As Harry tells the reporter McCord in a later chapter, his initiation into sex, which "would have been two seconds at fourteen or fifteen" (p. 139), did not occur until he was twenty-seven. The difference between him and the older doctor is that once awakened to passion, Harry chooses to pursue it.

The second chapter introduces the tall convict. In his own way he is as much a victim of romance as are Harry and Charlotte. Sentenced to a fifteen-year prison term at the age of nineteen for attempted train robbery, the tall convict believes that he has been defrauded by literature, for his decision to attempt the robbery was influenced by his reading of adventure stories about desperadoes and their heroic deeds. "He had saved the paper-backs for two years, reading and rereading them, memorising them, comparing and weighing story and method against story and method" (p. 24). When his attempt ends in ludicrous failure and he is sent to jail, the tall convict shows no resentment against his captors; but he rages within at the writers whom he "did not even know were not actual men but merely the designations of shades who had written about shades" (p. 25). In time, the tall convict becomes accustomed to and even dependent upon the prison routine. References to the progress of the flooding Mississippi River anticipate the force of nature that will yank him out of his accustomed pattern of life as violently and suddenly as passion yanks Harry Wilbourne out of his.

The first two chapters establish the general conditions from which the two parallel and counterpointed plots of the novel issue. The remaining "Wild Palms" chapters tell us how Charlotte and Harry meet and fall in love; how they define their relationship, and to what lengths they will go—literally (they are constantly moving from place to place) as well as emotionally—to be together on their own terms. However,

the terms of the relationship are dictated primarily by Charlotte. The "Old Man" chapters relate the tall convict's story.
At first his being swept away as he attempted to rescue flood
victims would seem a fortuitous event: he is given his freedom,
and the prison officials assume he has drowned. But the tall
convict does not desire freedom, and his experiences with
nature are cast in terms of violent upheavals (the flood, his later
fights with alligators). What he desires more than anything is
security; so, as Harry and Charlotte pursue their single-
minded bid to escape conventionality at all costs, the tall
convict is equally determined to return—bringing with him the
boat he was originally sent out in to rescue stranded flood
victims—to the security of the most rigidly structured conventionality imaginable: prison.

Michael Millgate has aptly summarized various parallels
between Harry and the tall convict. He notes that both "start
out from somewhat parallel situations":

> both are secure and content, though not precisely happy,
> in the simple, spartan, ordered, almost monastic, exter-
> nally controlled life of the hospital on the one hand and
> the prison on the other. . . . They are approximately the
> same age . . . and at the beginning of their stories each has
> abjured sex . . . each, however, is led by unusual cir-
> cumstances . . . to break away from the familiar pattern
> of his life and to embark, in company with a strange
> woman, on an adventure of extraordinary violence and
> diversity.[8]

In the last of the "Old Man" chapters, another parallel is
revealed between the tall convict and Harry. Before the attempted train robbery the tall convict had had a sweetheart, "a
girl a year or so younger than he, short-legged, with ripe
breasts and a heavy mouth and dull eyes like ripe muscadines"
(p. 338). Just as Harry sacrifices everything for love, so the tall
convict is motivated to commit his crime, at least in part, by

similar feelings. Harry ends up in prison for homicide when Charlotte bleeds to death, but his imprisonment is radically different from the tall convict's. The convict cannot handle freedom. He shuns it, and his whole fantastic adventure is the story of his attempt to return to the security of captivity. Scrupulous in his performance of assigned duty—to rescue a man and a woman stranded by the floodwaters—his every effort is bent toward the time when he can turn himself in, telling the deputy to whom he surrenders, "Yonder's your boat, and here's the woman. But I never did find that bastard on the cottonhouse" (p. 278). Harry Wilbourne's choice, however, is a choice of life over death. He rejects a cyanide tablet offered by Francis Rittenmeyer, Charlotte's husband, deciding that "*between grief and nothing I will take grief*" (p. 324). Dead, even memory ceases to exist; and Harry realizes that as long as he is alive, he will be able to preserve something of the love that he and Charlotte have shared.

The beginning of Harry and Charlotte's love affair, and the establishment of some of the premises on which it is based, is developed in the second "Wild Palms" chapter. Serving his internship at a New Orleans hospital, Harry is persuaded to celebrate his birthday by attending a party in the Vieux Carré section of the city where he meets Charlotte. Their suddenly falling in love and Harry's finding in a garbage can a sum of money that makes it possible for them to go away together may appear as highly improbable events. Yet they are consistent with the overall context of the novel. As Cleanth Brooks has written, "This love at first sight must be accepted as a *donné* of the novel. . . . given such a situation . . . the author asks us, what would happen to the young man? to the young woman with whom he fell in love?"[9] Brooks observes that Harry and Charlotte pursued "an impossible goal; they ask of human life a great deal more than it can provide."[10] For their love to survive, they must eschew conventionality and respectability, for these are the two things that most dissatisfied Charlotte before she met Harry. As she tells Harry, "it's got to be all honeymoon, always. Forever and ever, until one of us dies. It cant be anything else. Either heaven, or hell: no comfortable safe peaceful purgatory between for you and me to wait in until good behavior or forbearance or shame or repentance overtakes us" (p. 83). Charlotte emerges early as the dominant partner, and Harry acknowledges that Charlotte is "a better man than I am" (p. 133). But there are negative aspects to Charlotte's character, too. Brooks points out that "there is more than a hint that Charlotte is half in love with death";[11] and Millgate notes that "She has, rather like Thomas Sutpen, a magnificent design, but the design, like Sutpen's, has a fatal flaw, the flaw of rigidity: the assertion of the will, of the needs of the design, is made irrespective of the demands of the human situation, of humanity, of life."[12] Though Charlotte's will is stronger than Harry's, her desire for an abortion—which ultimately kills her, and may be yet another expression of a personal death wish—"is seen to be, quite specifically, life denying."[13] Critics have also noted that the "rules" by which their affair is conducted contain the seeds of self-defeat. Insisting that the fire of their passion be stoked at the level of white heat, Harry and Charlotte actually spend a substantial amount of their time working on different schedules (and therefore not sleeping together), in the company of friends, or in periods of self-imposed abstinence, as when they share the Utah mining cabin where Harry manages to get a job as the camp doctor.

Harry Wilbourne gradually assumes a stronger and stronger role in the relationship. He complains that there is no place in the modern world for love. "We have eliminated it," he says. "It took us a long time, but man is resourceful and limitless in inventing too, and so we have got rid of love at last just as we have got rid of Christ" (p. 136). But Harry is not permanently embittered by his experiences, and by the end of the novel he is actually a stronger person than Charlotte. He not only refuses the cyanide tablet, he also resists Charlotte's insistence that he save himself by escaping, another opportunity that is presented to him by her husband after Charlotte's death.

Though the "Wild Palms" sections dominate the novel, the stories of the tall convict and Harry Wilbourne ultimately work together to achieve meaning; as McHaney concludes: "In two complementary modes of expression, in two complexly related stories, Faulkner explores and dramatizes the ultimate questions of man's fate. What can man do in the face of the inevitable oblivion of death to which he and his kind are irrevocably doomed?"[14] *The Wild Palms* suggests that one thing man can do is to make a choice—between captivity, security, and vegetation on the one hand, and freedom, responsibility, and the burden and pain of memory on the other.

The reception of *The Wild Palms* was influenced by a *Time* magazine cover story on Faulkner that coincided with the book's publication. Not only was the *Time* feature a measure of Faulkner's solid literary reputation, it was also a potent stimulus to sales. In June 1940, an earnings report for Faulkner's four books published up to that time by Random House showed that he had been paid royalties of $5,560 on *The Wild Palms*, some seventy-five percent more than any of his other Random House books. Aside from the respectful *Time* article by Robert Cantwell, reviews were predictably mixed. As usual, Clifton Fadiman had support for his criticisms of Faulkner's novel among such critics as Ben Ray Redman in *Saturday Review*. But Faulkner had his advocates, too, among them Peter Munro Jack who referred to Faulkner's "genius" in his review for the *New York Times*.

Though literary critics have been more attentive to Faulkner's Yoknapatawpha novels, it is generally agreed that *The Wild Palms* is a significant novel in the Faulkner canon. In addition to the secondary sources already cited, the reader may wish to consult W. T. Jewkes's "Counterpoint in Faulkner's *The Wild Palms*" and Nancy Dew Taylor's "The River of

Faulkner and Mark Twain," which places *The Wild Palms* in context with other, earlier writings about the Mississippi River.[15]

---

[1]Vickery, *The Novels of William Faulkner*, p. 156.

[2]*Lion*, p. 247.

[3]McHaney, *William Faulkner's The Wild Palms: A Study* (Jackson: University Press of Mississippi, 1975), pp. xiii-xiv. Another source for the "Jerusalem" title is suggested by Brooks in *Toward Yoknapatawpha and Beyond*, pp. 406-407.

[4]Millgate, p. 179.

[5]McHaney, *William Faulkner's The Wild Palms*, pp. xvii-xviii.

[6]McHaney, *William Faulkner's The Wild Palms*, p. 26.

[7]*The Wild Palms* (New York: Random House, 1939); Quote is from the 1964 Vintage reissue, p. 4. Subsequent references to this edition are placed within text.

[8]Millgate, p. 176.

[9]Brooks, *Toward Yoknapatawpha and Beyond*, p. 209.

[10]Brooks, *Toward Yoknapatawpha and Beyond*, p. 219.

[11]Brooks, *Toward Yoknapatawpha and Beyond*, p. 215.

[12]Millgate, p. 172.

[13]Millgate, p. 172.

[14]McHaney, *William Faulkner's The Wild Palms*, p. xv.

[15]W. T. Jewkes, "Counterpoint in Faulkner's *The Wild Palms*," *Wisconsin Studies in Contemporary Literature*, 2 (Winter 1961): 39-53; Nancy Dew Taylor, "The River of Faulkner and Mark Twain," *Mississippi Quarterly*, 16 (Fall 1963): 191-199.

The Snopes Trilogy

(The Hamlet, The Town, The Mansion)

Published over a period of seventeen years, *The Hamlet* (1 April 1940), *The Town* (1 May 1957), and *The Mansion* (13 November 1959) form a trilogy which tells the story of the Snopes clan in Yoknapatawpha County, and particularly of the rise of Flem Snopes. Faulkner's work on *The Hamlet*, the first volume of the trilogy, started much earlier than 1940, however. In a 1957 interview at the University of Virginia, he stated that the novel was written "in the late twenties. . . . It was mostly short stories. In 1940 I got it pulled together."[1] In a 1945 letter to Malcolm Cowley, Faulkner had given a fuller explanation: "THE HAMLET was incepted as a novel. When I began it, it produced Spotted Horses, went no further. About two years later suddenly I had THE HOUND, then JAMSHYD'S COURTYARD, mainly because SPOTTED HORSES had created a character I fell in love with [Suratt, later changed to V. K. Ratliff]. . . . Meanwhile, my book had created Snopes and his clan, who produced stories in their saga which are to fall in a later volume."[2] Because it was conceived and written over a long period of time, some of Faulkner's ideas about his material changed as the work progressed. In this regard his prefatory remarks to *The Mansion* are instructive:

> This book is the final chapter of, and the summation of, a work conceived and begun in 1925. Since the author likes to believe, hopes that his entire life's work is a part of a living literature, and since "living" is motion, and "motion" is change and alteration and therefore the only alternative to motion is un-motion, stasis, death, there will be found discrepancies and contradictions in the thirty-four-year progress of this particular chronicle . . . contradictions and discrepancies due to the fact that the

author has learned, he believes, more about the human heart and its dilemma than he knew thirty-four years ago; and is sure that, having lived with them that long time, he knows the characters in this chronicle better than he did then.[3]

The contradictions Faulkner speaks of are matters of narrative detail, consisting primarily of discrepancies in dates and reported events. Characterization and thematic development are consistent throughout the trilogy.

The predominant themes of the trilogy are economic and social, and they are used to explore human nature's tendency toward acquisitiveness, manifesting itself in avarice, greed, and outright rapacity. Counterpointing, but by no means balancing, these unattractive tendencies are occasional examples of altruism, sympathy, and compassion. The themes of the trilogy are first presented in *The Hamlet* which is structured in four separate units, "Flem," "Eula," "The Long Summer," and "The Peasants." The "Flem" section introduces and establishes the Snopes clan in the Frenchman's Bend community. The first rise of Flem Snopes is seen as he gradually usurps Jody Varner's place in his father's (Will Varner's) store, and the section ends with Flem moving into Will Varner's home as a boarder. The "Eula" section presents Will Varner's daughter, Eula, as a fertility goddess living in a community of eunuchs; that is, there are no males in Frenchman's Bend who possess the masculinity to match Eula's overpowering and completely unselfconscious sensuality and fertility. When Eula becomes pregnant by Hoake McCarron, Will Varner arranges a business deal whereby Flem agrees to marry Eula. "The Long Summer" takes place while Flem and Eula are in Texas on what is supposed to be their honeymoon. This section reveals some of the most sterile and negative aspects of the community, and develops in considerable detail contrasting themes of love and respectability. The final section, "The Peasants," begins with the return of Flem and Eula from Texas and concentrates initially on the sale of a herd of wild Texas ponies. By the end of the section, Flem has conquered, in his view, all that is worth conquering in Frenchman's Bend, and is ready to begin his conquest of Jefferson. There is, then, a linear development in the novel: the ascendancy of Flem Snopes. But the richness and complexity, as well as the unity, of *The Hamlet* lies in Faulkner's own masterful blend of disgust and amusement with the human condition, in the portrayal of character and motivation, and in the development of interlocking and contrasting themes.

The Hamlet concentrates almost entirely on the white yeoman and tenant farmer class of Yoknapatawpha County. These are the people who migrated into Mississippi "from the northeast, through the Tennessee mountains by stages marked by the bearing and raising of a generation of children. They came from the Atlantic seaboard and before that, from England and the Scottish and Welsh Marches. . . . They brought no slaves and . . . what they did bring most of them could (and did) carry in their hands."[4] This is the class of the Snopeses, and it is the class of the Varners and of the sewing machine agent V. K. Ratliff, even though the Varners and Ratliff have advanced beyond this status. Frenchman's Bend is the white man's domain. "Strange Negroes would absolutely refuse to pass through it after dark" (p. 5). Economic, political, and social power in the region are controlled by Will Varner, a shrewd patriarch who—among other extensive holdings—owns the property that gives the area its name. He is described as "the largest landholder and beat supervisor in one county and Justice of the Peace in the next and election commissioner in both" (p. 5). Social and economic issues are introduced at the outset. Varner owns or holds mortgages on considerable amounts of property in the county and in the little crossroads community of Frenchman's Bend; and the nature of the power he wields is strongly implied by the fact that "it was considered, to put it mildly, bad luck for a man of the neighborhood to do his trading or gin his cotton or grind his meal or shoe his stock anywhere else" (p. 5) other than Varner's store, gin, mill, or blacksmith shop.

Among the important disclosures made in the first chapter is a reference to the legend of buried gold at the Old Frenchman's place which will emerge as an important element of plot later on. The basic concept of what some Faulkner critics have referred to as the phenomenon of Snopesism—the negative, antisocial behavior most frequently associated with Snopeses—is established in the first chapter and is elaborated in the "Flem" section. What some critics of the novel failed to observe is that Snopesism is not an attribute found only in Snopeses. Those tendencies toward mindless and sometimes rapacious acquisitiveness are a part of general human nature; and they appear sometimes even in a positive character like V. K. Ratliff, a man with a definite sense of moral standards and who, on a selective basis, is protective of community values. The person who initially displays the most repugnant Snopes-like attributes is Will Varner's son Jody. When Ab Snopes (Flem's father) is first moving his family into the neighborhood, Jody learns that he is suspected of being a barn burner. He begins to plot immediately how he can use this information to cheat Ab out of the cotton crop that he will be growing as a sharecropper on Will Varner's property. As Jody explains to his father, "I'll just let him find a couple of rotten shingles with a match laid across them on his doorstep the morning after he finishes laying-by and he'll know it's all up then and aint nothing left for him but to move on. That'll cut two months off the furnish bill and all we'll be out is hiring his crop gathered" (p. 12). But Jody is not as good at Snopesism as Flem is. Flem gains a foothold in the community by using his father's reputation as a barn burner as a psychological lever to pressure Jody into hiring him as a clerk in the store. His ploy is completely passive; he makes no threats but merely allows Jody's imagination to run away with itself. Thus Flem begins a rapid economic advance in Frenchman's Bend and soon takes over Jody's place in the store.

Ironically, it is V. K. Ratliff who helps the Snopes family to establish itself in Frenchman's Bend. Ratliff grew up on a farm adjacent to one worked by Ab Snopes, and he understands how Ab became "soured" as the result of a horse-trading experience with Pat Stamper. Thus, when Ab shows up in Frenchman's Bend some twenty-three years later, Ratliff does what he can to help Ab get a "new un-Stampered start" (p. 49). He does this by instilling in Jody such a fear that Ab might burn the Varners' barn that Jody becomes almost irrational and is willing to go to extreme lengths to placate his new tenant. However, Ratliff quickly recognizes the threat of unbridled rapacity represented by Flem and judges correctly that only he and Will Varner are a possible match for him. This judgment is further substantiated in the goat-trading episode where Ratliff surprises and briefly manages to get the upper hand on Flem. Nonetheless, by the end of the section Flem is firmly established in the community and is bringing other Snopes relatives into it as he extends his control over more and more enterprises.

The Hamlet is dominated by men and by the commerce and business of men, which are viewed by Faulkner as essentially sterile activities. Men prove their masculinity not through their virility and vitality, but by owning things. In this sense, the community of Frenchman's Bend is another of Faulkner's wastelands. Counterpoised against this wasteland is the figure of Eula Varner, a girl who:

> though not yet thirteen years old . . . was already bigger than most grown women and even her breasts were no longer the little, hard, fiercely-pointed cones of puberty or even maidenhood. On the contrary, her entire appearance suggested some symbology out of the old Dionysic times—honey in sunlight and bursting grapes, the writhen bleeding of the crushed fecundated vine beneath the hard rapacious trampling goat-hoof (p. 95).

There is no masculine counterpart in Frenchman's Bend to the feminine principle of fertility represented by Eula Varner. Her presence completely destroys the schoolteacher, Labove, who, despite his learning and his hermitlike ways, comes from the same yeoman farmer stock that most of Frenchman's Bend men do. Though Eula loses her virginity to Hoake McCarron and becomes pregnant, she is not seduced by him. Rather, after she and Hoake have beaten off an attack by a group of jealous local youths, and after Will Varner splints Hoake's broken arm and goes back to bed, Eula responds to the moment and the situation and makes love with Hoake. When he learns she is pregnant, McCarron runs off to Texas to escape the wrath of the Varners, and Flem Snopes agrees to marry Eula. The uniqueness of Eula is implied frequently throughout her section; but nowhere else is it made more clear than in Faulkner's description of Frenchman's Bend at the time of Eula's marriage to Flem: "a little lost village, nameless, without grace, forsaken, yet which wombed once by chance and accident one blind seed of the spendthrift Olympian ejaculation and did not even know it" (p. 149).

Eula's marriage to Flem is significant on a number of different levels. In confirms ironically Labove's earlier vision that Eula's husband would be "a dwarf, a gnome, without glands or desire, who would be no more a physical factor in her life than the owner's name on the fly-leaf of a book" (p. 119). And in fact Flem — who is impotent — is described at the moment when the marriage deal is being executed as "the froglike creature which barely reached [Eula's] shoulder" (p. 149). The motive forcing Will Varner to make the marriage deal with Flem is social respectability — Eula is pregnant and must therefore have a husband, any husband, to be a father for her child — and respectability as a force in determining human affairs is one of the major themes of the novel. But what Eula's marriage to Flem represents more than anything else is waste; the waste of passion on impotence, of love on indifference. This overwhelming sense of waste prompts Ratliff to imagine Flem in hell, where Ratliff perceives him as such a cold-blooded arch-conspirator that even the devil is no match for him.

"The Long Summer" is a season of death in a wasteland from which Eula has been withdrawn. The idiot Ike Snopes's relationship with Jack Houston's cow is another variation on the theme of the sterility and perversion of romantic love. This relationship once more brings V. K. Ratliff into combat against the forces of Snopesism. By convincing the school-teacher, I. O. Snopes, that it is in his own economic interests to do something about Ike and the cow—a public scandal might cost him his job—Ratliff is successful in bringing public viewings of Ike's lovemaking sessions to a close. Ratliff is, however, sickened by the entire business, and he tells the boardinghouse operator, Mrs. Littlejohn, "Maybe all I want is just to have been righteouser, so I can tell myself I done the right thing and my conscience is clear now and at least I can go to sleep tonight" (p. 201).

The chief characters of "The Long Summer" are Jack Houston and Mink Snopes. The exact reasons for Mink's murder of Houston are not revealed until *The Town*; but more important than the question of motivation is the contrast es-tablished between the two men, especially in terms of the women in their lives. Houston marries Lucy Pate, who evi-dently elected Houston to be her eventual husband while they were in school together, and who was willing to wait for thirteen years while Houston roamed around the country.

Houston is the victim not of love or grief but of respectabil-ity. He left Frenchman's Bend to escape the smothering ubiquity of Lucy Pate: "He fled, not from his past, but to escape his future" (p. 214). During his travels he lives with an ex-prostitute for seven years, though he never marries her. This woman loves Houston and lives with him unquestion-ingly. She is described as being "loyal, discreet, undemanding, and thrifty with his money" (p. 215). Yet, when Houston's father dies and he returns home, he will not take his common-law wife with him. Houston's Protestant code of respectability is the force that pulls him back to Frenchman's Bend where he finally marries Lucy Pate, whom he does not dislike but for whom he evidently feels no passion. Shortly after their marriage Lucy is killed by Houston's stallion.

Both Houston and Mink are men of principle, and their principles are expressed in specific codes of behavior. Houston impounded a milk cow of Mink's that had been grazing on his property. He took advantage of the law to exploit Mink, and Mink killed him for it. After the murder, Mink accepts responsibility for the fact that he has set in motion a chain of events that he must see through to the end. "It was no blind, instinctive, and furious desire for flight which he had to combat and curb. . . . What he would have liked to do would be to leave a printed placard on the breast itself: *This is what happens to the men who impound Mink Snopes's cattle*, with his name signed to it. But he could not, and here again, for the third time since he had pulled the trigger, was that conspiracy to frustrate and outrage his rights as a man and his feelings as a sentient creature" (p. 222). Mink's cousin Lump is wrong in his assumption that Mink killed Houston for money. Mink may be an insignificant sharecropper whose material possessions will never amount to much; but he has a strong sense of pride in his own manhood and individuality, and will brook no violation of either. His pride is shown by his relationship with his wife. She is the daughter of a man in the timber business who uses convict labor as loggers, and before meeting Mink she was in the habit of having the foreman bring to her bed any of the men she wanted. Mink, who does time at the logging camps, realizes that "when he did approach her at last he would have to tear aside not garments alone but the ghostly embraces of thirty or forty men" (p. 242). Yet he is able to do just that; there is a quality of passion in him that the woman has never experienced before. After they are married she tells him, "I've had a hundred men, but I never had a wasp before. That stuff comes out of you is rank poison. It's too hot. It burns itself and my seed both up" (p. 243). The contrast is an interesting one. Jack Houston, the man with most of the ingredients necessary for a full and reasonably happy life, cannot overcome his own in-grained sense of respectability; while Mink, who never con-fuses respectability with principles, is led by his code of be-havior to commit an act that will remove him completely from the life he has known.

In the last chapter of *The Hamlet*, "The Peasants," V. K. Ratliff shows that he too is vulnerable to the influence of Snopesism. He is not tempted at all by the sale of wild Texas ponies in which townsmen are taken advantage of by an out-sider who accompanies Flem back from his honeymoon. But Ratliff becomes convinced that there is buried money at the Old Frenchman's place, which Will Varner deeded to Flem in exchange for his marrying Eula, and the lure of unearned wealth is too much of a temptation for Ratliff to resist. In exchange for an interest in the property Ratliff, in partnership with two other men, gives Flem his half-share of a Jefferson restaurant, and this is what gives Flem his first toehold in Jefferson. After much fruitless digging, Ratliff realizes there is no buried treasure to be found.

The moral focus of *The Hamlet* is one of the primary elements—in addition to theme and character—serving to unify the work. Writing to critic Warren Beck in 1941—and confirming Beck's judgments about Faulkner's moral concerns—Faulkner stated: "I have been writing all the time about honor, truth, pity, consideration, the capacity to endure well grief and misfortune and injustice and then endure again."[5] Faulkner went on to say, "I believe there are some, not necessarily many, who do and will continue to read Faulk-ner and say, 'Yes. It's all right. I'd rather be Ratliff than Flem Snopes. And I'd still rather be Ratliff without any Snopes to measure by even.' "[6] Such a statement might be taken as evi-dence that V. K. Ratliff is somehow the moral center of *The*

Hamlet and of the trilogy as a whole, a position that is not necessary or even warranted. As can easily be seen, Ratliff has weaknesses of his own; and because he comes from the same social class and is in a position to understand them, he is not always unsympathetic to Snopeses. The trilogy is concerned with moral values, especially when they come into conflict with economic and social values. But it is far too complex a work to have a locus of positive or negative values seated in one character, either V. K. Ratliff or Flem Snopes.

The narrative structure of *The Town* is quite different from that of *The Hamlet*. Rather than being divided into separate sections, and told generally from a third-person point of view, the events in the novel are reported from the first-person perspectives of Charles Mallison, Gavin Stevens, and V. K. Ratliff. The focus on economic and social values in conflict with moral and ethical ones remains the same as in *The Hamlet*, though the scene of action has shifted from the country to the town. Charles Mallison explains in the first chaper, "when I say 'we' and 'we thought' what I mean is Jefferson and what Jefferson thought."[7] Perhaps more than in *The Hamlet*, community attitudes are of extreme importance and thus the force, influence, and desire for respectability are all the stronger.

In the first chapter Charles ("Chick") Mallison reports on events which he did not witness himself, but which were reported to him by his cousin, Gowan. Chick explains how Flem, Eula, and the infant Linda first arrived in Jefferson, and gives a detailed account of Flem's attempt to steal brass from the city, an episode described not as a monument to his cupidity but as a footprint in his ongoing path: "A monument only says *At least I got this far* while a footprint says *This is where I was when I moved again*" (p. 29). The brass-theft episode is Snopesism in its purest form, requiring the careful manipulation of people and the setting of individual interest against individual interest.

The process by which Snopeses have spread throughout the

county is also described. After Flem has left the restaurant he
got from Ratliff and has become superintendent of the power
plant, he is "replaced . . . by another Snopes accreted in from
Frenchman's Bend into the vacuum behind the first one's next
advancement by that same sort of osmosis by which, according
to Ratliff, they had covered Frenchman's Bend, the chain
unbroken, every Snopes in Frenchman's Bend moving up one
step, leaving that last slot at the bottom open for the next
Snopes to appear from nowhere and fill" (pp. 8-9). Eula has the
same aura that clothed her in Frenchman's Bend. As Chick
Mallison reports:

> She wasn't too big, heroic, what they call Junoesque. It
> was that there was just too much of what she was for any
> one human female package to contain, and hold: too
> much of white, too much of female, too much of maybe
> just glory . . . so that at first sight of her you felt a kind of
> shock of gratitude just for being alive and being male at
> the same instant with her in space and time, and then in
> the next second and forever after a kind of despair because
> you knew that there never would be enough of any one
> male to match and hold and deserve her . . . (p. 6).

As in Frenchman's Bend, there is no man in Jefferson whose
masculinity is commensurate with Eula's womanhood. The
man who comes closest is Manfred de Spain, bank president
and mayor of Jefferson, a man of courage and considerable
vitality; but even he cannot dominate Eula or be an adequate
mate for her.

Gavin Stevens makes his first appearance as a major character in *The Town*. In dramatic terms the first section of the novel
concludes with the conflict involving Eula's place in
Jefferson—as a lady deserving of respect or as Manfred's
whore—that takes place between Gavin and de Spain. Gavin is
an idealist, a well-meaning and sometimes courageous man
who believes in justice and duty and honor, but who, for all his

good intentions, is not effective. He is not always a good judge of character and his complicated reasoning about the forces influencing or determining human events is frequently in error. All Snopeses are alike to him, and for that reason he does not understand them as well as Ratliff does. He maintains, "they none of them seemed to bear any specific kinship to one another; they were just Snopeses, like colonies of rats or termites are just rats and termites" (p. 40). To Gavin, Snopeses are the constant "other" and he never comprehends Snopesism as a general principle operating within society.

Because of his idealism, Gavin can be seen as a human crucible for the testing of some of the moral and ethical themes in *The Town* and *The Mansion*. In his excellent book-length study of the trilogy, Warren Beck describes Gavin as a protagonist "of a humanistic ethic."[8] Gavin's tendency to sometimes attribute to people higher motives than they possess is characterized as "the humane man's most dangerous vulnerability; yet its alternative, a complete defensive cynicism, must be worse, according to Faulkner's treatment of the question."[9] Beck makes a more positive evaluation of Gavin's character than does Cleanth Brooks or Michael Millgate; and of those critics who see Gavin as a positive force in the trilogy, Beck's argument for him is the strongest. But neither Beck, Millgate, nor Brooks identify—as some critics have—Gavin as a reflector of Faulkner's own ethical, moral, and social views. Issuing his own caveat against such an interpretation in his discussion of *The Town*, Brooks warns that the reader will be "very likely to miss the tone and even the basic meaning of the novel. For if any one thing about this novel soon becomes clear, it is that Gavin, and not for the first time in Faulkner's fiction, is treated as a figure of fun—almost as the butt of the author's jokes."[10]

Though no specific evidence is cited, it is generally known that Eula and Manfred de Spain are having an affair. By pretending not to notice, Flem advances himself to positions of increasing power and influence. Ratliff apparently understands what Flem is doing and explains it to Gavin: "Not catching his wife with Manfred de Spain yet is like that twenty-dollar gold piece pinned to your undershirt on your first maiden trip to what you hope is going to be a Memphis whorehouse. He dont need to unpin it yet" (p. 29). Gavin is concerned about the affair for another reason: he is obsessed with Eula and he wants her to have respectability, though he never bothers to find out whether that is important to Eula or not. As he often does, Gavin is defending an abstract principle, in this case "the principle that chastity and virtue in women shall be defended whether they exist or not" (p. 76). He does not understand, as his sister Maggie does, that the womenfolk of Jefferson are not really interested in whether or not de Spain and Eula are having an affair. She tells Gavin, "Women are not interested in morals. They aren't even interested in unmorals. The ladies of Jefferson dont care what she does. What they will never forgive is the way she looks. No: the way the Jefferson gentlemen look at her" (p. 48).

The Christmas cotillion, to which Gavin manages to get Eula invited, prompts the finely drawn comedy of Mrs. Rouncewell's flower panic when, in order to give Eula a corsage and not violate the rules of propriety, both Gavin and de Spain give every lady in the cotillion a corsage, forcing their husbands to give them flowers as well. The cotillion ends in a fight between Gavin and de Spain, which Gavin loses. Eula makes a forthright assumption about Gavin's motives, comes to his office one night shortly after the dance, and offers herself to him. But Gavin cannot deal with this direct and intense reality, and he sends her away. He does continue to fight with de Spain by bringing suit over the matter of the brass missing from the power plant. He hopes to put de Spain in a position where he will be forced to resign as mayor, but he fails in this also. The episode ends with Gavin, about as soundly defeated as a man can be, pathetically asking his father, who is a judge, "What must I do now, Papa? Papa, what can I do now?" (p.

99). He leaves Jefferson and goes to Germany to study at Heidelberg, telling Ratliff that he will have to look after the Snopeses until he gets back.

After the outbreak of World War I, Gavin joins the YMCA and serves in France. (Before American involvement in the war, he had been a stretcher bearer with the French at Verdun until he caught pneumonia and was forced to come home.) During this time a relationship is formed between Ratliff and Chick's cousin Gowan, Flem becomes vice president of the Sartoris bank, Wallstreet Panic Snopes—who does not act like a Snopes at all—sets up in Jefferson in the grocery business, and Linda Snopes, Eula's daughter, makes her first appearance. Following his return from Europe, Gavin transfers to Linda the compulsive, frustrated idealism he had wasted on her mother. Though attractive, Linda has nothing of her mother's aura; and Gavin reasons that "very Nature herself would not permit that to occur, permit two of them in a place no larger than Jefferson" (p. 133). Nevertheless, as he had once resolved to save Eula from de Spain, he now resolves to save Linda from her father.

While Gavin is thinking about Linda Snopes, V. K. Ratliff is acting effectively to help one Snopes against another. When Wall Snopes's grocery business begins to show signs of prospering, Flem begins looking for ways to buy into it. It appears that he might have his chance when Wall overbuys his stock for the store. By using his influence to prevent the two local banks from loaning Wall any money, Flem plans to put Wall into a position where he will have to accept a personal loan and thus give Flem the leverage to buy into the business. However, Ratliff provides Wall with the money he needs and thereby forestalls Flem's plans. As Ratliff tells Gavin, "All I wanted was jest a note for [the loan]. But he insisted on making me a partner" (p. 149). After Wall has expanded his business to include wholesale activities, Ratliff is in a position to turn a profit on his altruism.

During the times that Gavin and Ratliff talk about the Snopeses, it becomes increasingly apparent that Gavin does not understand their character or what motivates them. This is especially true of his judgments regarding Flem. When it is learned that Flem has withdrawn his money from the Sartoris bank, of which he is vice president, and deposited it in the Jefferson bank, Gavin guesses that Flem had "arranged himself for his profit to be one hundred percent, that he himself was seeing to it in advance that he would not have to steal even one forgotten penny of his own money" (p. 141). But Ratliff, who admits he does not know why Flem transferred his money, insists Gavin's interpretation is incorrect: "you got Flem all wrong, all of you have. I tell you, he aint just got respect for money: he's got active . . . reverence for it. . . . the last thing he would ever do is to insult and degrade money by mishandling it" (p. 142). When almost a year later Ratliff suggests that Flem's ultimate goal is to become president of the Sartoris bank, Gavin rejects the possibility outright, refusing to believe that Flem's motives can extend beyond rapacity, greed, or money.

Gavin never perceives Flem's need for something as abstract as respectability, a necessary attribute if he is to become a president of the bank and secure his stature in the community. When Flem makes certain that Montgomery Ward Snopes is sent to prison—not on the pornography charge of which he is guilty, but for dealing in bootleg whiskey, which Flem plants in his studio—he is not, as Gavin suspects, just getting rid of another Snopes competitor. Flem is quite serious when he tells Gavin, after the planted liquor has been found, "I'm interested in Jefferson. . . . We got to live here" (p. 176). To live in Jefferson Flem must have respectability. It is what Ratliff describes as "this-here new thing he has done found out it's nice to have. . . . It's got to be out in the open, where folks can see it, or there aint no such thing" (p. 175). In Jefferson, Mississippi, in the early twentieth century, bootlegging is illegal, but being sent to prison for it is not disrespectable; being sent to prison for trading in pornography is. In *The Hamlet* the same motive, the desire for respectability, causes Flem to refuse to help Mink Snopes during his trial for murdering Jack Houston. In Flem's scheme of things, he cannot afford to have a relative known to be guilty of murder wandering free in the county.

In both obvious and subtle ways the force of respectability exerts itself throughout the novel. But the chief dramatic event that takes place after Gavin's experience with Eula and his return from the war is his attempt to liberate the mind of Linda Snopes and therefore make her free of her father, a goal which no one but Gavin seems to think is important. As he explains to his sister, "To save a Snopes from Snopeses is a privilege, an honor, a pride" (p. 182). Gavin begins his project to save Linda when she is sixteen by having talks with her over ice cream at the drugstore and by giving her books to read. Later, when she is preparing to graduate from high school, he sends her college catalogues and offers to discuss plans for her college education. Gavin is surprised when Linda tells him that she has changed her mind and will not be attending college.

The problem is Flem, who needs Linda in order to control Eula. Flem cannot afford to have the affair between his wife and de Spain become visible, which might happen if Eula and de Spain were simply to go away together. The only weapon that Flem has to use against Eula—to bind her to him—is Linda, who is unaware that Flem is not her real father. Eula would also be hesitant, for Linda's sake, to create a public scandal. The threat to Flem is that if Linda were to go away to college she would be beyond the range of his supervision; then, if Linda were to meet someone and get married, he would lose all his leverage with Eula, who, in turn, is all the leverage that Flem has with Will Varner. Thus, the position that Gavin's well-intentioned meddling puts him in is quite precarious.

The person with the best grasp of the overall situation, and with a solution for it, is Eula. She knows that Linda ultimately will simply not defy the man whom she thinks is her father, and that it would be a very bad mistake to tell her the truth. She tries to explain to Gavin: "Women aren't interested in poets' dreams. They are interested in facts. It doesn't even matter whether the facts are true or not, as long as they match the other facts without leaving a rough seam" (p. 226). And it is a "seamless" fact in Linda's life that Flem is her father. Twice Eula tells Gavin that the solution to the problem is for him to marry Linda. But Gavin, never a man to solve a problem by direct action, resists such a solution.

After his initial opposition, Flem changes his position and tells Linda she may go away to school. To express her gratitude, Linda has a document drawn up giving any inheritance she stands to receive from her uncle Will Varner to her father. Flem then plans to use this document, as well as Eula's adultery, as the means to force de Spain out of the bank, thus clearing the way for him to become president. Still, the only way Linda can be freed absolutely from Flem's influence is for Gavin to marry her, but the best Eula can get from Gavin is a conditional promise. After she and de Spain have left Jefferson, Gavin says: "if or when I become convinced that conditions are going to become such that something will have to be done, and nothing else but marrying me can help her, and she will have me, but have me, take me. Not just give up, surrender" (pp. 332-333). Shortly after this scene, Eula kills herself—not out of defeat but as the ultimate sacrifice she can make for Linda, making it impossible for Flem any longer to manipulate mother and daughter for his own purpose, and hoping perhaps that her act might create a "condition" that will cause Gavin to marry Linda. It does not; and Gavin never has any real notion what the reasons for Eula's suicide were. The monument that is finally placed over her grave is the apotheosis of Flem's desire for respectability: "A Virtuous Wife Is a Crown to Her Husband/Her Children Rise and Call Her Blessed" (p. 355).

After the monument is uncovered, Linda goes to New York, to Greenwich Village; Flem is ready to ascend the final rung of his ambition's ladder; and the stage is set for the concluding volume of the trilogy.

Fittingly, the initial focus of *The Mansion* is on Mink Snopes; for it is he who at the end of the novel will act as the instrument of fate, bringing Flem's career and life to a close. Thus, the first five chapters of *The Mansion* are centered on Mink. The first chapter, beginning with the moment of Mink's sentencing for the murder of Jack Houston, gives us some insight into his notions of justice and society. All during his trial, Mink keeps looking for his kinsman Flem, even though he knows he is in Texas with his new wife and that the couple will have to stay there "long enough for what they would bring back with them to be able to call itself only one month old."[11] It is probably not likely that Flem, even if he had been in Frenchman's Bend at the time and had been disposed actively to help Mink, could have kept him from going to prison or have had any influence on the actual sentence. After all, the evidence against Mink is conclusive and the crime he is guilty of is murder. But it is also possible that Mink does not expect Flem to get him off. He does expect him to try, however, recognizing a duty to family and blood. Flem's absolute passivity then becomes a sin against the code of family loyalty, and leads to Mink's decision to kill him when he gets out of prison.

Mink identifies with no specific class. Because he views himself as living outside the boundaries of any particular society, his sense of pride, honor, and independence is ultrasensitive. His concept of justice is one that has him pitted by himself against amorphous and powerful forces referred to as "they," "them," "it":

By *them* he didn't mean that whatever-it-was that folks referred to as Old Moster. . . .
He meant, simply, that *them–they–it*, whichever and

whatever you wanted to call it, who represented a simple
fundamental justice and equity in human affairs, or else a
man might just as well quit; the *they*, *them*, *it*, call them
what you like, which simply would not, could not harass
and harry a man forever without some day, at some
moment, letting him get his own just and equal licks back
in return. . . . maybe in fact They were even testing him,
to see if he was a man or not, man enough to take a little
harassment and worry and so deserve his own licks back
when his turn came (pp. 5, 6).

Jack Houston finds himself on the receiving end of Mink's
sense of justice. Characterized as "arrogant and intolerant" (p.
7), Houston is the kind of man to whom Mink would naturally
take a strong disliking. The seed of disaster is sown when Mink
intentionally lets his cow winter with Houston's herd; for
Houston demands that the increased value of the fattened cow
be paid before she is released. Will Varner, in his capacity as
justice of the peace, rules that Mink must work off the value of
the cow by setting fence posts for Houston. Mink views this
ruling as yet another machination of "them" against him; but
he resolves to meet his obligation to the letter and he rejects all
attempts to ease the hardships of working for Houston at the
rate of fifty cents a day, at the same time trying to tend to his
own crop. Houston then makes the mistake of adding unnecessary injury to what Mink considers the original insult by
demanding, after Mink believes he has worked off his obligation, the dollar per pound fee allowed by the law for any stray
animal that goes unclaimed by its owner before dark on the day
it strays. To Mink, this is an unforgivable violation of
principle—compounded by the fact that Houston has no need
to claim the fee—and thus it is sufficient reason for Mink to kill
Houston.

It is only after his trial is over that Mink realizes that Flem is
not going to help him. He thinks to himself: *"He aint coming.
Likely he's been in Frenchman's Bend all the time. Likely he*

heard about that cow clean out there in Texas and jest waited till the word come back they had me safe in jail, and then come back to make sho they would do ever thing to me they could now that they had me helpless" (p. 42). Though sentenced to life imprisonment, Mink will be eligible for parole in twenty years and he is a man patient enough to wait a long time to bring justice to Flem. Realizing that Mink is planning to kill him after his release, Flem must figure a way to keep him in prison the longest possible time. Adept at using whatever material he has available, Flem convinces Montgomery Ward, whom he has had arrested for bootlegging, to arrange a bungled escape attempt for Mink. When he is caught, disguised as a woman, Mink's sentence is increased.

The core of the novel—the story of Gavin Stevens and Linda Snopes—is sandwiched between the two sections dealing with Mink, who is the most dramatically engaging character in the novel. Millgate contends that though the novel itself is a competent performance, the Gavin and Linda section "becomes tedious and even, in the New York and Pascagoula episodes, imaginatively unpersuasive."[12] The voices that carried the narrative weight of *The Town* are heard again in this section: Chick Mallison, Gavin Stevens, and V. K. Ratliff. The combined picture that is presented of Gavin and Linda is not a cheerful or a reassuring one. Linda is nowhere near the equal of her mother. She returns from her experience in the Spanish Civil War deafened and in a state of emotional debilitation; she is unable to find a meaningful focus for her life in Jefferson. Gavin is even to a greater degree the idealistic but ineffectual man he was in *The Town*, and by the end of the novel he has become, through sheer passivity, an accomplice to murder.

Moreso than in *The Town*, Gavin's failures are cast in sexual terms. In *The Mansion*, Millgate sees Gavin as reaping the results of his not marrying Linda earlier. He reasons that such a marriage, though not a panacea, might still be "an eminently practical way of resolving a number of difficulties."[13] And in

Gavin's aversion to dealing directly with sexual matters, Millgate detects a certain parallel with Flem: "Where Flem is impotent through physical disability Stevens seems no less effectively to emasculate himself through his inhibitions and intellectualisations."[14] Less harsh in his criticism than Millgate, Brooks sees Gavin as "the optimist, the romanticist, the believer in the more tidy decencies of life" who "is to be shaken by forces which he always manages to underestimate and to misunderstand."[15]

The Mansion deals with social issues much more overtly than *The Town* did. Linda is a Communist and when she learns that there are two other Communists in town (Finnish immigrants), she invites them to her house. The description of their meetings is heavily ironic: "the two Finnish immigrant laborers and the banker's daughter, one that couldn't speak English and another that couldn't hear any language, trying to communicate through the third one who hadn't yet learned to spell" (p. 222). Linda also interests herself in the affairs of Negroes, but her efforts only stir the ire and suspicion of Jefferson's whites. The principal of the black school tries to explain the situation to Gavin, telling him, "we have got to make a place of our own in your culture and economy too. Not you to make a place for us just to get us out from under your feet" (p. 224). In all of her activities the impression is given that Linda is more interested in serving herself than any other person or thing. Her capacity for taking is much greater than her capacity for giving, and that is one of the most crucial differences between her and her mother.

The counterpoint to Linda and Gavin is Mink, who despite his faults is identified with important, elemental things, and who has the courage and endurance to rise above adversity (he is in prison for thirty-eight years and is sixty-three years old at the time of his release). Cleanth Brooks is correct in judging Mink's character to be of heroic proportions, even though he has "all the prejudices of people of his breeding and education.

He is suspicious of Negroes and townsfolk. He is in no way presented as an exemplar of the downtrodden proletarian, the hardworking and oppressed laboring man, or a put-upon peasant. Faulkner has not made it easy for us to see Mink in a heroic light and yet . . . he manages to do just this."[16] Mink's stature derives from the quality of spirit he maintains despite the fact that his life as a tenant farmer is expended on a bleak treadmill of poverty and harsh labor. The land he farms is "an inimical irreconcilable square of dirt to which he was bound and chained for the rest of his life" (p. 90). In a strong and moving interior monologue it is made clear that Mink will not be defeated by the land:

> *You got me, you'll wear me out because you are stronger than me since I'm jest bone and flesh. I cant leave you because I cant afford to, and you know it. Me and what used to be the passion . . . of my youth . . . will be here next year . . . and you know that too. . . . And not just me, but all my tenant and cropper kind that have immolated youth and hope on thirty or forty or fifty acres of dirt that wouldn't nobody but our kind work because you're all our kind have. But we can burn you. Every late February or March we can set fire to the surface of you until all of you in sight is scorched and black, and there ain't one god-damn thing you can do about it* (pp. 90-91).

There is a fierceness of pride in this statement that certainly elevates Mink's character. Faulkner makes no apologies for his weaknesses or his viciousness; but he insists that there is a core of integrity in Mink, an adherence to a small set of rigorous standards that sets him apart from others. Even Flem acknowledges the principle of Mink's code when he makes no effort to prevent Mink from killing him.

Taken as a whole, the Snopes trilogy is a vast and imposing body of work. Conceived early in his career and completed only three years before his death in 1962, it is marked by a consistent statement of ethical concerns, whether the episodes dramatizing those concerns are accomplished through pathos or comedy. Critics generally agree that the three volumes comprised by the trilogy are not all sustained on the same high level. Judged purely on its own terms, *The Hamlet* is considered to be one of Faulkner's major works. And of the remaining two volumes, *The Town* is superior to *The Mansion*. At the same time there are no inferior performances in any of these works, and the trilogy itself stands coherent and unified. Millgate says Faulkner's Snopes trilogy is "the work with which he had lived the longest and in which he had concerned himself, more consistently than elsewhere . . . with the ordinary, the humble, and even the abject representatives of mankind."[17]

Faulkner had hoped *The Hamlet* would sell well enough to relieve some immediate financial pressures, but, though the novel was well received, its sales record did not meet Faulkner's expectations.[18] Reviews in the *New York Herald Tribune*, the *New York Times*, and the *New Republic* were particularly strong. *The Town* was not reviewed favorably. Concerning the negative reviews it received, Blotner writes, "After [Faulkner's] fears during the novel's composition—that it had no fire or force, that what remained was only empty craftsmanship—it was good that he did not read the reviews."[19] Reviews of *The Mansion* were much more favorable than those of *The Town*, but still they were not as strong as those given originally to *The Hamlet*. Scholarship has tended to address the novels individually; and, as already indicated, rates *The Hamlet* as the best of the three. Warren Beck's *Man in Motion*—which places Gavin Stevens in a more positive light than some other scholars have—is an excellent book-length study of the trilogy.

---

[1]*Faulkner in the University*, pp. 14, 15.
[2]*Letters*, p. 197. For additional information on the composition of *The*

Hamlet and a useful discussion of "Barn Burning," the novel's deleted first chapter, see Millgate, pp. 180-186.

[3]*The Mansion* (New York: Random House, 1959), p. ix.

[4]*The Hamlet* (New York: Random House, 1940). Quote is from the 1973 Vintage edition, p. 4. Subsequent references to this edition are placed within text.

[5]Warren Beck, "A Preface and a Letter," *Yale Review*, 52 (October 1962): 159.

[6]Beck, "A Preface and a Letter," p. 159.

[7]*The Town* (New York: Random House, 1957). Quote is from the 1961 Vintage edition, p. 3. Subsequent references to this edition are placed within text.

[8]Beck, *Man in Motion: Faulkner's Trilogy* (Madison: University of Wisconsin Press, 1961), p. 11.

[9]Beck, *Men in Motion*, p. 52.

[10]Brooks, *The Yoknapatawpha Country*, p. 194.

[11]*The Mansion* (New York: Random House, 1959). Quote is from the 1965 Vintage edition, p. 4. Subsequent references to this edition are placed within text.

[12]Millgate, p. 245.

[13]Millgate, p. 246.

[14]Millgate, p. 247.

[15]Brooks, *The Yoknapatawpha Country*, p. 220.

[16]Brooks, *The Yoknapatawpha Country*, p. 221.

[17]Millgate, p. 252.

[18]See Blotner, pp. 1039, 1041.

[19]Blotner, p. 1663.

Go Down, Moses

In her discussion of *Go Down, Moses*, Olga Vickery remarks that the work, comprising revised versions of seven stories previously published between 1935 and 1941, has "unifying features which give the book the character of a loosely constructed novel."[1] Published originally on 11 May 1942 as *Go Down, Moses and Other Stories*, the title was altered in the second printing at Faulkner's request, dropping *and Other Stories*.[2] Using published as well as unpublished short-story material for larger fictional purposes was a practice Faulkner resorted to frequently throughout his career and there is no doubt that Faulkner conceived of *Go Down, Moses* as a novel. Writing to Robert Haas in April 1940, Faulkner said that he was planning a book "in method similar to THE UNVANQUISHED, but since the chapters which I have written and tried to sell as stories have not sold, I haven't the time to continue with it."[3] The notion of converting chapters into stories for economic reasons is a good indicator that what Faulkner had in mind in 1940 was a single, unified work. Later, in 1957, responding to a question about the place of "The Bear" in the novel, Faulkner said, "That novel was—happened to be composed of more or less complete stories, but it was held together by one family, the Negro and the white phase of the same family, same people."[4]

The unity of *Go Down, Moses* lies not so much in the development of plot as it does in the exploration of certain interrelated themes which are demonstrated through characterization and Faulkner's examination of family relationships, as well as by events which frequently assume symbolic significance. The chief character in the novel is Isaac McCaslin, though there are some chapters in which he does not appear or does not figure (for example "The Old People" and "Pantaloon in Black"). In one way or another, however, all of the thematic material in the novel relates to his development; inasmuch as *Go Down, Moses* is the story of Isaac McCaslin, we see him as a person locked in a struggle to come to terms with the past—both as it was and as he imagines it to have been—so he may cope with the present. The degree to which Isaac is successful in reconciling the past to the present has been the subject of considerable critical debate.

The McCaslin family thread that runs through the novel is not the only unifying factor. There are complex interrelationships made up of thematic materials—for the most part, the same materials appearing in different guises—that help to bind the chapters, though in some instances such realizations must be discovered in retrospect. In the first chapter of the book, "Was," for example, there is no way of being sure that the Negro Tomey's Turl is the son of Carothers McCaslin and his slave Tomasina and therefore a half brother to Buck and Buddy McCaslin. We learn in subsequent chapters that Tomey's Turl's marriage to Tennie Beauchamp produces the line of black Beauchamps paralleling the white line of descent from old Carothers, which will be extended by the confirmed bachelor Buck McCaslin, who later fathered Isaac. Thus the large question of black-white relations is one of the dominant themes of the novel. Other important themes concern man's relationship to nature, the nature of freedom, the importance (and danger) of ritual in human affairs, relations between men and women, the concept of property, and the importance of coming to terms with the racial and social realities with which one lives.

The question of land and ownership of land—a theme that frequently merges with the question of man's relationship to nature—is established at the outset. Of Isaac it is said that he "owned no property and never desired to since the earth was no man's but all men's"[5]; and of his kinsman McCaslin Edmonds it is remarked that though he was the descendant of Carothers McCaslin's daughter, and therefore not in a direct line of inheritance from his grandfather, he was "not-withstanding the inheritor, and in his time the bequestor, of that which some had thought then and some still thought should have been Isaac's" (p. 3). Thus a basic thematic tension is introduced which cannot be resolved until the events leading to Isaac's repudiation of his inheritance are revealed and the reasons for that repudiation examined. In a way, Isaac's action is the nucleus around which all other thematic materials in the novel cluster.

The theme of the hunt, the pursuit of quarry, is also introduced in the first chapter, albeit in comic fashion, in the pursuit of a tame fox by the McCaslins' dogs, and in the pursuit of Tomey's Turl by Buck McCaslin and the boy Cass Edmonds. There is a sense, as with other hunts in the novel, of something unnatural in these chases. Dogs are not supposed to track and chase the same tame fox over and over, as the McCaslins' dogs do. In nature, a hunt should have a purpose and a conclusion; to perpetuate the chase simply for the sake of the chase goes against nature and is sometimes simply a way of avoiding reality, of denying movement, change, and death. In contrast, the periodic escape and pursuit of Tomey's Turl is in perfect accord with nature. When Tomey's Turl runs away, he has a definite purpose in mind—getting to see his sweetheart Tennie, whom he wants to marry—and he will be happy to have the ritual chase come to a conclusion when he is finally successful in getting Tennie for his wife. His motives are wholesome and healthy, especially when compared to those of his white half brothers, who seem resolved to a sterile bachelorhood. There is also an ironic reversal here in that the quarry, Tomey's Turl, is in control of the situation and not the hunters; and though the chase of Tomey's Turl is comic, there are also more serious matters implied. As Cleanth Brooks writes, "The judgment passed upon slavery generally in *Go Down, Moses* is a withering one"; and in dramatizing from a humorous perspective what is often treated as a stereotype in writing about the Old

South, Faulkner is "giving human depth to what is too often treated as melodramatic abstraction . . . if, by 'humanizing' slavery, he seems to make it more tolerable, the same process makes it more terrible and anguishing."[6] The attempt of Sophonsiba Beauchamp to capture Buck McCaslin for a husband may be considered a third kind of hunt or chase. Certainly the bedroom trap she lays for him is as carefully conceived and placed as that of any woodsman; and the incident, which sets up a dramatic poker game as a means of settling questions of property and family honor, serves to introduce another aspect of the theme of man-woman relationships at that period.

"The Fire and the Hearth" focuses on the black descendants of Carothers McCaslin, especially Lucas Beauchamp, one of three children born to Tomey's Turl and Tennie and the only one who remains on the plantation. All of the themes introduced in the first chapter are developed further, but there is particular emphasis placed upon the theme of family and of black-white relations, and of the destructive effects of lust for wealth. The present inheritor of the McCaslin property is Carothers Edmonds, great-grandson of Carothers McCaslin and grandson of McCaslin Edmonds, who inherited the property when Isaac renounced it. The title of the chapter refers to the fire that is laid in Lucas and Molly's cabin at the time of their marriage, and is intended "to burn on the hearth until neither he nor Molly were left to feed it" (p. 47). The symbol is associated generally with black families in the novel—it appears in the "Pantaloon in Black" and in the "Go Down, Moses" chapters—and symbolizes the sacredness and endurance of marital and family bonds. Here and in "Pantaloon in Black" is seen, as Michael Millgate notes, "that intensity and longevity of family loyalty and love in which the Negroes of the novel show themselves to be so much the superior of their white relatives and neighbours."[7] The contrast is particularly strong in "Pantaloon in Black" where the white deputy is completely incapable of understanding the quality and intensity of Rider's grief for his dead wife.

The fact that Rider does not appear to be related to any of the primary family groupings in the novel has been the source of confusion among critics. Malcolm Cowley, for example, noting that the story "fell outside the novelistic pattern," got an equivocal response from Faulkner: "Rider was one of the McCaslin Negroes."[8] Of course, whether Rider is or is not related to the McCaslins is not the point. Again, Millgate demonstrates that the story "is satisfactorily integrated into the novel, despite its lack of narrative links with other chapters; indeed, Faulkner's refusal to make the few minor changes in names and relationships which would have made Rider a McCaslin has the effect not of isolating the episode in which Rider is the major character but actually of expanding, beyond the limits of the single McCaslin family, the whole scope and relevance of the book."[9] Unable to bear the loss of his wife Mannie—to whom he has been married only six months— Rider's grief leads him on a course of self-destruction which culminates in his killing a white man, an act that brings a lynch mob down on him. It is the motive for this action, and the actions that lead to it, that the white deputy does not understand—he concludes merely that blacks "ain't human" and are devoid of "normal human feelings and sentiments" (p. 154)—and his attitude fits into the general pattern of white misunderstanding of black emotion and family ties.

But Faulkner does not intend to draw any easy stereotypical comparisons between blacks and whites in the novel; and at times Lucas is shown to have a number of unattractive, mendacious qualities. Lucas's sense of pride and self-worth is at once a positive character trait and a rather unpleasant aspect of his personality, leading him into vanity, stubbornness, and greed. He is very proud that he descends from the male bloodline of Carothers McCaslin, and for that reason he holds himself superior to the Edmonds line. As a young man he plays a deadly game with Zack Edmonds when he believes he may have been cuckolded by his white kinsman. The scene in Zack's bedroom is extremely tense. A number of gambits are made; finally, the two men face each other, kneeling on opposite sides of the bed, the white man's pistol between them, on terms of absolute equality. Earlier, Lucas had discarded his razor, which is identified as a weapon black men use on each other. In Lucas's view, the confrontation is between a McCaslin and an Edmonds, not just between a black man and a white man. Zack proves to be a man of courage, a worthy opponent. At one point he flings Lucas's challenge back at him: "Do you think I'm any less a McCaslin just because I was what you call woman-made to it? Or maybe you aint even a woman-made McCaslin but just a nigger that's got out of hand?" (p. 55). The scene is resolved when Lucas gets the pistol, pulls the trigger, and the weapon misfires. Later he realizes that, had the weapon fired, he would not have taken the relatively easy way out by committing suicide or by trying to run away: *"I would have paid. I would have waited for the rope, even the coal oil. . . . So I reckon I aint got old Carothers' blood for nothing, after all"* (p. 58). The themes that are involved here are simultaneously of family and race, and the racial question ends the section: "How to God," Lucas asks, "can a black man ask a white man to please not lay down with his black wife? And even if he could ask it, how to God can the white man promise he wont?" (p. 59).

Lucas's beliefs about his racial inheritance lead in several instances to narrow thinking and incorrect assumptions. When Lucas thinks of his contact with the past, he thinks of the time of old Carothers "when men black and white were men" (p. 37); and he compares his own longevity to that of Isaac McCaslin "who lived in town, supported by what Roth Edmonds [Zack's son] chose to give him, who would own the land and all on it if his just rights were only known" (p. 36). This is an incorrect assumption. Lucas does not know that

Isaac actually renounced his inheritance over the objections of
Cass Edmonds, Zack's father, and he would probably not be
able to comprehend it if he did. For Lucas has within him a
strong acquisitive streak, a lust for ownership which, combined with prideful stubbornness, brings out his worst
qualities—qualities which he in turn attributes to Cass Edmonds. His search for nonexistent gold with a metal detector is
a meaningless game, as empty as the illusory rituals that are
pursued by several of the novel's white characters. The almost
monomaniacal nature of this pursuit is emphasized by the fact
that Lucas has no use for the money; he simply wants to own it.
Yet for this chimera he is willing to risk his marriage to Molly,
and he capitulates only when he realizes that Molly—
appearing with Roth Edmonds before the chancery judge in
the Jefferson courthouse—is within moments of divorcing
him.

The central white character in *Go Down, Moses* is Isaac
McCaslin, grandson of old Carothers and, since childless, the
end of the male McCaslin line. Observing that "The Old
People," "The Bear," and "Delta Autumn" are designed
primarily to tell the life story of Isaac McCaslin, Warren Beck
rates these chapters of the novel as "one of the most impressive
novellas in modern fiction," an achievement all the more remarkable because their virtuosity does not "eclipse the book's
other four sections or minimize their essential intrication
within the novel as an orchestrated whole."[10] Beck offers a
thoughtful, well-reasoned, and highly detailed analysis of
Isaac McCaslin, who he maintains "is sometimes condescend-
ingly viewed, and even superciliously judged, without regard
for his situation, upbringing, and emergent nature as a
youth."[11] Beck's view of Isaac is a positive one:

> To the youth of sixteen situated and conditioned as Isaac
> was, his discovering evidence of his grandfather's mis-
> cegenation and incest, offenses entered into as a land-

holding slaveowner's *droit* and with the most arrogant assumption of the Negro's natural subservience, was so massive a shock that it could be countered with no less outright an answer from Sam Fathers' disciple than repudiation of the inheritance upon reaching his majority. . . . But such absolutists [as Isaac] make their morally less strenuous fellows uncomfortable, and incline them to evade the fact that some traitors to their class have proved themselves friends to mankind, and not all apostates become professing cynics, some have turned up as saints.[12]

Other appraisals of Isaac's character are less favorable. Questioned in 1955 as to whether Isaac did the right thing or not in rejecting his inheritance, Faulkner replied, "I think a man ought to do more than just repudiate. He should have been more affirmative instead of shunning people."[13] Brooks believes that Isaac, by "divesting himself of his legacy . . . has thereby reduced his power to act," and Millgate views Isaac's decision as arising out of a desire to escape, an inability to deal with the past.[14]

Whatever ultimate view may be taken of Isaac, it should be recognized that his is a complex character, not reducible to the simple classifications of saint or coward. To understand his character, it is necessary to look at the kind of education he receives from Sam Fathers. Sam's blood is combined from three races: white, Negro, and Indian. Fathers is the most independent character in the novel, but his racial inheritance from his Indian chief father and Negro slave mother puts him in a kind of cage that severely limits his freedom. As McCaslin Edmonds explains to Isaac, "His cage aint McCaslins" (p. 167), but is rather the trace of bondage that comes to him through his quadroon mother's portion of his black blood: "Not betrayed by the black blood and not wilfully betrayed by his mother, but betrayed by her all the same, who had bequeathed him not only the blood of slaves but even a little of the very blood which had enslaved it; himself his own battleground, the scene of his own vanquishment and the mausoleum of his defeat" (p. 168). It is possible that the limits of Sam's freedom might also prescribe his limits as a teacher.

To be sure, Isaac learns respect and reverence for nature from Sam, and a code of behavior based on humility, pride, acceptance, and courage; but he appears limited in his ability to transfer what he learns from one area of experience to another. This is seen in the position Isaac takes relative to two of the novel's major themes, black-white relationships and the destruction of the wilderness. As Millgate states it, "the wilderness disappears to make way for a system based on physical or economic slavery, and [Isaac's] education in the wilderness fosters a sense of values which prompts him to a repudiation of that system and of the concept of land-ownership upon which it is based."[15] What Isaac learns in the wilderness he is unable to apply in a positive sense that will help him cope with the realities of the past or the conditions of the present. At question is the lesson Sam is trying to teach and the kind of existence that Isaac wants to prevail.

Sam Fathers indoctrinates Isaac into the ritual of the hunt, and part of that indoctrination is to absolve Isaac "not from love and pity for all which lived and ran and then ceased to live in a second in the very midst of splendor and speed, but from weakness and regret" (p. 182). To understand and grow from what Sam teaches, Isaac must be able to accept change and finality. The object of the ritual, the ultimate hunt, is the pursuit and killing of Old Ben, a large bear with a trap-ruined foot. This hunt has great ceremonial significance for Sam and he is grooming young Isaac for it. But Isaac cannot kill Old Ben; that job falls to Boon Hogganbeck who also has Indian blood—though not that of chiefs, like Sam—and who kills Ben not with a gun (a white man's weapon with which Boon is totally inept) but in the more elemental fashion of his Indian forebears, with a knife. Of Sam Fathers it might be said that he has misjudged both his pupil and the conditions necessary for the killing of Old Ben. The ideal but impossible condition Isaac wants is revealed when, near the end of "The Bear," he visits the wilderness where Sam and the dog Lion and Old Ben are buried. He thinks of Lion and Sam, "not held fast in earth but free in earth and not in earth but of earth, myriad yet undiffused of every myriad part, leaf and twig and particle, air and sun and rain and dew and night, acorn oak and leaf and acorn again, dark and dawn and dark and dawn again in their immutable progression and, being myriad, one: and Old Ben too, Old Ben too; they would give him his paw back even, certainly they would give him his paw back: then the long challenge and the long chase, no heart to be driven and outraged, no flesh to be mauled and bled" (pp. 328-329). Isaac does not want the chase or the hunt to end; he desires instead a nirvana where there is no pain, no death, and no emotional risk. When he cannot find anything approximating this condition in the realities of his world, he chooses a course of withdrawal and repudiation.

In a long colloquy with McCaslin Edmonds, Isaac finds each of his reasons for rejecting his inheritance being rebutted effectively. As each island of moral justification—the Bible, slavery, the war—disappears beneath him, he jumps to another one. Finally, Isaac is left in the position of having followed a course of repudiation for repudiation's sake; by choosing a negative to cancel out a previous negative, Isaac deceives himself. He does not like the way things are, but he makes no sustained attempt to substitute another more acceptable condition. Thus he is unsuccessful in setting himself free at all; for as the novel demonstrates time and time again, there can be no freedom without responsibility, and responsibility marks the difference between freedom and license.

Discussing the organization of the novel, Millgate writes, "it would be unwise to assume that the apparently episodic structure of Go Down, Moses is the result or reflection of any lack, on Faulkner's part, either of interest or of effort: it is more fruitful to see that structure as a logical step in his persistent effort to hold in suspension a single moment of experience, action, or decision and to explore the full complexity of that moment."[16] In this fashion, in Faulkner's "disposition of large blocks of material,"[17] the novel comes full circle in the final two chapters. The black and white threads of the McCaslin family, having wound in various directions, are brought dramatically together in "Delta Autumn." There is considerable irony in the confrontation between Isaac and Roth Edmonds's mistress, whom he does not at first realize is black. But even Roth does not realize that his mistress is also a kinswoman, the granddaughter of Tennie's Jim. This resurfacing of miscegenation—the girl brings into the tent with her the child she and Roth have produced—is too much for Isaac. He tells her, "Get out of here! I can do nothing for you! Cant nobody do nothing for you!" (p. 361). Earlier, when Isaac first thought he had discovered the incest of old Carothers, he tried to convince himself that *"there must have been love. . . . Some sort of love. Even what he would have called love: not just an afternoon's or a night's spittoon"* (p. 270).[18] But now Isaac is totally incapable or unwilling to consider that there might be love between Roth and his mistress, or that marriage is a possible alternative. The gulf that stands between them is not entirely racial, and the girl seems to realize this when she asks Isaac, "Old man . . . have you lived so long and forgotten so much that you dont remember anything you ever knew or felt or even heard about love?" (p. 363).

The theme upon which the novel concludes—white misunderstanding of black emotions and motives—is treated briefly but effectively in the final chapter, "Go Down, Moses." Fittingly, the burden of misunderstanding is given to Gavin Stevens to carry. Asked by Molly Beauchamp to locate her grandson, Stevens discovers that he is about to be executed at an Illinois prison. In typical Stevens fashion, he thinks, *"And that's who I am to find, save"* (p. 372). He completely misunderstands Molly's wish to bring the boy's body home for burial, murderer or not, and he is equally incapable of dealing directly with family grief, though Miss Worsham, an old white woman, is not. The final picture is a somber one, consisting of the related character impressions given by Isaac McCaslin, a well-intentioned man incapable of acting, and by Gavin Stevens, a well-intentioned man willing to act, but incapable of acting effectively.

Though the sales of *Go Down, Moses* were inhibited by the perception among readers and reviewers that it was a collection of stories, which traditionally do not sell as well as novels, the notices were more favorable than Faulkner was used to. He was called "The most gifted of living U.S. writers" by *Time* and "One of the few writers of our day who deserve increasing respect and admiration" by Horace Gregory in the *New York Times*. There were still complaints about the difficulty of his style and the complexity of his technique, but these objections were becoming less prominent as Faulkner's literary stature increased.

For discussions of the unity and structure of *Go Down, Moses*, see Stanley Tick, "The Unity of *Go Down, Moses*" and James M. Mellard, "The Biblical Rhythm of *Go Down, Moses*."[19] An excellent discussion of "The Bear" chapter is provided by John W. Hunt in "Morality with Passion: A Study of 'The Bear.' "[20] As James Meriwether points out, the chief obstacle standing in the way of a comprehensive assessment of *Go Down, Moses* was the failure of scholars to approach the work as a novel.[21] This deficiency has been largely corrected by the work of Millgate, Beck, and Brooks. "The Bear" chapter of *Go Down, Moses* has been frequently misread as an independent short story and sometimes published as such. However, Faulkner himself made it clear that the novel and short-story treatments of "The Bear" were not the same.[22]

[1]Vickery, *The Novels of William Faulkner*, p. 124.

[2]See Millgate, pp. 202-203, 328.

[3]*Letters*, p. 122.

[4]*Faulkner in the University*, p. 4.

[5]*Go Down, Moses* (New York: Random House, 1942), p. 3. Subsequent references are placed within text.

[6]Brooks, *The Yoknapatawpha Country*, p. 248.

[7]Millgate, pp. 205-206.

[8]*Faulkner-Cowley File*, p. 113.

[9]Millgate, p. 204.

[10]Beck, *Faulkner*, pp. 335-336.

[11]Beck, *Faulkner*, p. 375.

[12]Beck, *Faulkner*, pp. 376-377.

[13]*Lion*, p. 225.

[14]Brooks, *The Yoknapatawpha Country*, p. 273; Millgate, pp. 208-209, 210.

[15]Millgate, p. 212.

[16]Millgate, p. 214.

[17]Millgate, p. 214.

[18]Meriwether points out that "there is no proof of old Carothers' incest (i.e., that he is the father of Tomasina); Isaac believes that, but he also believes that Eunice was a virgin when old [Carothers] (he thinks) had her. That is, Ike needs to believe such dramatic stuff. He might be right; he might not." Meriwether to Cox, 2 July 1981.

[19]Stanley Tick, "The Unity of *Go Down, Moses*," *Twentieth Century Literature*, 8 (July 1962): 67-73; James M. Mellard, "The Biblical Rhythm of *Go Down, Moses*," *Mississippi Quarterly*, 20 (Summer 1967): 135-147.

[20]Hunt, *Art in Theological Tension*, pp. 137-168.

[21]See *Sixteen Modern Authors*, p. 250.

[22]See *Faulkner in the University*, p. 273.

Intruder in the Dust

If *Intruder in the Dust*, published 27 September 1948, was conceived by Faulkner in mid-1941 primarily as a detective story, his concept broadened considerably before he actually began writing it in January 1948. As he explained in 1957: "It was the notion of a man in jail who couldn't hire a detective, couldn't hire one of these tough guys that slapped women around, took a drink every time he couldn't think of what to say next. But once I thought of Beauchamp, then he took charge of the story and the story was a good deal different from the idea . . . of the detective story I started with."[1] Though Lucas Beauchamp is a pervasive presence throughout the novel, the "different idea" Faulkner spoke of may have had to do with Chick Mallison and the maturity he gains as a result of his experiences. In this way, *Intruder in the Dust* becomes less a detective novel and more a Bildungsroman, depicting an educational process in which the lessons Chick learns are not from school but from life.

At the outset the reader learns that Lucas Beauchamp has been accused of murder; whether justly or unjustly is not made clear. The remainder of the narrative in the first two chapters establishes the relationship between Lucas and Chick Mallison. Sixteen years old at the time of the present action, Chick has known Lucas for four years, and the acquaintance has not been altogether pleasant. At the age of twelve, hunting one winter on the property of Roth Edmonds, Chick falls off a log into an icy stream. Climbing up the bank, Chick sees Lucas for the first time and remarks about the expression on his face: "it had no pigment at all, not even the white man's lack of it, not arrogant, not even scornful: just intractable and composed."[2] Though he is a Negro, nothing in Lucas's outward expression acknowledges a racial identity. He is the same independent, sometimes willfully stubborn character he showed himself to be in *Go Down, Moses*.

Taken to Lucas's cabin to dry and warm himself, Chick feels that he has no power to do other than what Lucas tells him to do, a feeling that makes him uncomfortable and resentful. When Chick attempts to pay for the meal provided for him, Lucas refuses to attach a cash value to what he considers the obligations of hospitality: "What's that for?" he asks (p. 15). Not knowing how to deal with the situation, Chick increases his embarrassment by dropping the coins on the floor and futilely ordering Lucas to pick them up. After his initial humiliation, Chick feels a compelling need to get even, to somehow cancel his debt; in doing so he acts out an attitude toward Lucas shared by the community for years: "*We got to make him be a nigger first. He's got to admit he's a nigger. Then maybe we will accept him as he seems to intend to be accepted*" (p. 18). When the boy sends Lucas's wife, Molly, a dress, Lucas sends some molasses in return, and Chick then realizes that he is no match for the older man: "This would have to be all; whatever would or could set him free was beyond not merely his reach but even his ken; he could only wait for it if it came and do without it if it didn't" (p. 23). More than a year after his first encounter with Lucas, Chick feels some measure of relief at the prospect, when Lucas passes him on the street without speaking, that Lucas has forgotten about him. Later he learns that that was shortly after Molly had died, and another of Chick's unthinking assumptions is revealed: "*That was why he didn't see me. . . . He was grieving. You dont have to not be a nigger in order to grieve*" (p. 25).

Now, in the present action of the novel, Chick must deal with the nemesis of Lucas Beauchamp once more. As a result, more of his assumptions about himself and his community will be challenged, bringing Chick to a new level of maturity. Lucas is accused of killing Vinson Gowrie, "youngest of a family of six brothers one of whom had already served a year in federal penitentiary for armed resistance as an army deserter and another term at the state penal farm for making whiskey, and a ramification of cousins and inlaws covering a whole corner of the county . . . a connection of brawlers and farmers and foxhunters and stock- and timber-traders" (p. 35). Lucas is found standing over the body with a recently fired pistol in his pocket; and, since Roth Edmonds has gone to New Orleans for surgery, there is no one in a position to help him.

It is consistent with Lucas's character that the shooting would have taken place under such adverse circumstances, because "apparently he had been working for twenty or twenty-five years . . . toward this one crowning moment" (p. 37); it seems as though the crime were as much an intentional affront to the community as a crime against an individual. Gavin Stevens ironically articulates a code of behavior by which community attitudes might be expressed: "and now the white people will take [Lucas] out and burn him, all regular and in order and themselves acting exactly as . . . Lucas would wish them to act: like white folks; both of them observing implicitly the rules: the nigger acting like a nigger and the white folks acting like white folks and no real hard feelings on either side" (pp. 48-49). Gavin does not approve of such actions; but in effect he instructs Chick that relations between the races must be conducted according to certain rules, and there is no reason for Chick to suspect that his uncle's presumption of Lucas's guilt might be wrong, either in fact or in principle. The point is made that though Chick may not be in total agreement with the actions of his society—a lynching is talked about but is never seriously threatened—he is nonetheless a member of that society and has a strong sense of loyalty to it.

When Chick goes to watch Lucas being taken into the jail, he is certain that the black man has forgotten all about him. He is wrong. As Lucas is being taken in, he stops and, though there is a large crowd, looks directly at Chick: "You, young man" he addresses him. "Tell your uncle I wants to see him" (p. 45). When Gavin and Chick go to see Lucas in jail, Lucas, knowing that his story will probably not be believed, is unwilling to tell Gavin all he knows. Gavin becomes irritated because he thinks he understands the situation and is rankled that Lucas is unwilling to take his advice. Chick, then, must find out what Lucas wants: to dig up the grave of Vinson Gowrie and examine the body. Lucas believes that an examination of the body—presumably Chick would have to bring it back into town—will prove that Vinson was not shot with the same caliber pistol Lucas owns. In making his request, Lucas voices a theme that is expressed often in Faulkner's work. He explains to Chick, "I mought have told your maw. But she would need help. So I waited for you. Young folks and womens, they aint cluttered. They can listen. But a middle-year man like your paw and your uncle, they cant listen. They're too busy with facks. . . . If you ever needs to get anything done outside the common run, dont waste yo time on the menfolks; get the womens and children to working at it" (pp. 71-72). Women and children do indeed get something done; for later that night Chick, along with his black companion, Aleck Sander, and the elderly Miss Eunice Habersham, goes out and digs up Vinson Gowrie's grave. But the body in the grave is not Vinson's; it is instead Jake Montgomery's. The ensuing action reveals that Vinson and his brother Crawford were operating a black market timber operation with which Montgomery was involved or of which he was at least aware. Crawford kills his brother and implicates Lucas, and later kills Montgomery.

Most strands of plot are resolved at a fairly early point. What follows is a lengthy and sometimes tedious discourse between Gavin and his nephew Chick on truth, justice, and the nature of relations between races and regions of the country. The picture of Chick is one of a boy in late adolescence on the verge of early manhood. His personality is integrated in a positive sense because he is able to identify and accept certain personal values without rejecting his region, at the same time recognizing the inequalities that exist. Riding with his uncle he reflects:

he seemed to see his whole native land, his home—the dirt, the earth which had bred his bones and those of his fathers for six generations and was still shaping him into not just a man but a specific man, not with just a man's passions and aspirations and beliefs but the specific passions and hopes and convictions and ways of thinking and acting of a specific kind and even race: and even more: even among a kind and race specific and unique . . . since it had also integrated into him whatever it was that had compelled him to stop and listen to a damned highnosed impudent Negro who even if he wasn't a murderer had been about to get if not about what he deserved at least exactly what he had spent the sixty-odd years of his life asking for . . . (p. 151).

For his part, Gavin appears capable of acknowledging and learning from his own error of judgment, and he encourages Chick not to let ambiguity about his region or the people in it weaken his sense of values.

Because of the proportion of *Intruder in the Dust* that is concerned directly with racial and regional issues, it has sometimes been interpreted as a polemical or reactionary work, depending upon what ideals critics assumed Faulkner to be arguing for or defending against. In this novel more frequently than in any other, Gavin Stevens has been identified as representing the views of William Faulkner. This interpretation appeared in contemporary reviews of *Intruder in the Dust* and has been an unfortunate hallmark of subsequent scholarship. But as Cleanth Brooks observes, "Gavin Stevens occupies no privileged position in Faulkner's novels: sometimes he talks sense and sometimes he talks nonsense. . . . But Gavin is not presented as the sage and wise counselor of the community. His notions have to take their chances along with those of less 'intellectual' characters."[3] It is true that Faulkner believed (as does Gavin Stevens) that the South should recognize and correct its own shortcomings, and thereby preempt the necessity of outside interference; however, to develop these similarities of belief into mutually held ideas is hardly responsible criticism. It is far more useful to see *Intruder in the Dust* as the story of Chick Mallison, a story that carries forward themes and characters from *Go Down, Moses* and, in its exploration of the themes of maturity and education, anticipates *The Reivers*.

----

[1]*Faulkner in the University*, p. 142.

[2]*Intruder in the Dust* (New York: Random House, 1948), p. 7. Subsequent references are placed within text.

[3]Brooks, *The Yoknapatawpha Country*, pp. 279-280.

Requiem for a Nun

Requiem for a Nun, Faulkner's fifteenth novel, which was begun in 1933 and published on 27 September 1951, took up the story of Temple Drake, part of whose story he had first told in *Sanctuary*, nineteen years earlier. Reference has been made in previous chapters to Faulkner's use of stage imagery, a familiar motif that runs through much of his work (see, for example, the previous discussions on *Flags in the Dust*, *Light in August*, and *Absalom, Absalom!*). In this regard, *Requiem for a Nun* might be considered an extreme development of what is elsewhere used on a more limited basis as a technical or stylistic device. Almost the entire novel is structured as a dramatic play. To Faulkner this was not merely a matter of experimentation:

> I felt that that was the best way to tell that story. That the story of those people fell into the hard simple give-and-take of dialogue. The longer—I don't know what you would call those interludes, the prefaces, preambles, whatever they are—was necessary to give it the contrapuntal effect which comes in orchestration, that the hard give-and-take of the dialogue was played against something that was a little mystical, made it sharper, more effective, in my opinion. It was not experimentation, it was simply because to me that seemed the most effective way to tell that story.[1]

The "contrapuntal" effect Faulkner tries to achieve through the alternation of sharply contrasting sections is the same effect he sought by contrasting the "Wild Palms" and "Old Man" sections of *The Wild Palms*, and, through various means and to various degrees, the effect he sought in most of his mature fiction.

At the same time, Faulkner does not abandon particular uses of stage imagery. In "The Jail" section, one of the three long narratives that preface the three "acts" of the novel, Faulkner describes the departure of Chickasaw chieftainess Mohataha from Yoknapatawpha County: "she vanished so across that summer afternoon to that terrific and infinitesimal creak and creep of ungreased wheels, herself immobile beneath the rigid parasol, grotesque and regal, bizarre and moribund, like obsolescence's self riding off the stage enthroned on its own obsolete catafalque"; and later, on an even more metaphoric level, the signing over of the Indian land to the whites has the impact of violently flinging the wagon (and the Indian people) "not only out of Yoknapatawpha County and Mississippi but the United States too . . . like a float or a piece of stage property dragged rapidly into the wings across the very backdrop and amid the very bustle of the property-men setting up for the next scene and before the curtain had even had time to fall."[2] The use of this and related imagery in the narrative interchapters serves to emphasize not so much the inevitability of fate as the inexorability of the movement and force of time and change on human affairs.

The narrative interchapters introduce the "acts" of the novel: "The Courthouse," the preface for act one, describes the history of the place where Nancy Mannigoe, the Negro who murders Temple Drake's child, receives her sentence; "The Golden Dome," preface to act two, describes the state capitol where Temple goes with Nancy's lawyer, Gavin Stevens, to meet with the governor; "The Jail," preface to act three, is about the prison where they visit Nancy on the eve of her execution. One of Faulkner's points is that any community (or civilization) is characterized by the institutions it creates, and in turn these institutions are created out of the shared values that society affirms as the principles upon which civilized existence should be based. Thus, the first interchapter, "The Courthouse (A Name for the City)," contains important implications for the rest of the book. As Noel Polk has pointed out, this beginning section "concerns the moral complications that prompt the beginning of the city of Jefferson," and as such deals with "the themes of freedom and responsibility . . . man's various relationships with his fellow man and with his government."[3] Three symbols dominate this section: the courthouse, the jail, and the lock on the jail door. Polk writes, "If we can tentatively identify the courthouse as the emerging symbol of all that is worthy in Man, of his dreams of a better world . . . and the jail, conversely, as the emerging symbol of the harsher realities of human existence—sin, suffering, anguish, and death—we are able to see in the gradual separation of the two buildings the metaphoric working out on a broad scope of one of the major themes of the novel [freedom and responsibility]."[4] The lock is not presented as a static symbol, but is associated with "numerous . . . symbols of civilization which accrete throughout the episode."[5] With the courthouse and the jail as contrasting symbols of the community, the citizens, at the moment they name their town, "become part of history, see themselves in relation to Time: they accept their individual and conglomerate pasts as burdens they must bear, and begin to look upon the future as something to be prepared for."[6] This can be difficult to do, however; for, as is made clear in the remainder of this section, change is concomitant with civilization; it occurs with increasing and finally breathtaking speed, so the future is something difficult and uncertain for man to deal with.

Set against the historical context and the sweep of progress delineated by the narrative interchapters are the three acts of the novel, which, though a continuation of the Temple Drake story, certainly does not have to be read as a sequel to *Sanctuary*. As Faulkner explained, "I began to think what would be the future of that girl? And then I thought, What could a marriage come to that was founded on the vanity of a weak man? . . . And suddenly that seemed to me dramatic and worthwhile."[7]

The dramatic event that begins the first act is the sentencing of Nancy Mannigoe for the infanticide of Gowan and Temple Stevens's child. The scene then shifts to the Stevenses' living room where there is an exchange between Gowan and Temple and Gowan's uncle Gavin Stevens, who defended Nancy at the trial. The Stevenses are planning to leave Jefferson with their son Bucky until after Nancy's execution, some four months later. The Stevenses' reason for giving Nancy a job in their home is discussed, and necessary background information about the couple—how they came to be married, the time Temple spent in a Memphis brothel—is presented through dialogue. Two general matters of significance are presented in the first act. First, the theme of suffering is introduced. It is obvious that Temple and Gowan, though their marriage is not a stable one, care about one another. They must suffer separately, however, because there is a chasm of guilt and resentment between them that they are not able to bridge. The second matter is raised by Gavin who asks Gowan why he thinks it necessary that Nancy die. These two topics are closely related, for Gavin's question has broad implications. Is it necessary for Nancy to die to ease the Stevenses' suffering by some measure of revenge? Should the suffering caused by Nancy lead Temple and Gowan to a better understanding of themselves and each other? Or does the nature of existence occasionally require people to suffer simply for the sake of suffering? In the first act Gavin questions Temple and Gowan in an unsuccessful attempt to get them to respond to these problems. The final scene of the act takes place on 11 March, two days before Nancy's execution. Unable to stay away, Temple has returned to Jefferson with Gowan and Bucky; and at this point Gavin tells her she must go and talk with the governor, ostensibly for the purpose of trying to save Nancy.

The second act takes place mostly in the governor's office at Jackson—though there are treatments of earlier events that serve to make clear the circumstances under which Nancy decides she must take the life of Temple's child. Temple reveals that her real reason for hiring Nancy was "to have someone to talk to" because "Temple Drake, the white woman, the all-Mississippi debutante, descendant of long lines of statesmen and soldiers high and proud. . . . couldn't find anybody except a nigger dopefiend whore that could speak her language" (p. 120). She questions sharply and bitterly the necessity for human suffering, "anguish for the sake of anguish" (p. 133) she calls it, and wonders how it is possible for any person to really be prepared to deal with the reality of evil in the world, because "You've got to be already prepared to resist it, say no to it, long before you see it; you must have already said no to it long before you even know what it is" (p. 134). As the second act proceeds, it becomes increasingly clear that Gavin's reason for bringing Temple to the capitol is not to save Nancy but, if possible, to save Temple and Gowan. In the third scene Gowan is seated in the governor's chair and the governor has left the room. Having told her complete story as she has never done before, there is no longer any pretense or illusion between the couple. Whether they will be able to build a strong and durable relationship on the basis of their new discoveries is not revealed, but they will at least have the opportunity.

The third act is brief and takes place entirely in the jail where Nancy is awaiting her execution. Temple addresses Nancy with her questions about the necessity for human suffering, and asks Nancy how she is to cope with the future. Temple acknowledges the lesson she learned in the governor's office, that her purpose is not to save Nancy but, if possible, herself: "not to save you," Temple says, "that wasn't really concerned in it: but just for me, just for the suffering and the paying: a little more suffering simply because there was a little more time left for a little more of it" (p. 275). The questions that Temple and Gavin put to Nancy are in a sense rhetorical because Temple realizes that Nancy does not have any of the answers. All of her questions ultimately turn back on herself.

To what end, then, does suffering lead? That is the question raised by Noel Polk in an article on *Requiem for a Nun* and *A Fable*. Rather than pressing a case, as some critics have done, for Nancy as the moral center of the novel, Polk argues that Temple is left finally in a position where "she will spend the rest of her life . . . trying to 'buy back,' atone for, her own sins."[8] What Nancy does "is give Temple the opportunity to continue the suffering she has tried to escape"; but the moral issue remains highly ambiguous for, as Polk observes, it is "very much a question whether Temple's marriage—any marriage, for that matter, even a happy one—was worth the double sacrifice Nancy made."[9] Yet in the last act of the novel that is precisely where Temple's case is left, with Temple asking, "why must it be suffering? . . . Why couldn't He have invented something else? Or, if it's got to be suffering, why cant it be just your own?" (p. 277). The point may be that the human situation is always in doubt, that the ability to endure suffering does not buy or guarantee anything. As Harry Wilbourne, faced with a choice between grief and nothing in *The Wild Palms*, selects grief—which is to say life—so Temple Drake Stevens, faced with a similar choice in *Requiem for a Nun*, may be willing to accept suffering and life as opposed to the suffering-free condition of nonexistence and death that Nancy Mannigoe is about to step into.

Initially, *Requiem for a Nun* was well received, but later reviews tended to be negative or questioning. Hal Smith's treatment of the novel in the *Saturday Review* was fairly typical: Faulkner's stature as a writer was not questioned, but the mixture of prose fiction with a dramatic format was held to be structurally unsound, needlessly confusing. Historically, *Requiem for a Nun* has not received the thorough scholarly study that it deserves, even if it is not considered up to par with Faulkner's major works. For critics and scholars alike, the structure of the novel has proved to be a problem; and some have been too ready to read *Requiem for a Nun* simply as a sequel to *Sanctuary*. A much-needed corrective to this neglect is Polk's book-length study *Faulkner's Requiem for a Nun: A Critical Study*, which includes in an appendix a thorough discussion of the novel's composition.[10]

---

[1]*Faulkner in the University*, p. 122.

[2]*Requiem for a Nun* (New York: Random House, 1951), pp. 217, 221-222. Subsequent references are placed within text.

[3]Polk, "Alec Holston's Lock and the Founding of Jefferson," *Mississippi Quarterly*, 24 (Summer 1971): 249.

[4]Polk, "Alec Holston's Lock and the Founding of Jefferson," p. 250.

[5]Polk, "Alec Holston's Lock and the Founding of Jefferson," p. 252.

[6]Polk, "Alec Holston's Lock and the Founding of Jefferson," p. 268.

[7]*Faulkner in the University*, p. 96.

[8]Polk, "The Nature of Sacrifice: *Requiem for a Nun* and *A Fable*," in *Faulkner Studies*, 1, edited by Barnett Guttenberg (Miami: University of Miami Department of English, 1980), p. 107.

[9]Polk, "The Nature of Sacrifice," p. 107.

[10]Polk, *Faulkner's Requiem for a Nun: A Critical Study* (Bloomington: Indiana University Press, 1981).

A Fable

A strong case might be made that *A Fable*, published 2 August 1954 and composed over a nine-year period from December 1944 to November 1953, is the most ambitious novel attempted by Faulkner during the latter portion of his writing career. However, while critics have admired certain aspects of this work set during World War I, they have on the whole judged that it fails to accomplish its literary goals. However, these critics seem at times uncertain of what Faulkner's goals may have been.

Despite the deliberate, meticulous use of Christian symbolism in *A Fable*, it is neither an elaborate, modernized retelling of Christ's passion nor was it intended as an antiwar tract. In a statement on the novel written in late 1953 or early 1954, but not published until 1973, Faulkner expressed his intentions clearly:

> This is not a pacifist book. On the contrary, this writer holds almost as short a brief for pacifism as for war itself, for the reason that pacifism does not work, cannot cope with the forces which produce the wars. In fact, if this book had any aim or moral . . . it was to show by poetic analogy, allegory, that pacifism does not work; that to put an end to war, man must either find or invent something more powerful than war and man's aptitude for belligerence and his thirst for power at any cost, or use the fire itself to fight and destroy the fire with; that man may finally have to mobilize himself and arm himself with the implements of war to put an end to war; that the mistake we have consistently made is setting nation against nation or political ideology against political ideology to stop war. . . .[1]

Faulkner identifies no primary character in the novel, but

points to a group of three characters as representative of "the trinity of man's conscience": "Levine, who sees evil and refuses to accept it by destroying himself . . . the old Quartermaster General who says . . . there is evil in the world; I will bear both, the evil and the world too, and grieve for them—the battalion runner . . . who in the last scene says . . . there is evil in the world and I'm going to do something about it."[2] Respectively, these characters represent positions of nihilism, passivism, and activism; and Faulkner seems to say that these forces operate simultaneously in all men. Whatever the ultimate evaluation of the novel may be, *A Fable* is a complex work, one about which simple or overly generalized judgments should not be made.

A Fable abounds in elaborate time shifts, one of the hallmarks of Faulkner's fictional technique. The first chapter, set within the fortress city of Chaulnesmont, takes place on Wednesday, two days after the mutiny of a French regiment that is described in a later chapter. The general time (May 1918) and the chief element of plot (a regiment of soldiers refuses an order to fight) are both established. It is immediately apparent that there is intense unrest in the city. The mutinous regiment has traditional ties to that area of France, and the people crowding into the town are at the same time angered over the regiment's behavior and relieved that there has been no further fighting and killing since Monday. The tension between these two reactions is so palpably felt that the crowd becomes "one vast tongueless brotherhood of dread and anxiety."[3]

Since the mutiny of the French regiment, there has been a general, undeclared cease-fire along both sides of the entire European front. The war is at an impasse and it must be decided what is to happen next; whether hostilities will resume or whether the cease-fire will turn into a general peace. Though the fate of the regiment and the war is not inevitable at this point, there is a certain inexorability to the events taking place which limits the possibilities of what can happen. As the regiment is being brought into Chaulnesmont, the men appear "like phantoms or apparitions or perhaps figures cut without depth from tin or cardboard and snatched in violent repetition across a stage set for a pantomime of anguish and fatality" (p. 14). Throughout the first chapter the emphasis is on crowd perceptions, not individual identity. The allied generals are seen from a distance; the crowd recognizes only their power. The regiment is only a mass of tin or cardboard men in trucks. The third group, the corporal and his twelve followers who have been segregated from the rest of the regiment, is identified as a source of anguish and fear; there is no individual animosity directed at them.

The detailed treatment of individual characters does not begin until the second chapter, which describes events on the day of the failed attack. The chief character in this chapter is General Gragnon, commander of the division to which the regiment belongs. It is revealed early that the attack the regiment refused to make was not intended to be successful. It is, Gragnon realizes, "a sacrifice already planned and doomed in some vaster scheme, in which it would not matter either way, whether the attack failed or not" (p. 23). In this way, the theme of sacrifice, which is central to the meaning of the novel and which operates on many levels, is introduced. Whether on the grounds of military necessity or expediency, or on the grounds of personal sacrifice for some universal ideal, the question constantly asked is to what end sacrifices are being made, and what is actually achieved by sacrifice. For Gragnon, order through discipline, the perfect and unquestioning functioning of the military chain of command, is a necessary condition of existence. To maintain that condition no sacrifice is too great; and he therefore recommends to his superior, Bidet, that the entire regiment be shot.

The other major development in the second chapter arises from the meeting between Bidet and Gragnon. Bidet has a larger grasp of the situation than Gragnon, and he tries to instruct him: "We can permit even our own rank and file to let us down on occasion; that's one of the prerequisites of their doom and fate as rank and file forever. They may even stop the wars, as they have done before and will again; ours merely to guard them from the knowledge that it was actually they who accomplished that act. Let the whole vast moil and seethe of man confederate in stopping wars if they wish, so long as we can prevent them learning that they have done so" (p. 54). Bidet addresses here a point that the old marshal affirms later on in quite a different context: the necessity for society, or civilization, to impose order and exact a certain level of obedience from its members. This is not to argue that the continuation of the war is a good thing or a bad thing. The military has become a microcosm of society; and if the body politic is to be swayed and buffeted by individual whims or beliefs, social order will be replaced rapidly by chaos. Several critics have pointed out the dualism that runs throughout *A Fable*, the simultaneous presence of good and evil, guilt and innocence, bravery and fear. This is another example of dualism, and it instructs us that any society that is alive and in motion is also, to some degree, at war with itself; social vitality depends upon a certain degree of tension. Those who have responsibility for maintaining the stability of society must be willing to resort to extreme measures to maintain that tension. Though this point may be far removed from Bidet's immediate self-interest—just as Bidet's self-interest is far removed from Gragnon's—it nonetheless upholds a general principle that operates throughout the novel.

The third chapter, which takes place on Tuesday night, introduces the sentry and the runner, who have no names but are only identified by the functions they perform. The influence of the sentry over the other men in his unit is outlined and the background of the runner—a dual personality who has been both officer and enlisted man—is given. At this point the runner is aware of the mutiny and he has known for some time of the French corporal and his twelve followers. Knowing that the mutiny has resulted in a general cease-fire, he is trying to seize an opportunity for further action and in doing so he speaks to the opposite side of the issue addressed by Bidet. He thinks to himself, *"They could execute only so many of us before they will have worn out the last rifle and pistol and expended the last live shell"* (p. 68). All that is needed is for one side to emerge from its trenches and walk, weaponless, into no-man's-land. To accomplish this the runner needs the sentry to exercise his influence over the other men in his unit; but the sentry, totally untouched by the runner's hope, absolutely refuses and finally, in his rage, attacks the runner.

The next chapter concentrates on the young pilot Levine, who, in his idealization of war and his despair that it might come to an end before he has experienced combat, resembles Cadet Lowe of *Soldiers' Pay*. The steady, relentless movement of larger events takes place in the shadow of Levine's frustration and disappointment. When, along with two other airplanes, he attacks a German aircraft, he can tell by the trajectories of the tracer rounds that direct hits are being made; yet, like the antiaircraft ammunition being fired from the ground, they have no effect. An elaborate ruse is revealed. Matters have reached a point where it is necessary for the opposing sides to confer, so each side is equipped with blank ammunition to mask the flight of the ranking German general to Villeneuve Blanche, from which point he travels to Chaulnesmont. Levine's disillusionment about war—intensified by the fact that the German general calmly shoots his pilot after they have landed—is too much for him. He rejects life at the point where it no longer coincides with his own preconceived conventions, and finally, in the depths of despair, he commits suicide.

The World War I focus of *A Fable* is broken by the nearly forty-page interlude about a stolen three-legged racehorse that the sentry and his black accomplice Tobe Sutterfield had successfully raced all over the South. Michael Millgate, commenting on the similarities between *A Fable* and *Go Down, Moses*, writes that the "outstanding structural peculiarity of *A Fable*, the intrusion of the long story of the lame racehorse, is in some measure prefigured by the relationship between the hunting episodes in *Go Down, Moses*. . . . The injured horse, like the crippled bear, old Ben, is apparently a symbol of natural freedom, and his story—which the groom's devotion marks as a kind of lovestory—is portentously heralded by the invocation of mythological and literary references."[4] The sentry—who is also the groom for the horse—and Sutterfield are operating outside the bounds of official society, represented by the law which is sworn to protect private property. In this regard their actions reflect the overall pattern of the novel. After hearing this story the runner goes to the sentry and tries to persuade him to take action that will capitalize on and extend the cease-fire brought about by the corporal's passivity.

This section also gives insight into the theological themes of the novel and provides further evidence that Faulkner is not interested in retelling a traditional Christian story. Asked by the runner if his purpose is to bear witness to God, Sutterfield replies, "God dont need me. I bears witness to Him of course, but my main witness is to man" (p. 180). He then elaborates: "Man is full of sin and nature, and all he does dont bear looking at, and a heap of what he says is a shame and a mawkery. But cant no witness hurt him. Some day something might beat him, but it wont be Satan" (p. 180). Sutterfield does not deny the existence or importance of God, so his theology is not a complete, secular humanism, nor is it based on mysticism or divine intervention in the affairs of men. It is a humanistic doctrine that asserts that man must be able to save himself by recognizing and accepting the contradictions inherent in his nature. This, in essence, is the broad moral backdrop which gives dramatic and thematic relief to the positions taken by the corporal and the old marshal. As will be seen, the old marshal, the supreme commander of the military establishment in Europe, takes a position that is close to the one voiced by Sutterfield.

When the narrative returns to present time, a look is taken at the old French marshal, who must finally decide the fate of the mutinous regiment. The focus of the plot is on the meeting of the German general with the allied generals for the purpose of deciding what to do about the cease-fire. There is a mood of inexorability present throughout much of the chapter that is voiced by Gragnon when he makes his speech before the marshal and the allied generals: "The speech was much older than that moment two days ago in the observation post when he discovered that he was going to have to make it. . . . it had become . . . a part of the equipment with which he would follow and serve his destiny with his life as long as life lasted" (p. 231). The mood is also voiced by the marshal when, discussing the fate of the corporal, he asks, "will he not merely inherit from me at thirty-three what I had already bequeathed to him at birth?" (p. 301). The primary narrative is constantly branching off in different directions as the old marshal meets with various people. As he does so, we learn a great deal more about the corporal (who is his bastard son), the corporal's wife and sisters, and about the quartermaster general and his relationship to the old marshal.

The old marshal is a study of contrasts between the things he has done in his life and the expectations of others. He takes advantage of none of the wealth and power that are his by birth. After graduating from St. Cyr (the military academy) at the top of his class, he takes a minor outpost in Africa. While on duty in Africa he averts an outbreak of war, but must sacrifice a man's life to do it. Following this episode the old marshal leaves the army and disappears for thirteen years in a Tibetan monastery. Of his peers, only Lallemont—the quartermaster general who finished second in the same graduating class as the old marshal at St. Cyr—pretends to have any understanding of the marshal's motives. Lallemont sees in himself a "seniority of hope in the condition of man" (p. 263); and as the marshal is about to leave the African outpost, Lallemont tells him, "I know that you are going wherever it is you are going, in order to return from it when the time, the moment comes, in the shape of man's living hope" (p. 263). He believes it is the destiny of the marshal to save mankind. He is wrong; for, as the novel illustrates in dramatic terms, it is impossible for man to be saved by any outside agency.

Like Tobe Sutterfield, the marshal bears witness to man; and in his meeting with his son the corporal he makes his position clear. Drawing for the corporal what he sees as the mechanical and materialistic progress of modern civilization, he expresses his belief in man's ability to endure:

> because he has that in him which will endure even beyond the ultimate worthless tideless rock freezing slowly in the last red and heatless sunset, because already the next star in the blue immensity of space will be already clamorous with the uproar of his debarkation, his puny and inexhaustible voice still talking, still planning; and there too after the last ding dong of doom has rung and died there will still be one sound more: his voice, planning still to build something higher and faster and louder; more efficient and louder and faster than ever before, yet it too inherent with the same old primordial fault since it too in the end will fail to eradicate him from the earth. I dont fear man. I do better: I respect and admire him. And pride: I am ten times prouder of that immortality which he does possess than ever he of that heavenly one of his delusion (p. 354).

Because the marshal believes in man he is willing—even sees the necessity as Lallemont does not—to sacrifice his son. Lallemont believes the significance of the corporal's act can only be affirmed by pardoning it; but the old marshal tells him: "if he accepts his life . . . he will have abrogated his own gesture and martyrdom. If I gave him his life tonight, I myself could render null and void what you call the hope and the dream of his sacrifice. By destroying his life tomorrow morning, I will establish forever that he didn't even live in vain, let alone die so" (p. 332). In this way, as Noel Polk points out in a useful discussion of A Fable, "the moral center of the novel lies much closer to the old marshal than to the corporal."[5] Compared to the marshal the corporal "has no definite program, gives . . . no direction . . . provides . . . inspiration but not . . . leadership."[6] Only the influence of civilization, despite its flaws, can do this, and without civilization "freedom would be meaningless."[7] By sacrificing his son for civilization, the marshal fulfills the prophecy Lallemont made for him, though not in the way Lallemont had conceived.[8]

The theme of duality in A Fable has been touched upon several times; and Millgate describes the work as one that deals with "two opposed attitudes towards the problems of existence."[9] In this regard, it is fitting that the last scene of the novel should take place between the runner and the quartermaster general on the occasion of the old marshal's funeral. The runner's plan to have unarmed German and British soldiers meet in the midst of no-man's-land was a total failure; a heavy artillery barrage was called in to disperse the soldiers. Having survived the barrage, the runner is now "not a man but a mobile and upright scar" with "one arm and one leg" and "one entire side of his hatless head was one hairless eyeless and earless scar" (p. 435). This is the way he appears at the funeral of the marshal. In defiance he throws the medaille militaire at the coffin, and as a result he is almost beaten to death by the crowd. Left lying in the street, he is comforted by the quartermaster general. Together the two men represent mankind's extreme answers to the problem of existence: frustrated and violent action on the one hand, hope and ultimate grief on the other. The force that stabilizes this "trinity of conscience" is embodied in the person of the old marshal, the breadth of whose influence is witnessed by "people who had never heard his name" and "did not even know that they were still free because of him" (p. 435).

Though *A Fable* received a number of favorable reviews at the time of its publication, the negative reviews soon piled up. Despite Harvey Breit's assurance to Faulkner that "the bouquets outweighed the brickbats by a comfortable margin,"[10] the novel was not well received. None of the reviews, however, was as negative as Ernest Hemingway's private assessment that made a comparison between *A Fable* and "the night soil [human feces] from Chungking."[11] The critical reception notwithstanding, *A Fable* was awarded the National Book Award for Fiction and the Pulitzer Prize in 1955. In terms of scholarship, the novel has suffered from critical approaches that interpret the work too narrowly as Christian allegory. Badly needed correctives are supplied by the work of Butterworth and Polk; but *A Fable* still stands as one of Faulkner's novels most in need of responsible study.

---

[1]"A Note on *A Fable*," *Mississippi Quarterly*, 26 (Summer 1973): 416.

[2]"A Note on *A Fable*," p. 417.

[3]*A Fable* (New York: Random House, 1954), p. 3. Subsequent references are placed within text.

[4]Millgate, p. 228.

[5]Polk, "The Nature of Sacrifice," p. 106.

[6]Polk, "The Nature of Sacrifice," p. 106.

[7]Polk, "The Nature of Sacrifice," p. 106.

[8]As Polk acknowledges, his assessment of the old marshal is based in part on A. K. Butterworth's exhaustive study of the novel, "A Critical and Textual Study of William Faulkner's *A Fable*," Ph.D. dissertation, University of South Carolina, 1970. Butterworth presents a very strong argument for the old marshal as the "heir and defender of modern civilization," p. 136.

[9]Millgate, p. 228.

[10]Blotner, p. 1502.

[11]Baker, ed., *Ernest Hemingway: Selected Letters, 1917-1961* (New York: Scribners, 1981), p. 864.

The Reivers

The Reivers is the only one of Faulkner's novels written entirely in the comic mode.[1] It is the story which Faulkner had first described to Robert Haas in 1940, twenty-two years before it was published on 4 June 1962, of how an eleven-year-old boy, Lucius Priest, takes his first major steps toward maturity and adulthood through a series of humorous adventures. Its form combines characteristics of the picaresque novel (the hero moves through a series of roguish adventures) and the Bildungsroman (the hero receives an education in the ways of the world as a result of his experiences). The novel is comic in the sense that it is clear from the outset that the action is intended to move toward a satisfactory conclusion, and the humor of the work is heightened by the exotic nature of Lucius's experiences: eleven years old and in the company and somewhat under the influence of two family retainers, one white and one black, he gets involved in the theft of the family automobile, travels to a Memphis whorehouse, through no fault of his own loses the automobile, and as a result must race a stolen horse in order to get the automobile back. The literal meaning of *The Reivers* is "The Stealers," which Faulkner had at one time considered using as the title.

The subtitle of *The Reivers* is *A Reminiscence*, and that is precisely the narrative frame of the work. Lucius Priest, now a grandfather, tells this story of his childhood to his grandson, who in turn tells the story to the reader. Thus the novel begins with the statement, "GRANDFATHER SAID."[2] Speaking as a grandfather, Lucius's purpose is to impart some knowledge of the world, though he probably realizes that his grandson cannot learn all he needs to know vicariously. Like him, his grandson will also have to learn through experience. That the grandfather/grandson relationship is established by the narrative structure of the novel is significant; for within the narrative

there is a similar relationship between Lucius and his grandfather, Boss Priest. The grandfather is presented as a source of
authority, wisdom, probity, responsibility, and love: a model
of correct behavior. One of the points Faulkner makes in *The
Reivers* is that life is various and people's behavior does not
always conform to expected norms. Thus there is only so much
that can be learned from models; one must also be able to
extract lessons from experience.

The narration begins about a year before the main events of
the novel take place, and Lucius is ten years old. One of the
primary themes of the novel is family cohesiveness, and the
first chapter serves to establish family connections, which
include the connection between Boon Hogganbeck and the
Jefferson families that accept responsibility for him. Boon
Hogganbeck is the same character who appears in *Go Down,
Moses*; and the Priest family is related to both the Edmonds and
McCaslin families. Lucius gives a concise description of his
companion Boon: "He was tough, faithful, brave and completely unreliable; he was six feet four inches tall and weighed
two hundred and forty pounds and had the mentality of a
child; over a year ago Father had already begun to say that at
any moment now I would outgrow him" (p. 19). Ned, who
works for the Priest family as a coachman, is descended from
the McCaslin line of Negroes. He is smarter than Boon, and
remarkably wiley, but hardly reliable. With Ned and Boon
Lucius makes his trip to Memphis.

The trip takes place during the early days of the automobile;
and as Lucius goes through a process of personal change, from
childhood toward adulthood, the automobile serves as a symbol both of manhood—women do not drive them—and of
cultural and social change. Boss Priest remarks on the nature of
the change of which the automobile is harbinger. He remarks
that Maury Priest (Lucius's father) will remain in the livery
business, "He will just have a new name for it. Priest's Garage
maybe, or the Priest Motor Company. People will pay any

price for motion. They will even work for it" (p. 41). The mobility provided by the automobile also makes it a symbol of freedom; but the concomitant of freedom is responsibility, and this is another lesson that Lucius must learn.

The event that makes the trip possible is the death of Lucius's maternal grandfather. Lucius's parents and grandparents plan to attend the funeral, occasioning a trip that will have them out of town for four days. The children, including Lucius, are to stay with relatives at the Edmondses' place. Boon wants desperately to take Boss's automobile to Memphis but realizes he needs an accomplice and begins persuading Lucius to go with him. Boon, however, is not capable of persuading Lucius to do something he does not want to do or knows is wrong. As Lucius tells his grandson, "I was smarter than Boon. I realized . . . that of we two doomed and irrevocable, I was the leader, I was the boss, the master" (p. 53). Lucius weaves the fabric of lies that makes it possible for the pair to get out of Jefferson, and in this way the young boy takes his first step down the road of experience.

Getting to Memphis on roads made for wagons rather than automobiles is no easy matter. Boon and Lucius encounter a particularly difficult obstacle at Hell Creek crossing, where an erstwhile farmer uses his mules and plow to keep a mudhole churned up as a trap for automobiles, then levies a fee to pull them loose with his mules. At this point the automobile is no match for nature. It is an "expensive useless mechanical toy . . . held helpless and impotent in the almost infantile clutch of a few inches of . . . two mild pacific elements—earth and water" (p. 87). Just before they get to Hell Creek crossing Ned is discovered hiding in the back of the car. "I got just as much right to a trip as you and Lucius" (p. 71), Ned proclaims, and since they are now too far from Jefferson to turn back, Ned is allowed to remain.

When the trio nears Memphis, Lucius experiences another rite of passage: he gets to drive the automobile on the highway leading to the city. Boon is vague regarding their destination. He explains, "We're going to a kind of boarding house. . . . You'll like it" (p. 95). But Miss Reba's place is not a boarding-house, it is a brothel; and it does not take Lucius long to figure out what kind of place he is in, even if he does not fully understand what goes on there. Miss Reba is a younger and more generous character than she is in *Sanctuary*. Mr. Binford—the man she mourns in *Sanctuary* when she is in her cups—is still alive and makes a brief appearance. From him Lucius gets his first inkling of Miss Reba's business. Other important characters are introduced at this point. Corrie is one of the girls in Miss Reba's house; she is a good, compassionate, and loving woman who happens to be a whore. She is also Boon's "girl friend" in the sense that he sees her every time he is in Memphis. Staying with her is Otis, her cousin from Arkansas, who Boon thinks will be a good companion for Lucius during their stay. For Lucius, things happen almost too fast; experience outstrips cognition. Recalling his first entry into Miss Reba's house, he remarks, "I think you should be tumbled pell-mell, without warning, only into experience which you might well have spent the rest of your life not having to meet" (p. 99). His instincts, which derive from his background and training, are more reliable than his mental processes. Thus he has a strong positive reaction to Corrie and an equally strong negative reaction to Otis. When he first sees Corrie he remarks that she "was a big girl. I don't mean fat: just big . . . with dark hair and blue eyes and at first I thought her face was plain. But she came into the room already looking at me, and I knew it didn't matter what her face was" (p. 102). Lucius senses that there is something wrong with Otis, who is already a small-time crook, but he cannot quite identify what it is. "That was something else about him," he reflects uneasily, "when you noticed him, it was just a second before it would have been too late" (p. 125).

Shortly after their arrival at Miss Reba's, Ned, who had

earlier insisted on going his own way, reappears, and it is learned that he has swapped Boss's automobile for a horse. By running this horse (which has been stolen) in a race at Parsham against another horse (Acheron) it has never been able to beat in previous races, Ned plans to win back Boss's automobile and some extra money besides. Not the least of their problems is how to get the stolen horse from Memphis to Parsham. They accomplish this with the help of a railroad conductor (one of Corrie's customers) who is able to get the horse on an empty box car. In the midst of these goings-on Lucius, defending Corrie against the slurs of her nephew, gets into a fight with Otis and as a result gets his hand cut by Otis's pocket knife. No one has ever defended Corrie's honor before; she is so touched that she promises Lucius to give up her trade completely. After Lucius's hand has been tended to and he is ready for bed, Boon observes: "Eleven years old . . . and already knife-cut in a whorehouse brawl. . . . I wish I had knowed you thirty years ago. With you to learn me when I was eleven years old, maybe by this time I'd a had some sense too" (p. 159).

At Parsham, Ned begins to test Lightning—which is the name they give the stolen horse whose registered name is Coppermine—for racing ability. Ned's secret for getting Lightning to run, not revealed until the end of the race, is that Lightning loves sardines, and with these offered as incentive the horse will run very fast. Also, while at Parsham Lucius broadens his range of experience. In the person of Butch Lovemaiden, the local constable, he witnesses the ugliness of racial prejudice and lust. The constable uses the power of his office to intimidate the blacks in his district. Lovemaiden also has designs on Corrie and, when Lightning is impounded after the first of the three heats the horses are to run, Lovemaiden makes Corrie's submission to him the price for freeing Lightning to run again. Initially hurt because Corrie has broken her promise to quit whoring, another measure of Lucius's maturity is that he eventually accepts the reason for her action.

In a situation laden with physical and emotional pressure,

Lucius has the experience of being a jockey in a horse race at the age of eleven. Acheron wins the first heat; it is part of Ned's strategy to let him do so. The second heat is thrown out on a technicality; and after Lightning has been impounded and the question of his ownership settled, all stakes are placed on the third heat. Ned's sardine ploy works and Lightning wins the race. At this point Lucius's world begins to show some vestiges of the reality he has known before the Memphis trip. Still sitting on Lightning after his victorious ride he sees the familiar figure of Boss Priest, waiting to take him home.

The relativity of time and mutability is underscored when Lucius returns to Jefferson and is surprised that *"It hasn't even changed*. Because it should have. . . . I don't mean it should have changed of itself, but that I, bringing back to it what the last four days must have changed in me, should have altered it" (p. 299). Once again, Boss Priest helps Lucius discover some final meaning and focus for his experiences. He intervenes when Lucius's father is about to whip him—and in a family structure such as the one in which Lucius lives a whipping is a solemn occasion. Lucius is ashamed because he has lied and has betrayed the trust of his family. Boss tells him that he must now be man enough to bear his shame because "Nothing is ever forgotten. Nothing is ever lost. It's too valuable" (p. 302). He explains to Lucius that "A gentleman accepts the responsibility of his actions and bears the burden of their consequences, even when he did not himself instigate them but only acquiesced to them, didn't say No though he knew he should" (p. 302). Boss's points of principle and behavior have more impact since they are reinforced by Lucius's own recent experiences. The teaching and the experience do not make up a complete lesson in manhood, but they rest on the two cornerstones for mature, responsible behavior that are encountered frequently in Faulkner's fiction: endurance—in this instance the ability to endure a burdensome memory—and the ability to cope with physical and emotional stress.

The Reivers, the last of Faulkner's novels, received the

Pulitzer Prize in 1963, awarded posthumously. Faulkner died on 6 July 1962, just over a month after the novel's publication. The work was generally well received by the popular press though, correctly enough, it was not accorded the high status of Faulkner's major productions. George Plimpton, in the *New York Herald Tribune*, compared *The Reivers* to other boys' adventure stories such as *Treasure Island*, *Huckleberry Finn*, and *The Rover Boys*. Blotner observes how at the end of Faulkner's career "journalistic criticism of his work had changed relatively little. . . . whereas the mass of early reviewers tended to say, He would be a great author if only he would learn to control his writing, many would say during the latter part of his career, It's too bad that a major writer can't control his writing."[3]

Understandably, scholars have not paid as much attention to *The Reivers* as they have to other works in the Faulkner canon; this is not because it is a poor novel but because it does not present the challenges of understanding that his more complex work does. Very good general discussions of the novel are provided by Brooks, Millgate, and Vickery; and Meriwether, in a 1970 article that represents one of the few scholarly disagreements about the novel, challenges Elizabeth Kerr's argument that *The Reivers* is the "Golden Book" of Yoknapatawpha County that Faulkner said he one day wanted to write.[4]

---

[1]For a discussion of this aspect of the novel, see Mellard, "Faulkner's 'Golden Book': *The Reivers* as Romantic Comedy," *Bucknell Review*, 13 (December 1965): 19-31.

[2]*The Reivers: A Reminiscence* (New York: Random House, 1962), p. 3. Subsequent references are placed within text.

[3]Blotner, p. 1826.

[4]Meriwether, "The Novel Faulkner Never Wrote: His *Golden Book* or *Doomsday Book*," *American Literature*, 42 (March 1970): 93-96, and Elizabeth M. Kerr, "*The Reivers:* The Golden Book of Yoknapatawpha County," *Modern Fiction Studies*, 13 (Spring 1967): 95-113. See also Blotner, pp. 791, 1187, and *Letters*, p. 197.

Short Stories

During his career, William Faulkner produced five volumes of short fiction: *These 13* (1931), *Doctor Martino and Other Stories* (1934), *Knight's Gambit* (1949), *Collected Stories* (1950), and *Big Woods* (1955). Other collections of published work, not compiled by Faulkner, are *Early Prose and Poetry* (1962), and *New Orleans Sketches* (1958, augmented 1968). *Uncollected Stories* (1979) contains unpublished as well as previously uncollected short fiction.

Though many of the individual stories that Faulkner submitted to various magazines were written in the hope of quick sales, he did not lower his artistic standards for them; this is one of the reasons his stories did not sell as well as he hoped they would. Next to poetry, Faulkner considered the short-story form the most demanding literary discipline;[1] and in the compiling of short-story volumes he adhered to the same literary standards he applied to his novels. Writing to Malcolm Cowley in 1948 about his plans for *Collected Stories*, Faulkner expressed his belief that "form, integration, is as important as to a novel—an entity of its own, single, set for one pitch, contrapuntal in integration, toward one end, one finale."[2] Thus, as Michael Millgate says, when considering Faulkner's short-story collections, "it is essential to think of them not simply as aggregations of individual stories but as volumes which may conceivably possess a discernible internal organization of their own."[3] The striving for unity and structural integrity is especially evident in *These 13* and *Collected Stories*, whereas in *Doctor Martino* it is difficult, as Millgate notes, "to discern any clear pattern either of a contrapuntal or of a straightforward sequential nature."[4] The six stories of *Knight's Gambit* all feature the character of Gavin Stevens and are written in the mode of the popular detective story; in each of them Stevens is involved either in the solving or the prevention of a crime, and we see him acting not just as a legal but as a moral force in the community of Jefferson. *Big Woods* comprises stories of the wilderness and of hunting, stories that are combined to place "the actions of men in the long and diminishing perspective of the land's permanence and ultimate inviolability."[5]

The stories discussed in this chapter—with the exception of "Barn Burning," which is collected only in *Collected Stories*—were first collected in *These 13* and subsequently in *Collected Stories*, and are broadly representative of Faulkner's artistry as a short-story writer. As mentioned above, these are the most carefully structured of Faulkner's collections, and it is thus reasonable to assume that Faulkner selected the stories for them with a definite purpose in mind. *These 13* is divided into three parts. The first part consists of four World War I stories that describe the physical and spiritual wasteland that is being created by the war. This global view is narrowed to the local setting of Yoknapatawpha in the second section. "Red Leaves," an Indian story and the first of the six stories in this section, provides a historical context. Another Indian story, "A Justice," is a tale of courtship that stands in ironic contrast to the modern but macabre necrophylic love story narrated in "A Rose for Emily." The remaining three stories are contemporary in setting and deal with the white and black communities of Jefferson. The three stories in the third section move out of Yoknapatawpha and back into the larger world. Two are set in Italy and the last one, "Carcassonne," while it is set in a place called Rincon, is both placeless and timeless in the sense that it attempts to render, with symbols and impressionistic imagery, the nature of the creative experience. The contrapuntal effect Faulkner desired is achieved through the stark contrast between the different sections, while the stories within each section are related by subject matter and locale. Thematic strains—race, the condition of modern man, family relationships—tighten the structure of individual sections and, at the same time, overlap among the three.

Collected Stories is structured along similar lines but is more complex. It is divided into six subtitled sections: "The Country," "The Village," "The Wilderness," "The Wasteland," "The Middle Ground," and "Beyond." The stories in the first section deal with the yeoman farmer class of Yoknapatawpha County, and are paired with stories set in Jefferson in the second section. "The Wilderness" section—consisting of four Indian stories—steps backward in time to establish a historical context for the Yoknapatawpha locale. The fourth section comprises five World War I stories, all of which have transatlantic settings. The stories of "The Middle Ground" are a mixture; some are set in Yoknapatawpha, but others are set in such diverse places as Virginia, New York, and California. The last section consists of six stories, three of which had been used to conclude the last section of *These 13*. These stories are "beyond" Yoknapatawpha not only in a literal sense, but also in the sense that some of them are invested with elements of the surreal and the supernatural. The most accessible source for Faulkner's collected fiction is *Collected Stories*, and of the forty-two stories it contains, Hans Skei has written that it "may be said to contain the stories Faulkner wanted to represent him as a short story writer."[6] The most available source for stories not included in *Collected Stories* is *Uncollected Stories*,[7] which includes short fiction that was later worked into novels.

Faulkner's short stories use many of the same techniques and deal with the same basic themes and ideas that occupied his imagination in his longer fiction. The best of his stories show Faulkner's mastery in the artful withholding of certain information, which serves to heighten the ultimate effect; and the words and actions of the characters themselves obviate the need for narrative "explanations" by the author. In this way compression, the essence of the short-story form, is achieved.

"That Evening Sun" is an exemplary story in several respects. It is about a Negro washerwoman and sometimes cook named Nancy who has come to work temporarily in the kitchen of the Compson family while Dilsey, the regular cook, is sick. The story also concentrates on the Compson children, Caddy and Jason, and is narrated by Quentin, though he is not actually named. This, of course, is the same Compson family that Faulkner deals with in *The Sound and the Fury*.

Nancy is a prostitute addicted to alcohol and cocaine, and she is mortally afraid of Jesus, the man she lives with. Jesus resents Nancy's traffic with the white world. When Mr. Compson makes him leave the family's kitchen, he tells Nancy, "I cant hang around white man's kitchen. . . . But white man can hang around mine. White man can come in my house, but I cant stop him."[6] Shortly after this scene it is reported that Jesus has left Jefferson and gone to Memphis; but Nancy becomes convinced that he is going to return and kill her with his razor. Her fear, which has no rational foundation, is all consuming. As Mr. Compson and the children walk Nancy to her cabin after dark, she insists, "I can feel him. I can feel him now, in this lane. He hearing us talk, every word, hid somewhere, waiting. I aint seen him, and I aint going to see him again but once more, with that razor in his mouth" (p. 295). Once Dilsey returns to work, there is no reason for Nancy to be any longer in the Compson home or to be escorted to her cabin. Promising that she will tell stories and play games, Nancy persuades the children to come to her cabin with her, where she hopes they will stay the night. However, Mr. Compson soon comes to take them home and at the end of the story Nancy is left alone with her terror, certain that she will be dead before the morning.

By choosing a first-person narration, Faulkner limits severely the opportunities for authorial comment. And the fact that the action of the story is taking place before the eyes of children and is being narrated by one of them means that the level of commentary will be neither sophisticated nor analytical. Thus Caddy is confused when she hears Jesus say that

Nancy has a watermelon under her dress, and can even less understand the meaning of Nancy's reply: "It never come off your vine" (p. 292). Observations are usually made in the form of simple declarative sentences as in the following: "Dilsey was still sick in her cabin. Father told Jesus to stay off our place. Dilsey was still sick. It was a long time. We were in the library after supper" (p. 292). Though Nancy's fear is irrational, it is very real; and the intensity of her predicament is heightened by contrast with the innocence of the Compson children. The reader, then, must perceive the story through the eyes and ears of children; in doing so one learns not only something about the elemental nature of fear but something as well about the Compson family and the larger community.

Another story that deals powerfully with a child's perception of the world, though it is narrated from a third-person point of view, is "Barn Burning." Originally written as the first chapter of *The Hamlet*, the central character in the story is Sarty Snopes. At the beginning of the story Sarty's father, Ab, is appearing before a local justice on charges of barn burning—one of the most serious crimes one can commit in a rural farming community. For a moment there is a possibility that Sarty will be called to testify, and he realizes in "frantic grief and despair" what his father expects of him: *"He aims for me to lie. . . . And I will have to do hit"* (p. 4). Caught in a moral dilemma between his own concept of simple justice and truth and feelings of intense family loyalty, the pressure on Sarty is overwhelming. He escapes the dilemma only when the plaintiff, Mr. Harris, withdraws his request to have the boy questioned.

As a result of the trial, the family is forced to move away. After they have made camp and had supper, Ab takes Sarty out onto the road and strikes him because he believes his son would have told the court the truth had Harris not relented. He tells Sarty, "You're getting to be a man. You got to learn. You got to learn to stick to your own blood or you ain't going to have any blood stick to you" (p. 8). Later in life, Sarty realizes "If I had said they wanted only truth, justice, he would have hit me again" (p. 8). But at this point he does not have sufficient maturity or experience to articulate what he feels.

The family's destination is the property of Major de Spain, where Ab will once more take up work as a sharecropper. After their belongings have been off-loaded from wagon to cabin, Ab takes Sarty with him to de Spain's house. The sight of the house, which seems to Sarty as big as a courthouse, lifts the boy's spirits; and emotionally it symbolizes for him a fusion of his youthful concepts of truth and beauty: *"They are safe from him. People whose lives are a part of this peace and dignity are beyond his touch, he no more to them than a buzzing wasp: capable of stinging for a little moment but that's all . . . even the barns and stable and cribs . . . impervious to the puny flames he might contrive"* (p. 10). The narrative method is similar to that used in *As I Lay Dying*: a character's thoughts are expressed in language that he would not actually be capable of speaking. As the scene continues, Sarty hopes that his father might feel the same thing: *"Maybe it will even change him now from what maybe he couldn't help but be"* (p. 11).

That is not to be the case. Walking up to the house, Ab steps in a pile of horse manure which he then tracks into the house and, in front of de Spain's horrified wife, grinds into an expensive rug. When he returns home and discovers what has happened, de Spain takes the rug to Snopes and orders him to clean it. In doing so, Ab intentionally ruins the rug, and de Spain states his intention of fining him the equivalent of twenty bushels of corn, to come out of the meager profit Ab had hoped to make. To de Spain's surprise and outrage, Snopes files suit, and after hearing the two sides the justice reduces the fine to ten bushels of corn. That still does not satisfy Ab's sense of justice, which is based more on vengeance than equity, and he and Sarty's older brother Flem prepare that evening to burn de Spain's barn.

Sarty then has to make the most difficult decision of his life. Left by Ab in the custody of his mother, he breaks loose from her and runs to warn de Spain. The warning given, he runs back out onto the road where he is soon overtaken and passed by de Spain, who is on horseback. Soon after he sees the upsurge of flame from the barn and hears shots from de Spain's gun. Sarty knows at that moment that his warning has come too late; and he assumes that his father—perhaps his brother, too—has been killed. He does not return home. Later that night he finds himself on the crest of a hill: "*Father. My father*, he thought. 'He was brave!' he cried suddenly, aloud but not loud, no more than a whisper" (p. 24). Believing his father is dead, Sarty needs to invest his memory with attributes Ab did not have in life. The story ends with Sarty having taken his first painful step into the difficult world of adulthood. It is a somber world, and to survive in it Sarty must be able to cope with conditions of isolation, grief, and despair.

A number of Faulkner's stories concern themselves with the wasteland themes that appear in his longer fiction, especially *Soldiers' Pay* and *Flags in the Dust*. All of his World War I stories fall into this category, particularly those that deal with fliers. The story "Ad Astra," for example, features a grouping of seven characters: Sartoris, Bland, Comyn, Monaghan, and an unnamed narrator; an Indian major; and a captured German pilot who Monaghan insists he is going to take home with him. At the beginning of the story the Indian major comments on the isolation of all the characters: "We are like men trying to move in water, with held breath watching our terrific and infinitesimal limbs, watching one another's terrific stasis without touch, without contact, robbed of all save the impotence and the need" (p. 407).

"Ad Astra" is a story of mood rather than plot. We watch the characters move through a single drunken evening, seeking in alcohol and violence a momentary anodyne to the terror of their existence. The Indian major, a philosopher of sorts, tries to interpret the meaning of their experience. At one point he says, "All this generation which fought in the war are dead tonight. But we do not yet know it. . . . Those who have been four years rotting out yonder . . . are not more dead than we" (p. 421). The death the Indian major speaks of is a kind of spiritual death. He means that those who survive the war will never be able to return to the lives they knew before, because the world has been irrevocably changed by the war. The impact of this truth may be less easy to appreciate now, after World War II, Korea, and Vietnam. But World War I was the first modern war in which technology—in the form of airplanes, tanks, gas, and automatic weapons—made it possible to achieve a level of destruction that man had not before imagined possible.

The story, which begins on a somber note, ends in a mood of outright depression. Midnight finds the narrator, the Indian major, Bland, and Sartoris outside together. A band can be heard in the distance, "brassy, thudding . . . forlornly gay, hysteric, but most of all forlorn" (p. 428). Like a series of stark photographs, each of the characters is pictured at the end, frozen in his own isolation: the Indian major in his self-imposed exile (he has been away from home for seven years and does not plan to return); Sartoris sick and vomiting; Bland weeping for an imaginary wife; the narrator lashing out aimlessly with impotent bitterness.

Another group of Faulkner's short stories deals with Indians and their place in the history of Yoknapatawpha County. In many of these stories the Indian people are revealed as being torn between their own culture and heritage and the culture and economy of the white man, by whom the Indians are gradually being replaced as they adopt the ways and values of white civilization. Such a story is "Red Leaves." It is built around a simple framing device: the chief of the tribe, Issetibbeha, has died; and Indian ritual requires that his horse, his dog, and his chief servant be buried with him. But Issetibbeha's chief servant, a Negro slave, does not want to die and has run away. The responsibility for getting the slave back falls to two Indian characters, Three Basket and Louis Berry; even in their names Faulkner indicates the way in which the white man's culture is creeping into the Indian's world.

The nature of this intrusion is made manifest in the dialogue that takes place between Three Basket and Louis Berry, through which Faulkner gradually reveals the essential facts of the story, allowing the dramatic tension inherent in the acting out of the ritual to build slowly but steadily. The Indian tribe is engaged in a plantation economy the Indians do not like. At the beginning of the story Three Basket complains that slavery "is not the good way. In the old days there were no quarters, no Negroes. A man's time was his own then. He had time. Now he must spend most of it finding work for them who prefer sweating to do"; and he reasons that "They are too valuable to eat . . . when the white man will give horses for them" (p. 314). The first Negroes were brought into the Indian tribe by Doom, Issetibbeha's father, who got them in New Orleans. Since the Negroes represent a valuable economic commodity, the Indians cannot simply wash the problem from their hands by killing them or eating them. They must do as the white man does: "clear the land and plant it with food and raise Negroes and sell them . . . for money" (p. 319). The master cannot free himself of his slaves, and in this way the Indians have become enslaved in a system that is not a natural part of their culture.

Another aspect of the story has to do with power and how desire for it corrupts human nature. Doom learned about the acquisition of power in New Orleans, and when he returned to the tribe he used murder and intimidation to become chief and bear the title of "the Man." After Doom's death, when Issetibbeha became chief, he sold some of his slaves to finance a trip abroad, and from Paris he returned with a number of utterly useless objects, among them "a pair of slippers with red heels" (p. 320). These became a symbol of supreme power in the tribe,

shoes that only the Man could wear; from childhood Issetibbeha's son, Moketubbe, showed an inordinate desire to possess the shoes. Now that his father is dead and he can wear the
slippers as much as he likes, Moketubbe's dissipated appearance seems intended to illustrate the principle that power corrupts. When we first see him after his father's death he is
completely inert: "He was maybe an inch better than five feet
tall, and he weighed two hundred and fifty pounds. He wore a
broadcloth coat and no shirt, his round, smooth copper bal-
loon of a belly swelling above the bottom piece of a suit of linen
underwear. . . . Moketubbe sat motionless, with his broad,
yellow face with its closed eyes and flat nostrils, his flipperlike
arms extended" (p. 325). The slippers are much too small for
Moketubbe's feet; they keep cutting off his circulation and
causing him to lose consciousness, and his servants must
periodically remove the slippers to revive him.

Against this backdrop, the flight of Issetibbeha's Negro
slave achieves a level of human dignity that we do not find in
the other characters of "Red Leaves." He is not engaged in a
meaningless ritual. He is trying to save his life; and his success
in eluding his pursuers shows him to be a better woodsman
than the Indians who are his masters. He appears to value life in
a way that the Indians do not, and on the sixth day of his escape
when he is bitten by a moccasin he thinks to himself, " 'It's that
I do not wish to die' . . . as though it were something that,
until the words had said themselves, he found that he had not
known, or had not known the depth and extent of his desire"
(p. 335). He is a complete reversal of the stereotypical view of
the Negro advanced by the Indians. And though the poison in
his system makes it impossible for him to take in food or water,
he keeps trying to perform these life-affirming acts until the
moment of his death.

Aside from his World War I fiction, Faulkner's "Mistral" is
one of the few stories he wrote with a European setting. Like
"That Evening Sun" and "Barn Burning," it is a story in which

a degree of youth and innocence is lost as a result of experience. The unnamed first-person narrator of the story and his companion, Don, both Americans who are traveling in Italy, are young men unsophisticated in many ways, particularly in terms of sexual relationships, and they are unprepared for what they experience in the story. There is also an implied cultural comparison that underlies the action of the story. As the narrator remarks, "away from home, some distance away—space or time or experience away—you are always both older and eternally younger than yourself, at the same time" (p. 856). Italian culture is much older in the ways of the world than the relatively unsophisticated American culture in which the two young men have grown up.

The title of the story derives from the name given to a cold and dry northerly wind that is common to the Mediterranean area, and repeated references to it establish a consistent, ominous tone. As the story begins, the narrator and Don are looking for a place where they can find shelter and food. They are directed by an elderly couple to a nearby church where they will be able to eat and rest in the parish house. Before arriving at the church, they learn from the couple that the priest is conducting a funeral service for the fiance of a young woman who, after the death of her mother, the priest took into his house at the age of six. The priest had originally intended for the girl to stay cloistered within the church, but "at fourteen and fifteen she was already the brightest and loudest and most tireless in the dances, and the young men already beginning to look after her, even after it had been arranged between her and him who is dead yonder" (p. 848). Before the marriage engagement to a prosperous older man was made by the priest, the girl had been secretly meeting a local boy named Giulio, "Before we had thought she was old enough for such" (p. 849). When the priest found out about these meetings, Giulio suddenly, and somewhat mysteriously, was called into the army; and it is at this point that the girl's engagement was arranged.

The marriage, however, was put off for three years; and now, with the wedding scheduled to take place after the current harvest, the prospective groom has suddenly died and Giulio has reappeared. Don asks the old couple why the wedding had been put off for so long and is told by the woman that it was because of the girl's willfulness and lack of piety. Her husband, though, suggests that the priest may have had his own reasons for not wanting the wedding to take place: "The priest looked at her, too. . . . For a man is a man, even under a cassock" (p. 850).

Both Don and the narrator are intrigued by all of this information, and they begin to speculate on the various motives that may have been involved in sending Giulio away and in delaying the wedding, and what might have been the cause of the fiance's death—questions that remain mysteries throughout the story. It is made clear that the priest's sexual desire for his ward has turned him into a voyeur. Though he has never tried to consummate his passion, he has fallen into the habit of almost constantly following and watching her. When the two young men finally meet the priest, he appears to be highly distracted. Bending his head to say grace over the meal, he repeats instead words from the burial service; and when Don and his friend leave the house they discover the priest pacing frantically beside the courtyard wall, silhouetted "against the sky . . . his head rushing back and forth like a midget running along the top of a wall" (pp. 867-868). Later, when the two Americans are leaving the village, they catch the priest in the act of spying on Giulio and the girl: "He was lying on his face just inside the wall, his robes over his head, the black blur of his gown moving faintly and steadily, either because of the wind or because he was moving under them. And whatever the sound meant that he was making, it was not meant to be listened to, for his voice ceased when we made a noise" (p. 875). By this time the narrator has seen the girl also—"all in white, coatless, walking slender and supple" (p. 869)—and he can understand something of the priest's torment.

But something else has happened to the narrator and his friend. In all of their speculations, they have been participating vicariously in the priest's passion. The final ironic twist occurs at the end of the story, where we see them as two young voyeurs watching a voyeur who himself is in the act of watching a young couple make love. The point is not lost on either Don or the narrator, and their reaction is mixed with shame and bitterness.

There is no shortage of studies of individual stories written by Faulkner, but comprehensive treatments of his short fiction and significant short-story collections are few and far between. Meriwether comments on the need for such studies: "No one has yet examined any of Faulkner's . . . miscellaneous collections of short fiction to see what formal unity they may possess. . . . Faulkner often drew upon previously published stories in the construction of his novels, and often drew upon novels in progress in the writing of short stories for the magazine market."[9] Of the collections, *Collected Stories* looms large in Faulkner's career. In this regard, Hans Skei writes that "Collected Stories . . . marks an important step forward in the general acknowledgement of Faulkner's total work, in the same way as *The Portable Faulkner* had been a decisive step towards general recognition a few years earlier. Many reviewers either stated or implied that recognition of Faulkner as America's leading novelist of his generation would soon come, and they did this on the basis of the variety and richness of the short story material found in *Collected Stories*."[10] Skei's book also includes a useful listing of published and unpublished studies of Faulkner's short fiction. Millgate gives a general discussion of Faulkner's work in the genre of short fiction; and among other studies worth consulting are Norman Holmes Pearson's "Faulkner's 'Three

Evening Suns,' " Jane Millgate's "Short Story into Novel: Faulkner's Reworking of 'Gold is Not Always,' " and Mary Dunlap's "William Faulkner's 'Knight's Gambit' and Gavin Stevens."[11]

---

[1]See *Lion*, pp. 217, 238; *Faulkner in the University*, pp. 145, 207.

[2]*Letters*, p. 278.

[3]Millgate, p. 259.

[4]Millgate, p. 265.

[5]Millgate, p. 282.

[6]Hans H. Skei, *William Faulkner: The Short Story Career. An Outline of Faulkner's Short Story Writing from 1919 to 1962* (Oslo: Universitetsforlaget, 1981), p. 106.

[7]Blotner, ed., *Uncollected Stories of William Faulkner*.

[8]*Collected Stories* (New York: Random House, 1950), p. 292. The texts of all the stories cited in this chapter are taken from *Collected Stories*.

[9]Meriwether, "William Faulkner," in *Sixteen Modern American Authors*, pp. 253, 257.

[10]Skei, *William Faulkner: The Short Story Career*, p. 106.

[11]See, respectively: Millgate, pp. 259-275; Norman Holmes Pearson, "Faulkner's 'Three Evening Suns,' " *Yale University Library Gazette*, 19 (October 1954): 227-232; Jane Millgate, "Short Story into Novel: Faulkner's Reworking of 'Gold is Not Always,' " *English Studies*, 45 (August 1964): 310-317; Mary Dunlap, "William Faulkner's 'Knight's Gambit' and Gavin Stevens," *Mississippi Quarterly*, 23 (Summer 1970): 223-240.

While it is true that William Faulkner's formidable writing talents were recognized in Britain and France before they were in this country, by the time of his death in 1962 his reputation was secure on both sides of the Atlantic. In the twenty years since his death, Faulkner's reputation has continued to grow; his work has been translated into more than twenty-five languages and is now accessible to a large portion of the world's population.

Interest in Faulkner's life has grown at least as rapidly as his critical reputation. In addition to Joseph Blotner's massive two-volume biography, there have been numerous other biographical investigations, to say nothing of those critics and scholars who have persisted in interpreting Faulkner's life and beliefs through his fiction. In 1980 Faulkner's life was the subject of a two-hour documentary on public television. It is hardly likely, if he were alive today, that William Faulkner would welcome such attention; this man who defended his privacy with such zeal, who told Malcolm Cowley in 1945, as forcefully and as eloquently as he ever expressed it, of his aversion to biographical inquiries: "I would have preferred nothing at all prior to the instant I began to write, as though Faulkner and Typewriter were concomitant, coadjutant and without past on the moment they first faced each other at the suitable (nameless) table."[1]

There is a fine irony here, one that would not be lost on Faulkner himself; because for all the pages of text and footnotes that have been amassed in pursuit of this writer, Faulkner the man remains elusive. As Joseph Blotner has observed, "He was too varied for a single image and at the same time too strong to fail to leave a powerful impression behind."[2] So in the end it is as Faulkner always wanted it. His life was his work—he wrote the books and then he died—and if we aspire not to discover a personality but to understand Faulkner on his own terms, it is to his work that we must turn.

---

[1]*Letters*, p. 222.

[2]Blotner, "Did You See Him Plain?," *Fifty Years of Yoknapatawpha: Faulkner and Yoknapatawpha 1979*, edited by Doreen Fowler and Ann J. Abadie (Jackson: University Press of Mississippi, 1980), p. 22.

25 September 1897: Born, New Albany, Mississippi;

1898-1902: Family lives in Ripley, Mississippi;

22 September 1902: Family moves to Oxford, Mississippi;

Fall 1915: Quits Oxford High School;

10 July-early December 1918: Serves in RAF (Canada) as cadet;

6 August 1919: Poem, "L'Apres-Midi d'un Faune," his first published work, appears in the *New Republic*;

September 1919-December 1920: Special student at the University of Mississippi; produces six hand-lettered copies of a verse play, *Marionettes*;

Fall-December 1921: Bookstore clerk in New York;

December 1921-31 October 1924: Postmaster at University of Mississippi post office;

15 December 1924: *The Marble Faun* published by Four Seas;

January-June 1925: Extended visit to New Orleans;

August-December 1925: Travels in Europe and England with an extended stay in Paris;

25 February 1926: *Soldiers' Pay* published by Boni & Liveright;

December 1926: *Sherwood Anderson & Other Famous Creoles*, by Faulkner and William Spratling, published by Robert H. True Company;

30 April 1927: *Mosquitoes* published by Boni & Liveright;

31 January 1929: *Sartoris* published by Harcourt, Brace;

20 June 1929: Marries Estelle Oldham Franklin;

7 October 1929: *The Sound and the Fury* published by Jonathan Cape & Harrison Smith;

April 1930: Stories begin being published in national magazines; buys Rowan Oak;

6 October 1930: *As I Lay Dying* published by Cape & Smith;

11 January 1931: Daughter Alabama born, lives nine days;

9 February 1931: *Sanctuary* published by Cape & Smith;

21 September 1931: *These 13* published by Cape & Smith;

7 May-10 August 1932; October 1932: MGM contract writer;

6 October 1932: *Light in August* published by Harrison Smith & Robert Haas;

20 April 1933: *A Green Bough* published by Smith & Haas;

24 June 1933: Daughter Jill born;

16 April 1934: *Doctor Martino and Other Stories* published by Smith & Haas;

July 1934: Works for Universal Studios;

25 March 1935: *Pylon* published by Smith & Haas;

10 November 1935: Brother Dean killed in plane crash;

10 December 1935-late August 1937: Works intermittently for Twentieth Century-Fox;

26 October 1936: *Absalom, Absalom!* published by Random House;

Mid-October 1937: Suffers severe back burn in New York;

15 February 1938: *The Unvanquished* published by Random House;

January 1939: Elected to National Institute of Arts and Letters;

19 January 1939: *The Wild Palms* published by Random House;

1 April 1940: *The Hamlet* published by Random House;

11 May 1942: *Go Down, Moses* published by Random House;

26 July 1942-September 1945: Works intermittently for Warner Brothers;

29 April 1946: *The Portable Faulkner*, edited by Malcolm Cowley, published by Viking Press;

27 September 1948: *Intruder in the Dust* published by Random House;

23 November 1948: Elected to American Academy of Arts and Letters;

27 November 1949: *Knight's Gambit* published by Random House;

May 1950: Awarded American Academy's Howells Medal for Fiction:

2 August 1950: *Collected Stories of William Faulkner* published by Random House;

10 November 1950: Notified he has won 1949 Nobel Prize for Literature;

1 February-March 1951: Does scriptwriting for Howard Hawks;

March 1951: Receives National Book Award for Fiction for *Collected Stories*;

27 September 1951: *Requiem for a Nun* published by Random House;

26 October 1951: Awarded Legion of Honor in New Orleans;

30 November 1953-January 1954: Works on *Land of the Pharoahs* for Howard Hawks;

February 1954-29 March 1954: Works for Hawks;

2 August 1954: *A Fable* published by Random House;

25 January 1955: Receives National Book Award for Fiction for *A Fable*;

Early May 1955: *A Fable* wins Pulitzer Prize;

29 July-23 August 1955: Makes State Department trip to Japan;

14 October 1955: *Big Woods* published by Random House;

15 February-March 1957: Writer-in-residence, University of Virginia;

March 1957: Accepts Silver Medal of Greek Academy;

1 May 1957: *The Town* published by Random House;

30 January-March 1958: Writer-in-residence, University of Virginia;

30 January 1959: American debut of *Requiem for a Nun* on Broadway;

13 November 1959: *The Mansion* published by Random House;

25 August 1960: Appointed to University of Virginia faculty;

24 May 1962: Awarded Gold Medal for Fiction of National Institute of Arts and Letters;

4 June 1962: *The Reivers* published by Random House;

6 July 1962: Dies of heart attack at 1:30 A. M.;

7 July 1962: Buried in St. Peter's Cemetery, Oxford, Mississippi.